Tarantino

By the same author in this series:

GEORGE LUCAS
GANGSTER FILMS

with J Clive Matthews:
TIM BURTON
LORD OF THE RINGS

with Stephen Lavington:
BOND FILMS

virgin

film

TARANTINO

Jim Smith

First published in Great Britain in 2005
by Virgin Books Ltd
Thames Wharf Studios
Rainville Road
London
W6 9HA

A catalogue record for this book is available from the British Library.

ISBN 0 7535 1071 5

Typeset by TW Typesetting, Plymouth, Devon
Printed and bound in Great Britain by Mackays of Chatham PLC

Dedicated to

Jim Sangster
– My Scott Spiegel –

&

Scott Bassett
– My Robert Rodriguez –

Contents

Acknowledgements

Kirstie Addis, Janhanara Begum, Mark Clapham, James Clive Matthews, Jane Eastwood, Gareth Fletcher, Ellie Gibson, Steve Lavington, Eddie Robson, Christian Slater, Matt Symonds, Helen Taylor, Harris Watson, Mom and Dad and Lou, the BFI, NFT and the British Library.

Introduction

The merits of the filmic output of Quentin Tarantino are, like most things to do with qualitative assessments of art, naturally open to debate. That his very presence in the industry has changed many cultural assumptions that surround filmmaking and altered the way that the general public sees writers and directors is absolutely inarguable.

The arrival of his 1992 picture *Reservoir Dogs* (which was premiered at the Sundance Film Festival that summer amongst an unusually strong field of independent Americana) prompted a flurry of debates on the nature of screen violence and the state and nature of independent cinema. It also, naturally, introduced Tarantino's own wildly eclectic, intensely visual, jackdaw-sensibility to audiences.

However, something else it did was introduce audiences to Tarantino himself. His face, his voice, his very manner of walking became imprinted on the public consciousness. He became a star.

Partially this was because of his small, but extraordinarily showy, role in the film, enthusiastically spitting out some of the *most* memorable dialogue in a film *packed* with memorable dialogue, but many, many actors have gained less fame for doing far more in equally successful movies. It was also partially because the story of his rise to prominence was so extraordinary, and so instinctively understandable and loveable. (He was born in Knoxville, Tennessee, is part Native American and used to work in a video store – Video Archives in Manhattan Beach. Knoxville, incidentally, was described by another former resident, comedian Rich Hall, as a town where 'to call the people white trash is an insult to polystyrene'.) Mostly, though, it was because of his sudden omnipresence on talk shows and in the kind of magazines that concern themselves with celebrity.

This is something that, fundamentally, doesn't often happen to behind-the-scenes people and certainly didn't happen at all more than a decade ago. He began to do cameos as 'himself' on TV comedies and his private life became the subject of casual gossip in the manner normally reserved for actors, not screenwriters.

Film directors who can be identified, on sight, by the mothers of the intended audiences of their films are few now and were fewer in 1992. Steven Spielberg, Francis Ford Coppola, Martin Scorsese, Tim Burton and George Lucas count as 'Maybes'. Even (the by then long dead) Orson Welles's towering presence in the popular consciousness of film is, sadly, as much down to his roles as an actor, and his appearances in advertising, as his body of creative filmwork. The late Alfred Hitchcock had successfully managed his fame to the point where he became an icon, but he was never a celebrity in the modern sense; Stanley Kubrick successfully managed his anonymity to the point where, famously, a man who looked nothing like him and knew little about his work was able to impersonate him, without difficulty, in London society for an embarrassingly long time.

Filmmakers, from journeymen hacks to creative firebrands, can be almost entirely invisible to the people who willingly pay money to see their output and therefore fund their projects. The James Bond film *Moonraker* (to pick an almost entirely random example) made an extraordinary amount of money in 1979. Could one per cent of one per cent of the people who've seen it pick its director, the genial Lewis Gilbert, out of a line-up or identify one or two of his many other (and often far worthier) pictures? Of course not. Not even if they've seen *Alfie* (1966) and have *Sink The Bismarck!* (1960) on tape.

Quentin Tarantino became an instant presence; a presence with a distinctive face, and a distinctive name, that made a distinctive kind of film. He became a celebrity for being a director – and the majority of even the film-going population don't really know what that is.

In the post-New Hollywood era of filmmaking it has become possible, seemingly, for virtually any A-list actor to direct a mediocre movie and pick up an Oscar for his trouble along the way. This is due, often, to them being more instantly recognisable to academy voters (who are, in theory, meant to be his peers) than faceless creative types. Bearing this in mind it's safe to say that being more than an often unread name on an ignored list isn't something which happens to a lot of filmmakers; and the early 90s were a pre-mass-internet age, where less information was less easily accessible than it is now. A time before www.imdb.com and lengthy 'making of' puff pieces on every single DVD; a time when information about films, filmmakers and filmmaking was not only more difficult to acquire, but in a lot of cases simply wasn't out there no matter how hard you looked. Yet, suddenly, back in 1992 people knew who Quentin Tarantino was. Even now he's one of the most recognisable filmmakers in the world and in this respect he is, and has been, very different from his fellow directors, right from the very beginning of his career.

Quentin Tarantino wasn't, nay isn't, merely a recognisable figure amongst film directors and screenwriters, he's something else again. He's the film director as superstar.

How To Use This Book

This book is, hopefully, a useful guide to Tarantino's career as the aforementioned Superstar. His directorial pictures receive lengthy chapters, of several thousand words each, which examine the films in some detail while relating information about their production, release and reception. Films for which Tarantino was the principal screenwriter are treated in a similar, if slightly less extensive, manner – with more emphasis placed upon looking at the screenplay the film was shot *from* rather than the film that the screenplay *became*, and with less discussion of the production process and the details of the camerawork. The episode of NBC's *ER* television series ('Motherhood' – transmitted 11 May 1995) that Tarantino directed but did not write is treated as if it were a directorial feature, as is the portmanteau *Four Rooms* (1995) of which he directed roughly one quarter. His other projects, including films he had a hand in scripting, those he's appeared in as an actor and his appearances on television are discussed in 'box outs' of varying lengths which you'll find littered through the book at appropriate places.

The larger chapters, as mentioned above, are divided into numerous categories. The idea behind this is to create the sort of book where you can find the information, or the *kind* of information, you're looking for easily. Some categories will repeat and some will only be used once or twice. Some are easily understood (i.e. **BOX OFFICE DATA**) others are perhaps more obscure (**SPURIOUS INTERTEXTUALITY**). Many individual chapters will have one-off categories named for quotations or incidents from the film under discussion. Some of the sub-headings used will be:

Title (Year)

Production Credits

CAST: Who plays who.

SUMMARY

DEVELOPMENT: How the film came to be made and why. Tarantino spent many years struggling to break into filmmaking before *Reservoir Dogs*, writing no less than three full-length unproduced screenplays all of which were eventually made *after* the brilliant success of his debut directorial picture. This means that if you wish to tell the story of Tarantino's career in terms of the films he's made and the order in which they've been released – and I do – you're faced with having to explain the background to

Project B, which was *written* before Project A but *made* after it, after explaining the background to Project A. Even though Project A could never have been written, never mind made, without some of the things that need to be explained in relation to Project B happening. On a positive note, this means the genesis of Tarantino's screenplays reads in a manner not dissimilar to his own anti-linear approach to plot structure. Reading this book in chronological order (which I'd strongly advise) means that you'll occasionally get the answers before the questions; which is, I suppose, actually a form-and-content thing.

SCREENPLAY: Information on the writing process, where the ideas in and behind the script came from and influences explored.

CASTING: Discussions of the prior and subsequent careers of the main players. This is particularly relevant with Tarantino for the simple reason that he so often seems to cast someone because of prior associations. Movie stars have carried personae with them from one project to the next for practically as long as there have been motion pictures, but Tarantino deals with this in a particularly self-aware and interesting way. It isn't just about finding the actors, it's about getting the audiences to access the right part of the cultural databank that is their brains. For example, John Travolta dancing with Uma Thurman reminds the audience that he's John Travolta and 99.9 per cent of them have been thinking about *Saturday Night Fever* (John Badham, 1977) since it was suggested that Vincent might deign to dance.

KEY SHOTS: Camerawork of particular note. How the shooting and editing together of a scene really gets across what it's about. Also the place for noting really clever bits of lighting and camera usage. You know, like when the camera pans away before Vic Vega cuts off Marvin Nash's ear. Things like that.

RECURRING ELEMENTS: Tarantino uses many recurring elements in his screenplays, from reused character names and lines of dialogue to a character in one film being related to a character in another. This is partially, although not entirely, because some – although not all – of Tarantino's films take place in a distinct shared universe. *Pulp Fiction*, *Reservoir Dogs*, *True Romance* and (probably) the unfilmed draft of *Natural Born Killers* take place in a special 'Tarantino World'. Characters from one piece refer to characters from another, and they all share various reference points. It would be easy to dismiss this as mere aping of the shared realities of comic books (Batman, for example, knows Superman and they are both members of the Justice League of America. Things which happen in a Batman comic will often affect, even if only tangentially, what happens in Superman's comic that month, or the month after) although there are other, more 'respectable', examples of this technique. The brilliant American novelist Bret Easton Ellis uses it, as does crime writer Elmore Leonard (whose novel *Rum Punch* Tarantino would film (as *Jackie Brown*) in 1997). Both of them have created elaborate fictional universes that all their characters inhabit. Events in one Ellis or Leonard book connect, often only tangentially, but also frequently on matters of substance, to those in another and characters in one novel are related to those in others. (Patrick Bateman, the eponymous anti-hero of Ellis's *American Psycho* has a brother who is a major character in Ellis's earlier *The Rules of Attraction*, for example. Patrick actually cameos in *Rules*).

SPURIOUS INTERTEXTUALITY: In Tarantino's work, and this is vitally important, absolutely nothing exists in a vacuum. Everything only exists in relation to other things. There are two aspects to this, which are distinct, but are often confused with one another, so it's worth elucidating them. Firstly his work is packed with references to films, books, plays and records he likes and numerous in-jokes related to popular culture and pastiches, homages and sly references abound. Secondly – see **RECURRING ELEMENTS** above.

CRITICAL REACTION: How the critics reacted. I will usually use the *New York Times*, *Rolling Stone*, the *New Yorker* and the ever readable Roger Ebert of the *Chicago Sun-Times* as between them they offer a good cross-section of quality, mainstream American journalism. Depending on the picture I will also throw in quotes from numerous other sources, including the *Village Voice* and a smattering of the British broadsheet press. There will be a few surprises in here too.

THE NUMBERS: Box office data. The number of screens the films was released on. Where it opened. How it opened. When it opened and who it opened to.

FINAL COMMENT

My Best Friend's Birthday (1987)

(Black and White, 16 mm, c. 39 minutes, incomplete)

Produced by Quentin Tarantino, Craig Hamann and
Rand Vossler
Edited by Quentin Tarantino
Directors of Photography: Roger Avary, Craig Hamann,
Rand Vossler
Written and Directed by Quentin Tarantino and
Craig Hamann

CAST: Craig Hamann (*Mickey Burnett*), Quentin Tarantino (*Clarence Pool*), Allen Garfield (*Entertainment Magnate*), Al Harrell (*Clifford*), Brenda Hillhouse (*Wife*), Linda Kaye (*Ex-Girlfriend*), Stevo Polyi (*DJ*), Alan Sanborn (*Nutmeg*), Rich Turner (*Oliver Brandon*), Rowland Wafford (*Lenny Otis*)

SUMMARY (PARTIAL): DJ Clarence Pool entertains his listeners with stories such as how he was saved from killing himself aged three by *The Partridge Family*. But when Clarence snorts a baggie full of drugs during a commercial break, he has an on-air meltdown. Other subplots include Mickey finding his ex-girlfriend in his apartment only to be crushed by the revelation that she's now with somebody else and has only come round to collect her possessions and Clarence hiring a call girl who has only been on the job for a few days as a birthday present for Mickey.

DEVELOPMENT: Made super-cheap and on super 16 mm film while Tarantino was still working at Video Archives, *My Best Friend's Birthday* was shot over a number of years on an ad-hoc and amateur basis and never completed or released. Asked about the project's gestation Tarantino commented that he had read, and indeed conducted, interviews with numerous directors and they had all seemingly made their first films when they were in their 20s, and he wanted to be able to say that too. Acquiring a 16 mm camera cheap he 'just started shooting it that way' thinking 'I'm going to make a feature . . . black and white'. He shot over weekends, usually blowing his weekly pay packet in the process. After three years of this stop–start production he began 'starting processing some of the footage' and realised 'It was "real" and not in a charming way either.'

CASTING: Craig Hamann was a friend of Tarantino's from his acting class at Beverly Hills' Acting Shelter. He later directed *Boogie Boy* (1997). Allen Garfield was one of their teachers. He appeared in *Beverly Hills Cop II* (Tony Scott, 1986), *The Majestic* (Frank Darabont, 2002) amongst many other films and TV shows and later worked with Tarantino in *Destiny Turns on the Radio* (Jack Baran, 1995). Crystal Shaw went on to write and star in *Have a Periwinkle Day* (Laurence Barbera, 1998) which won awards at New York film festivals.

RECURRING ELEMENTS: The 'I'd fuck Elvis' speech as eventually used in *True Romance* was originally written for this project. The idea of hiring a call girl for a single friend also recurs in *True Romance*. There's a martial arts showdown between Mickey and Clifford that could be seen to, very loosely, pre-figure *Kill Bill*.

SPURIOUS INTERTEXTUALITY: Posters for *The Fury* (Brian De Palma, 1978), *Sisters* (Brian De Palma, 1973), *Black Oak Conspiracy* (Bob Kelljan, 1977) and *The Ninth Configuration* (William Peter Blatty, 1980) are seen. Misty's choice of profession (call girl) is said to have been inspired by De Palma's *Dressed to Kill* (1980). De Palma is discussed at length and called a 'genius'. Elvis Presley's limited abilities as an actor are pilloried.

MUSICAL NOTES: The Sweet's 'Ballroom Blitz' is heard. It was a US and UK top five hit in 1973. Tarantino intended to use it for the torture and murder of Marvin Nash in *Reservoir Dogs* but opted for another track instead.

AVAILABILITY ISSUES: Amateur, incomplete and never released, Tarantino's celebrity has ensured that copies are often 'offered' on the internet.

FINAL COMMENT: 'I worked on it for three and a half years' Tarantino was once moved to comment, and when he edited it together 'I didn't have what I thought I had'. However, he considers the process he went through making *My Best Friend's Birthday* to be essential to his evolution as a filmmaker and dramatist. 'I was able to look at it in a realistic way . . . after being horribly depressed for a little bit.' By the end of it he knew how to make a film even though he'd not actually wound up with a film at the end of the process of trying to make one. Next time, he knew he'd be able to do it properly.

Quentin's Novel . . .

Tarantino never intended to become a screenwriter-for-hire in Hollywood, always only intending to write films for himself to direct as he saw – and sees – himself as a director, not a writer, first and foremost. Since his breakthrough with *Reservoir Dogs* he's never written a screenplay for another director to shoot, although he has performed uncredited 'script doctoring' duties on a small number of movies. *True Romance*, *Natural Born Killers* and *From Dusk Till Dawn* all pre-date, in their original forms, the production of *Reservoir Dogs*. The first two were written by Tarantino for himself to direct and the latter was work-for-hire written to fund *Reservoir Dogs*; Tarantino later chose not to direct them because they were all written to be his first film and having made his first film in *Reservoir Dogs* they no longer held any interest for him as a director. Tarantino has also often said that if he really considered himself a writer rather than a director he would write novels, not screenplays. What he's said less often is that at a point in the late 1980s when he felt that he would never get a filmmaking career off the ground he did contemplate writing a novel and attempting to sell that, reasoning that in order to create a finished novel all a writer needed was a pencil and some paper, not a budget from backers. Inspired by 'All my friends will be strangers' by Larry McMurtry he set out to write a novel about his years working at Video Archives. He spent several months drafting and redrafting the first two chapters of the book before abandoning it to write more spec-screenplays for his putative directorial debut, realising that, while the idea of being a novelist appealed, he was fundamentally a filmmaker, even if he was as of yet one who hadn't made any films.

Sundance Institute Film Lab Reservoir Dogs (1991)

Written and Directed by Quentin Tarantino

DEVELOPMENT: Shot on video with a small cast this short (just over eleven and half minutes) consists of two scenes from Tarantino's then work-in-progress screenplay for what became his debut feature. The first scene is the meeting between Larry/Mr White and Joe which would serve, reshot in the completed film, as the 'Mr White' flashback. It details how Mr White becomes involved in Joe's planned heist and establishes the relationship between them. In a more traditional script it could easily be the opening scene of a motion picture and its positioning as such in the short version makes sense. It's an instantly engaging conversation and given that it's a scene in which a great deal of information is presented it does feel like an opening. No audience is going to be alienated or put off by it. Given the other limitations afforded to the piece, this is an obvious advantage. This version of Mr White's and Joe's conversation also contains dialogue which isn't present in the film as released, including a discussion of the power of Sylvia Plath's (frankly, magnificent) 1963 novella *The Bell Jar*.

The second scene in the piece is a version of the argument that, in the completed film, Mr White and Mr Pink have at the lock-up shortly before Mr Blonde arrives. In this version Buscemi delivers dialogue that belongs, in the finished film, to Mr Pink and he addresses a character played by Tarantino himself as Mr White. This, coupled with Buscemi's role in the previous section, suggests either that names and plot functions for all the characters weren't nailed down at this stage or that the scenes were done so that the best available actors got to say the most dialogue (Buscemi is the best actor here, by far, and he gets the most to say and do).

KEY SHOTS: Even with the aforementioned strictures placed on Tarantino by the small number of scenes he shot and the small number of actors available to him, the would-be director's skill at creating involving, noticeably showy camera set-ups which nevertheless mesh thematically with the underlying sense of the action taking place is already in evidence. A good, early example is the effect of sunlight streaking into the small room in which Joe and Larry meet. This is impressively achieved with a stage-lighting pattern that suggests the presence of an absent set wall and window.

In the second scene shot, the camera is initially placed on the floor and the viewer sees a pair of boots walking from left to right and back again in extreme close-up, while the 'real' meat of the scene – a discussion between Buscemi and an injured man (in the finished film this character would be Mr Orange) – is taking place in the extreme background, almost out of sight. Later, as Tarantino and Buscemi's characters move into the lavatory area of the lock-up the camerawork becomes even more inventive. For most of their, increasingly fraught, discussion, the camera lurks in a low position while the actors converse in front of a mirror with Tarantino and Buscemi both visible in the glass. The audience's focus is pointedly drawn to the reflection of one and the actual other. At no point do we see the 'real' Buscemi and the 'real' Tarantino in the same shot. It's always the 'real' one and the image of the other in the glass. While they're always in the same shot they're never on the same plane. Visually this emphasises their isolation from each other and the atmosphere of mistrust engendered between the two of them.

This isolation is further emphasised by the next camera set-up. The two actors walk outside to smoke and the camera is once again positioned on the floor. This time it's pointing to the door of the building they are in. Buscemi remains centred in the far back of the shot, Tarantino walking out of shot so that Buscemi can talk to him as he stands off camera.

SPURIOUS INTERTEXUALITY: During the Mr White and Joe conversation there is a reference to a female thief called Alabama, a character from a then unmade Tarantino script which would eventually become *True Romance*. Mr White has previously worked with Alabama, but says that the two of them stopped collaborating on crimes because a man and a woman can only work together for so long if they aren't a couple. The reference makes it into the theatrical version of *Reservoir Dogs* but, thanks to alterations made to the screenplay of *True Romance*, the events it refers to never occur (see **True Romance**).

It seems inconceivable that, given how much of this short version of *Reservoir Dogs* takes place in a lavatory, Tarantino wasn't thinking, on some level, of *Psycho* (Alfred Hitchcock, 1960), famously the first American film in which a toilet is seen to be flushed on screen.

'I KNOW EVERYONE THINKS I'M A CHUMP, BUT THEY'RE WRONG AND I'M RIGHT': At one point in this short Buscemi's character says the above line. It's dialogue that doesn't make it into the version of *Reservoir Dogs* that got to cinemas but it's the most striking line in the short. There's an almost palpable sense, in Buscemi's delivery, that he's channelling Tarantino's ambition as he speaks. The would-be director is absolutely sure of himself and his destiny. This sudden intrusion of accidental subtext is just one of the many striking moments in the short *Dogs* which remains an absolutely fascinating glimpse at a work in progress from a talent on the rise.

Reservoir Dogs (1992)

LIVE America Inc. Presents
A Lawrence Bender Production
In Association with Monte Hellman and Richard N Gladstein
Casting: Ronnie Yeskel, CSA
Music Supervisor: Karyn Rachtman
Costume Designer: Betsy Heimann
Editor: Sally Menke
Production Designer: Adrian Wasco
Director of Photography: Andrej Sekula
Co-producer: Harvey Keitel
Executive Producers: Richard N Gladstein, Ronna B Wallace
and Monte Hellman
Produced by Lawrence Bender

TAGLINES: 'Let's go to work.'

'Four perfect killers. One perfect crime. Now all they have to fear is each other.'

'Every dog has his day.'

'Let's get the job done.'

'Five total strangers team up for the perfect crime. They don't know each other's name. But they've got each other's number.'

CAST: Harvey Keitel (Mr White/Larry), Michael Madsen (Mr Blonde/Vic Vega), Chris Penn (Nice Guy Eddie), Steve Buscemi (Mr Pink), Lawrence Tierney (Joe Cabot), Eddie Bunker (Mr Blue), Quentin Tarantino (Mr Brown), Tim Roth (Mr Orange/Freddie Newendyke), Randy Brooks (Holdaway), Kirk Baltz (Marvin Nash), Rich Turner (Sheriff #1), Steven Wright (Radio Host), David Steen (Sheriff #2), Tony Cosmo (Sheriff #3), Stevo Polyi (Sheriff #4), Michael Sottile (Teddy), Lawrence Bender (Young Cop), Linda Kaye (Shocked Woman), Robert Ruth (Shot Cop), Suzanne Celeste (Shot Woman)

DEVELOPMENT: By early 1991 Quentin Tarantino was attempting to gain funding for a movie script entitled *Reservoir Dogs*. This was an on-spec self-penned screenplay which he had written in longhand and on a manual typewriter in just under a month. The finished script was touted to possible financiers and backers as a putative writing/directing debut. By this time Tarantino had already abandoned two earlier self-penned scripts, entitled *True Romance* and *Natural Born Killers* respectively, as too expensive to make on the kind of funds he felt he could realistically acquire. He eventually chose to sell them to other hands in order to provide some of the capital necessary to produce his third screenplay as an extremely low-budget independent picture (which he estimated he could make for $30,000 in a garage, shooting on super-16 mm film, should he absolutely have to). Some additional funds had also come his way through a work-for-hire assignment turning a Robert Kurtzmann outline, provisionally entitled *From Dusk Till Dawn*, into a screenplay draft at the behest of Scott Spiegel. Spiegel was a writer and director whom Tarantino admired and whom he'd met through a mutual contact. Spiegel had been impressed by *Natural Born Killers* in particular and introduced Tarantino – whom he believed was so talented it bordered on unbelievable that he was not making movies already – to producer Lawrence Bender. Bender had produced Spiegel's own first movie *Intruder* (1988), a terrific, small-scale horror movie set entirely in a grocery store which cost a paltry $100,000 to make. Bender and Tarantino immediately hit it off and together formed their first company Dog Eat Dog in order to produce *Reservoir Dogs*. Bender was, at this time, attending an acting class that was taught by a relation of the actress Lily Parker. Parker was, like Harvey Keitel, a member of the Actor's Studio in New York. Keitel was a former shoe salesman, soldier and court stenographer who had appeared in an extraordinary number of films in his career, including *Who's That Knocking at My Door?* (Martin Scorsese, 1968),

The Duellists (Ridley Scott, 1977) and *Mean Streets* (Martin Scorsese, 1973). He had also been Quentin Tarantino's favourite actor since childhood. Bender successfully managed to get a copy of Tarantino's screenplay to Keitel through this convoluted linked sequence of people. Keitel was so impressed by the screenplay he read (he later called it a 'well-written piece [that] deals with issues of betrayal, trust and instinct') and so seized by the desire to play Mr White, that he agreed to come aboard the film. It was a move which, as he knew it would, greatly assisted Tarantino and Bender in their search for funding. After the many years that Tarantino had spent trying to break into filmmaking the turnaround on this project was almost alarmingly fast. The script, with Keitel's name attached, was read by Richard Gladstein of LIVE America Inc. who was principally intrigued by the idea of making a film with Keitel in the cast. He liked the screenplay, met with Tarantino and Bender, and six months after Tarantino's completion of the first draft of his script he was shooting the film. For Keitel's help in getting the project off the ground and his enormous participation in the process of casting other actors for the film he also received a co-producer credit.

SCREENPLAY: 'I came up with the idea of having a heist film where you never actually see the heist,' said Tarantino when asked about his inspiration for *Reservoir Dogs*, adding that in it 'everything that can go wrong, goes wrong'. It's a great line, a bold inspiration for a screenplay and a decent 'high concept' summary of the film's essence, but, of course, the screenplay itself is more complex than that.

In terms of technique, *Reservoir Dogs* – the first Tarantino screenplay produced but not the first written – depends on four central strands that would come to be considered hallmarks of his writing, even though they stand in brute defiance to the 'realism' Tarantino's scripts have been accused of. These four techniques are, in roughly ascending order of importance: the dramatic monologue, the very long, slow scene, the sudden dramatic reversal of tone and a generally anti-chronological structure. These techniques are so linked in Tarantino's style of screenwriting that dealing with them entirely separately isn't terribly practical. They all impact on each other too much. However, to start with the last of those, *Reservoir Dogs*'s plot would – if written down in chronological order – look like this:

1. Joe and Eddie Cabot assemble a gang, the members of which are unknown to each other, to do a jewellery store heist.

2. An underground policeman is trained to, and succeeds in, getting into said gang.

3. The gang, including Joe and Eddie, meet to plan the robbery. They remain anonymous to each other responding to colour-coded names.

4. The robbery ends in a bloodbath, partially because the police are lying in wait and partially because one of the gang, Mr Blonde, cracks under pressure and begins killing people for fun. Some of the gang (and many civilians and police) are killed; others of the group escape.

5. Mr White and Mr Orange – who is also the underground cop – flee to the pre-arranged warehouse rendezvous point where they meet Mr Pink. Mr Orange is unconscious, Mr White and Mr Pink quarrel over whether they were set up or not and if so, who by.

6. Mr Blonde arrives at the rendezvous. He has a policeman as a hostage.

7. Nice Guy Eddie arrives at the warehouse, learning that Mr Pink has stashed a bag of jewels. When Eddie, Mr White and Mr Pink leave to get the stash, Mr Blonde tortures the cop for fun. Mr Orange kills Mr Blonde to save his colleague.

8. Nice Guy Eddie, Mr Pink and Mr White return and Eddie kills the cop that Mr Blonde has tortured in order to demonstrate how unimportant he is and tells Mr Orange that he doesn't believe Mr Orange's (admittedly false) story about how Mr Blonde intended to kill them all and run away with all of the loot.

9. Joe Cabot arrives and announces that Mr Orange is the rat, an undercover cop. Mr White protests that this cannot be true and draws a gun on Cabot when Cabot goes to shoot Mr Orange. Eddie defends his father but both Cabots are killed by Mr White who is also badly wounded. Mr Pink runs away.

10. The police arrive and Mr Orange tells Mr White that he is a cop. Mr White kills Mr Orange and the police kill Mr White.

This is the order that the scenes are in in the picture: 3.3; 4.4; 5.1; 4.3; 5.2; 6.1; 1.1; 7.1; 7.2; 7.3; 2.1; 2.2; 2.3; 2.4; 2.5; 2.6; 2.7; 4.1; 3.1; 2.6; 3.2; 4.1; 8; 9; 10.

Interestingly this is not as non-chronological as a first-time audience might initially assume. There are large stretches of the picture (the whole sequence of 2.1–2.7 and the earlier 7.1–7.3, for example) that do occur in what could be considered normal chronological order. What this clearly illustrates is that the film isn't non-linear for the sake of it, it's non-linear in order to advance its characters and plot. It's non-linear in order to achieve specific, desired effects. One of these is the advanced disorientation of the audience; Tarantino is, as screenwriter and director, a great showman who once opined 'There's no problem in [the audience] being confused if you feel you're in safe hands.' He wants the audience to acquire only information he wants them to have and only in the order he wants them to receive it. This 'answers first, questions later' approach is key to the *Reservoir Dogs* script. It allows us, for example, to get to know and understand what we think the Mr White/Mr

Orange relationship is before we discover that Mr Orange is an undercover policeman. It creates possibilities for manipulation of the audience's sympathies and responses that simply aren't there in an entirely linear narrative.

To deal with the idea of the long, slow scene: conventional screenwriting wisdom holds that no scene should – except in exceptional circumstances – last longer than three minutes. In *Reservoir Dogs* scenes which last longer than three minutes are the norm rather than the exception. Tarantino sustains these long scenes in two principal ways (indeed these two techniques are the reason the scenes are so long). One is that the many monologues in these long scenes work through a particular idea or point thoroughly and from numerous angles, almost as an essay might. The second is that these long, talky scenes, thanks to the non-chronological structure, are able, at their end, to cut backwards and forwards in time to other scenes featuring the same characters but in dramatically different situations.

The audience can plunge from comedy to drama to violence and back again with alarming frequency. The extensive use of declamatory dialogue (you might even term it rhetoric) is useful in that it can create a particular mood that the shock transitions the structure makes possible are then able to disrupt. It can also engage an audience to the point where the disruption is even more shocking than it would have been otherwise.

Here the audience sees how the anti-chronological structure, the long scene and the sudden change of tone can all work together to totally confound an audience or – and this is even more impressive – astound them not by creating confusion but by dispelling it. The best example of the three working together comes when Mr Orange guns down Mr Blonde in order to save Marvin Nash's life. The audience don't expect it. The bullets themselves are actually a shock to the audience. The audience is almost immediately cut away from this scene – the long scene of Mr Blonde torturing Marvin – to another long scene as they begin to learn about Mr Orange's past. The sequence being cut into will contain one of Tarantino's longest monologues (the 'marijuana drought of 1986' story) and also some of his most virtuoso directorial tricks (see **KEY SHOTS**). The sequence cut *from* also contains a very fine example of the kind of dramatic reversal of tone which doesn't depend on the anti-chronological structure of the film's screenplay, although this is more a directorial matter than something strictly relating to the screenplay (see **KEY SHOTS**).

What is particularly extraordinary about the placing of these scenes, the Mr Orange sequences, in this place and at this time is that they force the audience to recontextualise and reassess the scenes viewed up to this point. After the Mr Orange flashbacks the audiences have gone from knowing about as much as Mr White does to knowing more than Mr White. He has gone from being the closest the audience has to an identification figure to someone they regard with pity – because he's so very wrong about what has transpired. Not only that, the audience look on him with a little bit more dread thanks to the revelations in the discontinuous scenes of what he is capable of ('break his nose with the butt of your gun', 'cut off one of his fingers'). It also allows the audience to come to an understanding of Mr White's finer qualities, his loyalty and compassion, before they see him indiscriminately slaughtering policemen. Despite these horrors it is Mr White's good points that stay in the audience's memory longest – just as the dramatist intended. When asked about using a non-chronological structure in his films in 1994 Tarantino told his interviewer that if he had written *Reservoir Dogs* or *Pulp Fiction* as novels this would never have become an issue. 'You would never bring it up . . . novelists have always had . . . complete freedom to tell their story any way they saw fit' and that both *Reservoir Dogs* and *Pulp Fiction* gained 'a lot more resonance being told in this kind of . . . way'.

To return to the subject of monologue in slightly more detail, even without descending into pop psychology it's easy to see how a dramatic screenwriting style in which characters declaim at one another, explain theories and detail plans at inordinate length without being interrupted would evolve in the mind of Quentin Tarantino as an exceptionally intelligent young man trapped working in retail. Monologues such as the one about 'Like a Virgin' or on the deconstruction of tipping have a real feel of being personal pet theories worked out by Tarantino while working behind a counter. Although their verisimilitude may come from Tarantino's skill at creating dialogue for his characters.

Those two monologues mentioned above are in one sequence, the opening scene in the diner. One single scene has two of the most memorable exchanges of 90s film in it. To take these in reverse order, in the latter Mr Pink successfully deconstructs the institution of tipping waiting staff. Initially accused of taking this position because he's mean, Mr Pink provides a dizzying barrage of reasons why he's right. This discussion is also a demonstration of Mr White's compassion as he argues that waitresses are poorly paid and depend on their tips, and that waitressing is the number-one job for female non-college graduates in the United States, the one job any woman can do in order to make a living. Mr Pink dismisses these with another barrage of reasons, ultimately blaming society and federal tax law for waitresses's situations. What this discussion says about Mr Pink is that he defers, and will not accept, *any* responsibility for anything and any action not directly committed by himself – as he basically later admits when arguing with Mr White after they both arrive at the warehouse.

Mr Brown's commentary on Madonna and the meaning of the song is of a different character entirely because the knowledge it contains has no demonstrable real-world content or effect. It's clever, but also entirely trivial. It is also very hard, as it is with the Roger Avary penned deconstruction of *Top Gun* (Tony Scott, 1986) that Tarantino later performed in the film *Sleep With Me* (see p.77), to dismiss the reading Tarantino's Mr Brown babbles out. Any glance at the lyrics written down would support it more or less entirely. What's surprising about the scene is, cleverly, not that it's shocking but that it's incredibly obvious that that's what the song means but that it took Tarantino to point it out. That Chris Penn, present throughout the scene as the yet unnamed Nice Guy Eddie, was once Madonna's brother-in-law, just makes the whole thing even more fun.

This scene is not just about these two rhetorical exchanges though. It also establishes the other characters, the ones who don't get the big speeches but who are much more important in the film to come (itself a small, yet cunning, bait and switch). The scene establishes the closeness of Mr White's relationship with Joe by defining it against his largely non-existent relationship with Mr Blonde. Mr White says, with a combination of humour and ill-concealed menace, to Mr Blonde that if he shoots him 'in a dream' he 'better wake up and apologise for it'. Yet he himself jokes about shooting Joe, to Joe's face and Joe doesn't comment on it at all. Mr Blonde generally keeps quiet. This is so that the first-time audience has a less clear idea of him than the other, now dead, characters do when Mr Pink and Mr White begin to discuss him at the warehouse two scenes later. The audience can't remember Mr Blonde clearly but they feel they *should* be able to, as it seems from Mr White and Mr Pink's conversation he's a horrifically memorable personality. This just builds up the anticipation for his eventual re-appearance. An appearance that, thanks to Michael Madsen's crackerjack performance, doesn't disappoint. (When Mr Blonde finally does appear, it's another, albeit smaller, example of Tarantino's reversals of expectation. Traditionally someone bringing in a hostage would bring in a hostage, not turn up, fight, eat, shout, bitch, moan and then tease his comrades with the idea that he has a gift for them, a gift which later turns out to be the hostage cop. It's unorthodox in script terms but completely in character for Mr Blonde, which is what makes it so very good.)

In summary, the whole of the opening scene in the diner is engaging, funny, distinctive and gives the audience an enormous amount of information. As opening scenes go, it's a triumph. And then? The audience are into the first, but not the last, of Tarantino's shock transitions and changes of mood as the sound fades up on Mr Orange screaming as he bleeds to death in the back of a stolen car.

The screenplay's good qualities are not restricted to Tarantino's signature unorthodoxies, however. He also makes very careful use of language in his dialogue. Words seem specifically, even exactly, chosen for their precise meaning. There doesn't appear to be a word wasted and every word has significance. That Joe Cabot calls his colour-coded robberies 'capers' tells the audience something about his slightly contemptuous attitude to the men he employs and how – despite his protestations to the contrary – the fact that he deals with them at a distance means that the robberies aren't quite as serious a matter to him as they are to his men. Equally his use of the term 'broads' to mockingly describe his (male) employees shows the audience that he is from a different era (it's antiquated slang) and that he regards emasculating someone through language as a way of restoring order.

The absolutely key word for the film and several of its protagonists however is 'professional'. It's bandied around like candy for much of the picture, particularly in the first half with more than one character saying 'Am I the only professional?' and Mr Pink bellowing 'What you're supposed to do is act like a fucking professional' to Mr White when he thinks his behaviour falls below a certain standard. (Steve Buscemi summed his character, Mr Pink, up as someone who 'likes what he does, does it well, tries to go about it in the most professional way he can'.) The use of this word 'professional' is interesting because it allows the characters to express pride in their work and behaviour without forcing Tarantino to condone the 'honour amongst thieves' cliché in his script. The audience can appreciate, thanks to this word, that these are people who have standards of behaviour, and ideal ways of going about their work – they aren't ciphers and they aren't distressed by their life of crime. For some 'professional' may mean doing something by a specific deadline or achieving a certain amount of 'work done'. The word 'professional' allows the characters' moral senses to function on a scale recognisable to the audience and also allows the audience to see the falsity of the criminal lives these people have constructed for themselves when the situation collapses into recrimination, counter-accusations and mass slaughter. The badge of 'professionalism' is merely a self-deluding cover, one which is necessary to someone like Mr White so that he can distinguish himself from Mr Blonde, who genuinely disgusts him. They might be tough guys, they might all consider themselves professionals but they can't cope with the desperation and disorientation that this one really bad day brings to them; and in a sense, that's almost the point of the film.

The question of moral centre is itself interestingly handled. Mr Orange who is – from society's point of view – rightly the hero of the piece is the villain to all the other speaking characters. The betrayer is the man trying to do good. The characters who insist they treat each other with respect and professionally are – even the best of them – murderous and selfish to the point of near sociopathy.

Mr Blonde is a stone-cold psycho, the most despicable man in a film full of despicable men. However, he's also the one member of the gang that Eddie can trust because he's just done four years inside. It is Eddie's greater knowledge of Mr Blonde's recent history that means he can be absolutely 100 per cent certain that Mr Orange is the traitor even before his father arrives and announces that this is his verdict also. This is interesting because, as we see in the Mr Blonde character scenes, Vic Vega (Mr Blonde's real name) is only involved in the robbery at Eddie's suggestion; a suggestion that is made directly contrary to, and in violation of, his father's edict that people that they both know well should not be involved in the 'colour-coded' jobs that they are planning. Had Nice Guy Eddie not known Mr Blonde so well he may have believed Mr Orange's story. Had someone other than Vic Vega been Mr Blonde then not only would Mr Blonde not have tortured Marvin Nash nor shot up the place during the robbery, but Eddie would not have been in a position to be certain of Mr Orange's guilt. Eddie's certainty comes from him breaking his own rules just as Joe using Mr Orange in one of the colour-coded jobs goes against his own. The situation is its own destruction; like any tragedy, and that is ultimately what *Reservoir Dogs* is, only a very small change has to be made to the chain of events to make the outcome so different as to be inconceivable.

Other words in the script that seem precisely picked are the characters' code names. Joe may insist that the colour-coded names he allocates to his employees have no special significance beyond guaranteeing anonymity, and maybe they don't, to him, but in the context of the piece as drama, Tarantino's choice is as significant as, say, George Lucas calling his loner 'Solo'.

Larry is 'Mr White' and he is the 'purest': the character who is exactly who he says he is, never lies and always does as he says he will. Equally, there's obviously something wrong with Mr Blonde from the off. Blonde isn't a colour in the sense that pink, brown or blue are. 'Orange' is the colour of warning on traffic lights. As Joe says at the end, 'I should have my fucking head examined for going forward when I wasn't one hundred per cent'. You don't go forward on an orange light unless you're absolutely certain. Pink is also, while not exactly 'queer' in the American political sense, certainly the least macho of the main characters, the effete, nervy one – a characterisation that's virtually shorthand for homosexuality in Golden Age Hollywood film.

There's also the distinct possibility within the film that Mr Pink is a homosexual. Unlike the other characters he never makes casually lecherous comments about women and when he asks why he's called Mr Pink and Joe says 'Because you're a faggot', he looks embarrassed and irritated, but he doesn't deny it, get angry or fight back. Is this the whole reason he's uncomfortable with this nom-de-guerre in the first place? He's certainly quick to dismiss the ensuing conversation, desperate to 'move on . . . forget it, it's beneath me'.

Highly noticeable is the use of homophobic and racist language. These twin evils of modern society or rather the phraseology associated with them, occur often in Tarantino's screenplays. This is not to suggest that Tarantino is himself a homophobe or a racist. The use of the word 'nigger' in *Reservoir Dogs* is reserved more or less exclusively for the most negative characters. Certainly Mr Orange never says it even while undercover – and the whole aspect partially has the sting taken out of it by Mr Orange's superior officer in the LAPD being played (superbly) by black actor Randy Brooks.

Far more salient is the repeated use of homophobic terminology by, in particular, Mr Blonde and Eddie – for example 'If I was a butt cowboy I wouldn't even throw you to the posse.' Ultimately though the reasoning behind, and excuse for, this is exactly the same as the above. Mr Blonde is a sentimental sociopath and when unconscionable things are said in fiction it matters a great deal less if they're said by characters who do many other unconscionable things too. The topic of racism would prove controversial later on in Tarantino's career.

There are, to be completely honest, a couple of moments in the screenplay which just don't work, but they are tiny. The line, given to Mr Orange, 'I swear on my mother's eternal soul' just doesn't work. It's a bit too hysterical, and Tim Roth struggles to deliver it. That the audience knows that Mr Orange is lying, and that this is a rare invocation of something 'spiritual', makes this uncomfortable viewing for the wrong reasons; it isn't very good. The other moment that doesn't work is the joke, in the 'Mr White' establishing scenes, where Mr White asks Joe where the diamonds are being shipped and then deadpans 'No they're not' when told. What he means, of course, is that they will never reach there because they're going to be stolen, but again the actors (Tierney and Keitel) struggle to make it. For a screenplay to contain only two kinks, and for them to be this small, is in itself an enormous achievement.

The main techniques of Tarantino's screenwriting style are presented to the audience in their complete form in this, his first publicly available work. The later release of *True Romance* and the (arguably butchered) *Natural Born Killers* wouldn't so much damage Tarantino's reputation as a screenwriter as make his work seem almost so common as to be commonplace. The fact that they are, for all their fine qualities, juvenilia when compared to *Dogs* didn't really help. But none of this takes away from the *Dogs* screenplay itself. With its anti-linear plot development that fluctuates between shock/action and leisure/rhetoric, its use of monologues to create or relieve plot tension while examining character and working through thematic points and its long, long scenes, it's an idiosyncratic, and ultimately massively influential, triumph.

CASTING: Considering that it's a cheaply shot ensemble piece requiring a small number of skilled actors to perform roles perhaps more akin to characters created for a theatrical production than a screenplay, *Reservoir Dogs*'s casting is surprisingly starry and impressively eclectic. In the small but significant role of Joe Cabot, Tarantino felt he was lucky to get Lawrence Tierney. Tierney had starred in numerous films, mostly in tough guy roles or as anti-heroic leads. Films in which Tierney played such roles include *Dillinger* (Max Nosseck, 1945) and the film noir classic *Born to Kill* (Robert Wise, 1947) although other, less well-remembered, projects saw him diversify slightly. For example, *Step by Step* (Phil Rosen, 1946) finds him as a square-jawed marine fighting Nazis and *San Quentin* (Gordon Douglas, 1946) places him

at the centre of a PR-heavy, redemptive tale which also
functions as a eulogy of the United States penal system.
Tierney also had a colourful personal history having done
time in prison and struggled with alcohol problems, both of
which had a negative impact on his career as an actor. In the
1980s he'd played – in a wickedly ironic piece of casting – a
recurring role as a police sergeant in the latter years of *Hill
Street Blues* (1986–7). He'd also appeared as a mob boss in a
1940s pastiche episode of *Star Trek: The Next Generation*
entitled 'The Big Goodbye'. Almost immediately before
Reservoir Dogs he'd made a remarkable comic appearance in
Seinfeld, playing regular character Elaine Benes's
idiosyncratic author father in 'The Jacket'. Producer Larry
David loved his performance but the cast and crew found him
so difficult to work with he was never asked back to the
show; Tarantino had similar issues with Tierney on set. While
he, and his entire cast and crew, became very fond of the
actor – and all talk glowingly of him personally – Tarantino
was also prompted to comment, 'he personally challenges the
entire concept of filmmaking . . . he's insane . . . he's that far
from a nervous breakdown' when asked about him on-set.

As Cabot's son Eddie, Tarantino cast Chris Penn who had
been part of the ensemble cast of Francis Ford Coppola's
Rumble Fish (1983) and appeared in *Mobsters* (Michael
Karbelnikoff, 1991). Penn had actually watched Tierney's
film *The Devil Thumbs a Ride* (Felix E Feist, 1947) on
television a few days before being cast and had found
himself idly wondering what happened to the actor who
would, unbeknownst to him, shortly be cast as his onscreen
father. Importantly, Penn and Tierney do look like they
could be father and son; it's an obvious aesthetic
consideration that surprisingly few movie directors and
casting agents pay attention to (and one that Tarantino
would seem to forget himself when being cast as George
Clooney's brother in *From Dusk Till Dawn*).

Michael Madsen, cast in the key role of Mr Blonde, had
had a chequered career path working as a hospital orderly,

in a petrol station and doing a lot of small, low-budget movies and guest appearances in episodes of popular television series such as *St Elsewhere* (1983) and *Quantum Leap* (1989) although the immediately pre-*Reservoir Dogs* period saw strong performances from him in *Thelma & Louise* (Ridley Scott, 1991) and *The Doors* (Oliver Stone, 1991). 'I never read anything like it . . . I never saw anything like it before' was his comment on the *Reservoir Dogs* screenplay, although he acknowledged that he could see the film's roots, commenting on the resemblance to films like *The Killing* (Stanley Kubrick, 1956). Madsen was friends with the reformed ex-con, turned crime novelist and screenwriter Eddie Bunker. Bunker had worked on the screenplay to *Runaway Train* (Andrei Konchalovsky, 1985) and his novel *No Beast So Fierce* had been turned into the movie *Straight Time* (Ulu Grosbard, 1978) starring Dustin Hoffman. Bunker was cast by Tarantino after a single phone conversation.

The process of casting Brit Tim Roth was lengthier and even more obscurantist. Roth, who had starred in *Rosencrantz and Guildenstern are Dead* (Tom Stoppard, 1990) and *Vincent and Theo* (Robert Altman, 1990) initially refused to read for Tarantino, citing his earnest belief that he was always terrible in read-throughs rather than ego as the reason for his refusal. The two men met in the Coach & Horse pub on Sunset Boulevard to discuss the role and proceeded to get very drunk in each other's company. By 2 a.m. the next day Roth was sufficiently drunk to agree to read for Tarantino who, equally drunk himself, cast the Englishman on the basis of that reading. Dialogue coach Suzanne Celeste (who also cameos as the woman Mr Orange kills while escaping) was hired to help Roth perfect his LA accent for the film.

Completing the cast was indie film veteran Steve Buscemi. Buscemi had been appearing in independent films for around a decade – including a stellar performance as a man dying of AIDS in Bill Sherwood's *Parting Glances* (1986) – while occasionally drawing mainstream attention for his roles in pictures such as *New York Stories* (Francis Ford Coppola/Woody Allen/Martin Scorsese, 1989), *Miller's Crossing* (Joel Coen, 1990) and *Barton Fink* (Joel Coen, 1991). His role as *Reservoir Dogs*'s sole survivor cemented his position as an actor loved by film fans everywhere, always noticeable, enjoyable and interesting even when acting in the smallest roles. Other films graced by Buscemi's presence include *Things To Do In Denver When You're Dead* (Gary Fleder, 1995), *Fargo* (Joel Coen, 1996), *Ghostworld* (Terry Zwigoff, 2002) and his own directorial debut *Trees Lounge* (1996).

QUOTES:

Mr Pink: 'The words "too fucking busy" shouldn't be in a waitress's vocabulary.'

Mr Pink: 'The world's smallest violin playing just for the waitresses.'

Mr Pink: 'Someone stuck a hot poker up our ass and I want to know whose name is on the handle.'

Mr Blonde: 'Eddie, you keeping talking like a bitch I'm going to slap you like a bitch.'

KEY SHOTS: The film is shot in widescreen in a ratio of 2:35, which is unusual for a film of its budget at that time. When questioned about his choice Tarantino said he thought that widescreen 'was perfect for this movie', opining that contrary to popular belief that widescreen was only good for epics and spectaculars, it in fact made 'things more intimate . . . it's so big and takes you so close. It takes you inside the people, inside their space.' He enjoyed the fact that a close-up in widescreen has, by definition, two thirds of the screen empty, feeling that this increased intimacy and decreased the distance between the audience and the characters rather than the reverse. Certainly few viewers can ever have felt 'pushed away' from the characters while watching *Reservoir Dogs* although conversely audiences don't feel all that close to them either. The camera takes the audience into the characters' space as Tarantino says, but it doesn't go quite as close as it's physically capable of doing. The Reservoir Dogs are 'enjoyable guys to watch from a distance' said Michael Madsen in a contemporary interview – and the camera seems to understand this, spending a lot of time hanging back and allowing the actors to be seen, full length, in a variety of lurking mid-shots.

Reservoir Dogs establishes a lot of what audiences would come to think of as 'trademark' Tarantino directorial elements. These range from the obvious (36 minutes in, there is a shot of the camera looking out of the boot of a car – something Tarantino has returned to frequently throughout his career) to the somewhat less immediately noticeable (extraordinary use of sound effects).

Key to Tarantino's directorial style is the very long take. It could be suggested that using numerous, unbroken long takes is the only way to effectively deal with Tarantino's writing style (which includes many monologues) but that would be erroneous. Robert Rodriguez and Tony Scott would later take far more straightforward, fast-cutting approaches to shooting a Tarantino screenplay (see **True Romance** and **From Dusk Till Dawn**) and keep the writer's worldview intact. Indeed, in *Pulp Fiction*, in the 'Captain Koons' scene (a scene which consists solely of a monologue) Tarantino himself would eschew the single long take in favour of a leisurely cut-together combination of three takes of a not particularly unusual length combined with reaction shots.

Initially, one could argue that Tarantino's use of this long shot has its origins in the very low-budget filmmaking that *Reservoir Dogs* represents. After all Orson Welles's *The Trial* (1963)has been praised for its long impressive takes but many of these were accomplished by Welles out of necessity; he didn't have the time, money or facilities to edit the film in anything like a complex manner. Of course the basic answer as to why Tarantino uses such long takes is discussed in relation to the screenplay: it's part of his directorial 'control' of the audience's emotion, his push-me, pull-me manner of relaying information. The longer a take is the more comfortable the audience gets and the more shocking the escape/release from the comfort becomes.

Take, for example, the opening scene, in which the camera spirals seemingly endlessly around the table in the coffee shop (actually Pat & Lorraine's Coffee Shop, 4720 Eagle Rock Blvd, Eagle Rock, LA, California) as the characters' talk. There are several opportunities for invisible edits in here (when the screen is black because it's focused solely on a character's black-jacketed back). By the end of the scene the audience is completely comfortable with these characters. There is implicit violence in the dialogue but no real suggestion that this is a gang of murderers (and Tarantino the director ignores Tarantino the writer's suggestion that the audience see that one of the Dogs is carrying a gun as they leave). Of course, the spiralling camera movement doesn't last for the whole of this scene (which is about nine minutes long). It couldn't really for purely technical concerns and so the scene moves into more traditional shot/reaction shot formula from about halfway in. If this scene is watched closely it's noticeable that Tim Roth's Mr Orange spends most of his time looking at Mr White, laughs louder at his witticisms than the others do and briefly looks deeply concerned when Mr Blonde jokingly threatens Mr White. He even has his arm around Mr White's chair a lot of the time creating a physical closeness that is an indication of their emotional connection. This is, of course, largely Tim Roth's work, but if he wasn't sitting next to Harvey Keitel it wouldn't be possible for him to work it in, and it's Tarantino's production that places him there and Tarantino's camera that lets the audience see this. (This is also echoed by the immediately following sequence in which Mr Orange has a panic attack in the back of the car he and

Mr White have stolen. There the camera moves freely between Mr Orange and Mr White, bouncing from the front to the back seat with speed and ease; another reflection of the closeness between Mr Orange and Mr White and also the establishment of a physical theme of camera movement that is returned to in a later-seen, earlier-set scene in a car.)

In the lengthy 'Mr Orange' flashback sequence, Tarantino shoots Mr Orange's extended monologue – in which he explains an incident from his past in order to bond with the group – in a defiantly odd, but instantly comprehensible, manner. The monologue begins as Mr Orange reads from a script in his apartment. The anecdote isn't even his originally, he's been given it – written out in script form – by another police officer. It's all part of his cover. Initially Mr Orange is seen in his home, drifting in and out of shot, repeating, rehearsing, learning the script he's been given. He then wanders out of shot, and into a different scene, but he continues the sentence he was speaking as he walked out of the previous scene. He's now talking to Holdaway on the roof of a building; this is obviously, in terms of the film's ostensible objective reality, a different occasion where he's saying the same, or similar, things. Later the monologue moves again, to Mr Orange, Joe, Nice Guy Eddie and Mr White sitting around a table in a bar. This is yet another occasion, a later occasion, where Mr Orange is saying the same thing – the occasion he's been rehearsing for in fact. Not only has the rehearsal paid off, (Mr Orange's story is working), but the tension here is considerable because Tarantino has let the audience know what the gang members do not. As Mr Orange continues the monologue, Tarantino adds even more visual variety by depicting the action of the story-telling as an imaginary flashback. By now Mr Orange is telling the story while appearing to the audience to be standing in the place where it ostensibly took place. But it didn't take place. It's made up. He's making it up. It never happened. The audience is now in some space inside Mr Orange's head as he struggles to make the group believe that this really happened. It's extraordinary and the audience simply understands and accepts it. So confident is Tarantino the director (and his editor Sally Menke deserves equal praise for this) by this point that he can cut in and out of the fantasy, from the telling of the story in the bar to the imagined action of the story, and back again at will. Tarantino then throws in some extra touches. Firstly, the dog barking in slow motion at Mr Orange and the deafening sound of the hand drier (which sounds more an aircraft engine being switched on than a lavatorial appliance). It's real showmanship from Tarantino and extraordinarily ambitious for a small-scale directorial debut from an unknown filmmaker.

There are other clever directorial moments in *Reservoir Dogs*, albeit none as virtuoso. For example all the flashback scenes which establish the characters take place in the same location, Joe's office, but each one is shot in a completely different way in order to emphasise the nature of each of the protagonists' relationship with Joe Cabot. For example in the 'Mr Blonde' sequence the camera starts outside the office and then, as Mr Blonde walks into the room in order to meet with Joe for the first time in four years, the camera drifts into the scene, into his office, into their mutual confidence. By lurking outside earlier it emphasises the years of their forced estrangement, while by charging in after him and then remaining in the office throughout the scene it emphasises their closeness. This is completely different to the 'Mr White' flashback, where the camera stays tight in and close throughout Mr White's and Joe's conversation, representing their professional trust and obvious affinity but without ever hinting at the almost familial intimacy that the 'Mr Blonde' flashback achieves.

Another technique common in the film is the use of the camera, either in its movements or through cutting, to keep characters physically separate in order to emphasise an emotional or character separation from each other. For example, when the audience sees Joe's gang travelling together in the car the camera is careful to keep Mr Orange out of the communal shot. This is not simply because he's in the back of the car (although he's partially in the back of the car to facilitate this) – Mr Pink manages to be in the communal shot and he's in the back of the car, too. No, it's because Mr Orange is the traitor. The camerawork is reflecting the story's truth that he isn't really part of the group.

This sort of work, the physical separation of characters who are in the same place with camera movement in order to emphasise separation of character, is quite common in the film. When Mr White and Mr Pink have their first long discussion of the film (at the lock-up when Mr White suggests they go to the 'other room' in order to not talk in front of Mr Orange) the camera makes a point of not allowing the audience to see the two men's faces at the same time. They take turns at staring into the mirror and are kept physically apart until they come to some agreement about the events they've just been through. Interestingly in this scene there are bottles containing coloured liquid on the side in the lavatory. The liquids they contain are coloured white, orange and pink with the orange bottles separate from the others, perhaps again a deliberate physical reflection of orange being 'separate', i.e. the police's plant.

Another really important shot, one that is in the sequence which chronologically precedes that one, is Mr Orange's pained face as Mr White kills the policemen in the car. It's not just his pain at the murder that Roth's expression conveys but also the horrible conflict of interest that he suddenly feels as his admiration and genuine affection for Mr White crash into his core values and his duty as a policeman with horrible urgency. This, effective as it is, however, is ultimately just set up for the terrific shot a few minutes later when Mr Orange kills the civilian woman in the car who has just shot him. It's not a long shot but it seems so terribly lingering on Roth's face as he puts his head back on the ground, in emotional as well as physical pain.

Tarantino's camera does just enough to make sure that even the least attentive viewer is suddenly aware of what has happened: a law enforcement officer has committed the murder of a civilian while ostensibly trying to prevent a crime.

The most famous scene in *Reservoir Dogs* is the ear-cutting scene in which Mr Blonde tortures LAPD officer Marvin Nash. A suggestion often made is that the camera's drawing away from Mr Blonde's razor-blade assault on Marvin's ear is a deliberate reference to Michael Powell and Emeric Pressburger's *The Life and Death of Colonel Blimp* (1943). While there does seem to be some similarity (in both, a key event is panned away from rather than shown), Tarantino has stated on a number of occasions that he'd not seen the earlier film when he made *Reservoir Dogs*. It is also true that the 'ear scene' is shot the way it is because the make-up for the severed ear did not prove effective during shooting, but the solution that Tarantino hit on has a touch of inspiration, partially because the shot of the wall accompanied by the sounds of Nash's screaming is a physical, emblematic version of the film's general attitude to violence – it is heard about, through dialogue and sound effects, but the audience very rarely sees it.

This scene also contains two superb examples of Tarantino's ability to disorientate and re-orientate his audience around his wishes. The first is the change of tone caused by the close-up on Marvin Nash's terrified face as Mr Blonde begins to sing and dance badly. Initially this scene, once Eddie and the others leave, is sinister and slightly sick making, but then it becomes funny despite itself thanks to the music and Madsen's miming of shaving himself with his cut-throat razor. This effect is partially achieved by Tarantino not cutting back to Marvin's terrified face. The audience is robbed of the physical evidence of the consequences of Mr Blonde's actions and can start enjoying the comic aspects of Madsen's performance. Then, just as it starts to become *really* funny – thanks to Madsen's deliberately bad dancing (the moment when he spins is hilarious) and comical facial expressions – Mr Blonde slashes Marvin's face with the razor and suddenly it really isn't funny at all, it's gut-tighteningly unpleasant. The rawness of the human emotion presented is the key and the staggering humanity of Baltz's performance as Marsh has not been commented on enough. This is the kind of reversal – indeed reversal on top of reversal – that is created purely through orthodox camera cutting and the performances of the actors.

The very end of this scene is, however, an outstanding example of the kind of reversal only made possible by the film's structure. Just as Mr Blonde is about to set Marvin on fire and the audience is absolutely fixated on this action, Mr Blonde is blown away by Mr Orange's gun. The audience has, by now, almost forgotten about Mr Orange. He hasn't spoken for the best part of an hour and for all they know may now be dead. More, given what has gone before the audience has no reason to think that Mr Orange would murder Mr Blonde to save a policeman's life. The initial audio shock (and the impact of Mr Orange's bullets is primarily due to the sound) and Mr Blonde's leap out of shot, is then emphasised by the camera cutting to show Mr Orange holding his gun outstretched, breathing desperately heavily and then craning around from being in front of him to behind him in one slow swing. It's a crane shot which lasts just long enough for the audience to register what has happened. It's perfectly done.

Ultimately what's really important about Tarantino's directorial style is that it's so defiantly unnaturalistic – the camera has a personality and an involvement in the events it observes. The camera moves, bounces and spirals telling the audience what to look at when and where in a commanding and almost dictatorial way. It's about as far from the static camera naturalism that most people would term 'realism' as you can imagine. People have only called Tarantino's films realistic because they contain blood and implicit violence, and just as there is an erroneous assumption that darkness is more impressive and adult than light and that drama is harder than comedy, because Tarantino's work is visceral people assume it's real. It isn't, it doesn't even seem it, nor does it try to. Even when the psychological truth of a scene is immense, a Quentin Tarantino movie is a movie first and last.

LONDON CALLING: There's a long and noble list of uniquely American things which have been 'broken' and become a successful part of mainstream culture through their popularity in Great Britain and, more specifically, in London. It's a roll of honour that runs from Jimi Hendrix to the White Stripes and beyond.

This is, largely, because it's easier to create a buzz in a single city that is the undisputed centre of the country that it's the capital of, although it's not entirely hubristic to suggest there is an element of distinctive discernment to London's media zeitgeist that allows it, collectively, to make wise choices about what to elevate to premier cultural status.

Reservoir Dogs is not, however, something that was a hit in Britain before it was a hit in America. What it is, is something that was initially a bigger hit in Britain than it had been in the country which produced it. London was the first place that *Reservoir Dogs* was 'the number one film'. Not an indie hit, not a cult film, not a big film, but the biggest film out there. As Tarantino himself said, coming to London for the second time, he knew what it must have been like to be the Beatles.

Tarantino felt that the British reaction was, in part, a reaction to the 'fairytale' nature of his success – his journey from video-store clerk to the writer–director behind the country's number-one movie. In this he was probably correct, although his subsequent statement that this was partially a reaction to the wonder of the 'American Dream' as opposed to the very stratified, class-bound society of Britain is as capricious as his occasional attempts to do a cockney accent (which his friend Tim Roth has been known to mock publicly and at length). More likely it was – and this is something that Tarantino himself recognised on another occasion – that much of *Reservoir Dogs* was reminiscent of a certain kind of hard, British gangster filmmaking (such as *Get Carter* (Mike Hodges, 1971)). That Tim Roth was the film's conceptual linchpin and could be sold by the British press as a British actor seemingly making it in Hollywood certainly helped too.

RECURRING ELEMENTS: In the Mr White introduction scene Alabama (from *True Romance*) is mentioned as is a Marsellus Spivey (presumably a relation of *True Romance*'s Drexl Spivey). Spivey is said to be doing twenty years in Susanville prison (for 'bad luck'). Susanville is the same prison where Mickey Knox spent time in the (unshot) screenplay for *Natural Born Killers*. Seymour Scagnetti is the name of Mr Blonde's parole officer. There's an Officer Scagnetti in the *Natural Born Killers* screenplay. The tortured policeman in *Dogs* is Marvin Nash. There's a Gerald Nash (a reporter) in *Natural Born Killers*. In a cut scene Nice Guy Eddie refers to a 'Bonnie Situation' – the title of one third of *Pulp Fiction* and the implication that the nurse Bonnie mentioned here is the same one later seen in *Pulp Fiction* is too strong to ignore. In another cut scene Holdaway uses the phrase 'according to Hoyle' to mean 'going well'. Jules says this in *Pulp Fiction* whereas Wayne says it in *Natural Born Killers*. This is, as the first Tarantino script made, the first, but not last, chance the audience gets to see a Tarantino film end with a Mexican stand-off.

SPURIOUS INTERTEXTUALITY: In contemporary interviews Tarantino quoted the films of Jean-Pierre Melville as the primary influences on *Reservoir Dogs*: *Bob le Flambeur* (1955), *Le Doulos* (1962 – starring Jean-Paul Belmondo) and *Le Samourai* (1967 – starring Alain Delon) cited as particular examples. What he particularly appreciated about these films was the way that Melville took the archetypes and story metaphors of (chiefly Warner Bros-produced) American gangster movies and filtered them through a European sensibility. For Tarantino, as an American, watching them was a remarkable experience because he was watching a film produced by a culture he was unfamiliar with trying to get to grips with the products of his own culture. *Reservoir Dogs* is an attempt to continue the circle: an American's take on a French take on American culture, albeit filtered through other, separate foreign takes of American culture, such as Hong Kong action cinema (although, of course, *Dogs* isn't itself an action film). 'I took those movies and threw an LA right-now into them,' said Tarantino during production. On the topic of Hong Kong cinema, *Dogs*'s obvious influences include John Woo's 1987 *Yinghung Bunsik II* (*A Better Tomorrow II*) which Tarantino had not seen when he wrote *True Romance* but had by the time he wrote *Reservoir Dogs*) it's worth refuting the suggestions that *Reservoir Dogs* is simply a remake, or outright pastiche, of *Long hu feng yun* (Ringo Lam, 1987). These suggestions are inappropriate and overstated. While there are some similarities between the basic plot of *Reservoir Dogs* and the final few minutes of *Long hu feng yun* and the latter is a film Tarantino is undoubtedly familiar with, that doesn't make them the same. As with the contention that *Star Wars* (George Lucas, 1977) is a remake/rip-off of *Kakushi toride no san akunin* (*The Hidden Fortress*) (Akira Kurosawa, 1958) the charge of wholesale copying is usually made by those who haven't seen the earlier film. It might as well be claimed that *Reservoir Dogs* is the same as *Captain Scarlet and the Mysterons* (Gerry Anderson, 1967) due to the colour-coded names of both's protagonists. (Which, in *Reservoir Dogs*'s case are probably a reference to Joseph Sargent's 1974 *The Taking of Pelham One Two Three* anyway.)

In terms of references rather than influences, the film is abundant. Mr Brown refers to porn actor John Holmes. He also refers to Charles Bronson 'digging tunnels' in *The Great Escape* (John Sturges, 1963). While Bronson is indeed in that movie, his character isn't actually one of those who did dig tunnels. Freddie describes Joe Cabot to Holdaway as looking like the ever-loving blue-eyed 'Thing' from Marvel Comics' *Fantastic Four* comic book (as played in the 2005 film by the brilliant Michael Chicklis). At one point Joe himself makes a vague comic book reference by asking the question 'What in the Sam Hill is going on here?' a question beloved of *Daily Planet* editor and Superman's boss, Perry White. Holdaway's first reference point for 'a great actor' is Marlon Brando. While telling his story about the Los Angeles marijuana drought, Mr Orange whines that he's 'trying to watch *The Lost Boys*', Joel Schumacher's semi-cool, mainstream cult teen vampire thriller/comedy. The line 'Breaking up is a major pain in the ass' is a less charming play on 'Breaking up is very hard to do' the Burt Bacharach/Hal David composition. Ann Francis, the star of the TV series *Honey West*, is mentioned. As Mr Pink correctly apprehends, she was white and was therefore obviously not Pam Grier. Pam Grier was, of course, not the star of *Get Christy Love!* (1974–5) although she could be said to be the basis for the character type that Teresa Graves (the actual name of the actress the *Dogs* can't remember) played on that show. Mr Blonde is a Lee Marvin fan, as is Mr White.

MUSICAL NOTES: In the early 90s, the 70s were anathema. In fact even the 60s revival hadn't even really begun to kick in (British culture en masse seems to have forgotten this, assuming that the things that are popular now have always been popular). Therefore the use of the fictional K-Billy's *Super Sounds of the Seventies* radio programme on 'the station where the 70s survived' is not only iconoclastic, it's deliberately uncool. It's Tarantino and his producer creating an atmosphere using things they like rather than things that are currently perceived to have any cultural value (something that is consistently true of Tarantino's career –

for example, his championing of 70s exploitation cinema or grindhouse). Records used in *Reservoir Dogs* include, most famously, the George Baker Selection's 'Little Green Bag' over the opening credits and Joe Egan and Gerry Rafferty's 'Stuck in the Middle with You' (recorded when they were a duo known as Stealer's Wheel). Interestingly the DJ says this record reached the US Billboard chart No 5 in April 1974. It didn't. It was 1973. Songs mentioned but not actually heard include the Partridge Family's 'Doesn't Somebody Want to Be Wanted' and Edison Lighthouse's 'Love Grows Where My Rosemary Goes' and 'Heartbeat is a Love Beat' by Little Tony Franco and the DeFranco Family as well as 'The Night the Lights Went Out in Georgia' (which Nice Guy Eddie has taken twenty years to understand).

Now that in the twenty-first century 70s retro has become mind-numbingly tiresome thanks to endless cheap documentaries/clipshows on cable television, it's difficult to remember how different, fresh and exciting the music in *Reservoir Dogs* was. What is much easier to still appreciate at the distance of a dozen years is the sound mixing. Consider the aforementioned torture scene – the way the music fades as Mr Blonde goes out of the lock-up into an ordinary street where there is ordinary ambient noise including the sounds of cars, people talking, children, the general gentle silence of urban play and car alarms is remarkably effective. In the 'naturalism' of its sounds the scene is reminiscent of the work of pioneering sound editor Walter Murch on *American Graffiti* (George Lucas, 1973) but more impressive is what it achieves in terms of the world-building exercise underway. Suddenly the audience is aware that all of this is taking place somewhere very close to what they'd consider 'normality'; it's an almost frightening 'monsters in our midst moment' and it plays tricks with the audience's perceptions. Normally a viewer would expect the music to keep going when Mr Blonde leaves the garage. Not because that makes any sense, but because that's what would normally happen in film.

Elsewhere smart sound mixing is used to great effect. Helicopters are never seen during the police chase, only heard as sound effects, but people remember seeing helicopters in the film – which is pretty much the intended effect in all likelihood. In a similar way the loud insistent ring of the diamond wholesaler's alarms also distracts the audience from the fact that they never see the robbery.

The 'Wilhelm scream', the Golden Age Hollywood sound effect of a man yelling in pain, rediscovered and re-popularised by Ben Burtt, is heard as Mr Pink flees from the cops about 20 minutes in. It's another clever piece of Tarantino appropriation – putting his film firmly into a heritage of filmmaking and not just the making of films akin to *Reservoir Dogs*, but all films.

Equally backwards-looking, but as charming as it always is, is Tarantino's use of what could be termed the standard 'diagetic music joke'. This is when a record that the audience has come to think of as being on the soundtrack and therefore only audible to them (in the way that a film score is normally only audible to a film's audience, not its characters) is revealed to be audible to the characters as well. In this case it's Mr Orange listening to 'Magic Carpet Ride' in his apartment before setting out on the day of the robbery.

WHO SHOT NICE GUY EDDIE?: The answer to this often asked question is actually very easy. It's Mr White (Harvey Keitel). No mystery. If you slow the film down (something a great deal easier now in the era of DVD) you can see Mr White turn and shoot for a second time, killing Nice Guy Eddie even as he himself falls as he takes the bullet fired by Joe. The 'mystery' has partially arisen because of a small technical defect where, during filming, some of Chris Penn's 'squibs' (small packs of stage blood designed to explode to create the illusion of someone being struck by a bullet) detonated prematurely meaning that Eddie seems to be hit by the bullet an infinitesimally small amount of time before Mr White fires it.

TORTURE: He might be a homophobic, racist, murdering career criminal but Nice Guy Eddie is smart enough to know that torture doesn't work. This doesn't matter to Mr Blonde who isn't interested in using torture to gain information – 'I'm gonna torture you anyway. It's amusing to me, to torture a cop,' he says and he means it. He also tells Marvin Nash that it doesn't matter what he says to him or how he pleads with him he won't spare his life – 'heard it all before'. In reality actor Kirk Baltz improvised some of his lines during the shooting of this scene; he was given dispensation by Tarantino to extemporise in order to make Madsen's/Blonde's reactions to his pleadings more spontaneous. Baltz's pleading that he has children did actually have an effect on actor Michael Madsen, himself a devoted family man with four sons, and he temporarily found it difficult to continue with the scene. Mr Blonde is an intriguing mix of the sentimental and the monstrous. His affection for both Joe and Eddie is obviously real and vast and he has done them a great service by serving four years in prison in order to protect them. He's also passionately, selfishly self-justifying, explaining his murder of bank staff with the phrase 'If they hadn't done what I told them not to do, then they'd still be alive' and his insistence in his own self-sufficiency ('I don't have a boss, nobody tells me what to do' could come from a sociopath's handbook, were there such a thing).

'I'M A COP, LARRY': The final few moments of *Reservoir Dogs* have proven controversial. This is not for violence or language or any of the other red flags that normally generate controversy around any work which isn't so anodyne it might as well not be there at all. The end of *Reservoir Dogs* is controversial in terms of *sense*. Mr White and Mr Orange are the only members of Joe's gang still alive. Mr White has just killed two friends for Mr Orange's sake. The police are about to arrive and arrest them. Mr Orange, the undercover cop, will be taken to hospital and possibly survive. Mr

White will be captured, arrested and tried. Mr White has accepted this fate for himself and expects Mr Orange to share it. 'Looks like we're going to do a little time,' he says, cradling Mr Orange's head. 'I'm a cop, Larry,' Mr Orange responds. Mr White begins to weep uncontrollably and manages to kill Mr Orange before the police charge in and kill him too. People's problem with this scene can, essentially, be boiled down to the question: 'Why does Mr Orange tell Mr White that he's a policeman, thus giving him enough time to kill him before the police arrive and kill Mr White?' Tarantino has gone as far as to say that anyone who even feels the need to ask this question has fundamentally misunderstood *Reservoir Dogs*. The reasoning behind a statement as strong as that is that the whole ending is the concept of 'Jingi' which underlies a lot of Japanese drama and had been encountered by Tarantino in his journeys through Japanese film. Tarantino defined the literally untranslatable term as 'honour and humanity' while insisting it was 'beyond' either. It might be more understandable, albeit more prosaic, to summarise it as 'Doing what you feel it is you feel you morally have to do even though it is personally disadvantageous, even to the point of being fatal.' In the final moment of the film, with only the possibility, not the certainty, of survival and freedom dangled in front of him Freddy Newendyke (Mr Orange) finds that his relationship with Mr White – who has just surrendered his freedom, possibly his life – for him is more important than his mission, more important than going on living. Telling Mr White the truth is the most important thing he can do. He does and he pays for it with his life.

CRITICAL REACTION: Roger Ebert of the *Chicago Sun-Times*, who would later become a firm fan of Tarantino's and interview him several times, was impressed but not bowled over by the writer–director's debut: 'Now that we know Quentin Tarantino can make a movie . . . it's time for him to move on and make a better one' was the substance of his review; he also said that Tarantino 'doesn't do much with his characters except let them talk too much'. Over in the *New Yorker*, Terence Rafferty was even less impressed – 'The movie runs off film school cleverness,' he opined although it was, at least, 'fairly engaging'. However the 'dramatic possibilities of infantile bullies goading each other to violence are sadly limited', apparently, and *Dogs* is thus a 'reasonably lively picture about nothing'.

THE NUMBERS: The estimated final budget for *Reservoir Dogs* was $1.2 million. On its first limited US release (to a mere 19 screens) it took $147,839 – and its total US take was rated at just under the $1.2 million budget as of 2004. However, it must be remembered that the studio's take of that money is just 50 per cent of that. Interestingly given the much smaller scale of the cinema audience and indeed general population in the UK – and the fact that it was on at a mere 11 screens – *Reservoir Dogs* took $268,597 over its opening weekend which began on 11 January 1993.

FINAL COMMENT: 'I don't know what you think you know, but you're wrong.'

To say that *Reservoir Dogs* seemed like nothing its audience had ever seen before when it came out is to openly invite ridicule, to virtually demand someone lists the films that it pays homage to, and others which have influenced it, but none of that matters. None of it. It was an immense, powerful, shocking, at times profound viewing experience for the vast majority of those who saw it, and it retains its power to shock, to entertain and to move its audiences. The first thing that happens in *Reservoir Dogs* is Tarantino himself, in the person of Mr Brown, explaining to his uninterested colleagues that for the narrator of 'Like A Virgin' the whole point of the song is that the shocking reminder of a lost innocence is perhaps as powerful as the original loss of that innocence. The adverb 'like' is the most important thing in the lyrics of that song and it's the most important thing about *Reservoir Dogs*. *Dogs* knocks you over and makes you absolutely feel like you've never seen anything like it before; the link between that initial discussion and the film's own self is a beautiful marrying of form and content. *Reservoir Dogs* is a great film and Tarantino's pride that the first film of his to be released was also his directorial debut is entirely appropriate.

'That Sundance'

Quentin Tarantino has said that he considers himself and the numerous other independent filmmakers who 'broke through' in the early 1990s as 'the class of 92'. It's certainly true that the 1992 Sundance Film Festival showcased a large number of very fine non-Hollywood pictures. While Tarantino's *Reservoir Dogs* was the festival's 'hottest' (and most controversial) ticket the selection that year also included Derek Jarman's, Anthony Root-produced, adaptation of Christopher Marlowe's 1592 play about King Edward II; Anthony Dresen's *Zebra Head*, Alison Anders' *Gas Food Lodging* and Michael Steinberg's *The Water Dance*.

In addition, there were screenings of Alexandre Rockwell's splendid low budget (c$900,000) *In The Soup* and Tom Kalin's determinedly brilliant *Swoon*. The former is about a filmmaker who, down on his luck, sells his script to a gangster who then decides to make it. Featuring Steve Buscemi and a gloriously memorable rooftop scene, it's a film which doesn't get enough respect or exposure a dozen years after its creation. The latter is a dramatisation of the 'Leopold and Loeb' case. Now forgotten, this was a crime which scandalised a community when, in 1924, two eighteen-year-old Jewish intellectuals in Chicago killed a thirteen-year-old boy as part of a project to commit the perfect murder. Another technically independent picture in competition was *Poison Ivy* (Katt Shae, 1992) starring Drew Barrymore and Sara Gilbert. This is a very, very silly film: a sort of teen take on the *Single White Female* (Barbet Schroeder, 1992) situation, it is notable only for the presence of some low-rent lipstick lesbian tension and is very lucky to be considered in the same paragraph as the other pictures above. Perversely it has done rather better than them in recent years, being a frequent presence on cable channels. Not something that can be said of 1992's far worthier indies.

Chris Munch's *The Hours and the Times* had been produced back in 1988 but it premiered that same year. Another brilliant piece of low-budget, high-quality filmmaking, it concerned itself with the ambiguous relationship between Beatle John Lennon and the band's manager Brian Epstein. It has a jaw-dropping central performance from Ian Hart as Lennon. One he'd recreate in the more mainstream *Backbeat* (Iain Softley, 1994). Shot in Spain and England in an eerie monochrome that added verisimilitude to its entirely conjectural events, it would have won a major prize but for the fact that at around an hour it wasn't technically 'feature length'.

Reservoir Dogs also failed to win any awards at Sundance, although not because of its length. Tarantino later opined that this was because the jury had decided that he didn't need the recognition that a Sundance prize would have brought as his career was already assured.

There's a valid argument there, certainly, but it can't have seemed particularly compelling to Tarantino. Across the four scheduled screenings of his film he had suffered seeing it projected using the wrong kind of lens, been in an audience subjected to a power cut during the film's climactic 'Mexican stand off', endured the lights coming up during another key moment and – heart-stoppingly – watched a print of the movie become caught in the projector and literally *burn*.

True Romance (1993)

James G Robinson presents
A Morgan Creek Production
A Tony Scott Film
Christian Slater, Patricia Arquette,
True Romance
With Dennis Hopper, Val Kilmer, Gary Oldman, Brad Pitt,
Christopher Walken
Casting by Risa Bramon Garcia, Billy Hopkins
Costume Designer: Susan Becker
Edited by Michael Tronick, Christian Wagner
Music by Hans Zimmer
Production Designer: Benjamin Fernandez
Director of Photography: Jeffrey L Kimball, ASC
Written by Quentin Tarantino
Executive Producers: Bob and Harvey Weinstein
Produced by Samuel Hadida
Produced by Steve Perry
Produced by Bill Unger
Directed by Tony Scott

TAGLINES: 'Stealing, Cheating, Killing. Who said romance is dead?'

'Not since Bonnie and Clyde have two people been so good at being bad.'

CAST: Christian Slater (Clarence Worley), Patricia Arquette (Alabama Whitman), Dennis Hopper (Clifford Worley), Val Kilmer (Mentor), Gary Oldman (Drexl Spivey), Brad Pitt (Floyd (Dick's Room-mate)), Christopher Walken (Vincenzo Coccotti), Bronson Pinchot (Elliot Blitzer), Samuel L Jackson (Big Don), Michael Rapaport (Dick Ritchie), Saul Rubinek (Lee Donowitz), Conchata Ferrell (Mary Louise Ravencroft), James Gandolfini (Virgil), Anna Thomson (Lucy), Victor Argo (Lenny), Paul Bates (Marty), Chris Penn (Nicky Dimes), Tom Sizemore (Cody Nicholson), Said Faraj (Burger Man), Gregory Sporleder (Burger Stand Customer),

Maria Pitollo (Kandi), Frank Adonis (Frankie), Kevin Corrigan (Marvin), Paul Ben-Victor (Luca), Michael Beach (Wurlitzer), Joe D'Angerio (Police Radio Operator), John Bower (Detective), John Cenatiempo (Squad Cop #1), Eric Allan Krame (Boris), Patrick John Hurley (Monty), Dennis Garber (Lobby Cop #1), Scott Evers (Lobby Cop #2), Hilary Klym (Running Cop), Steve Conzales (I.A. Officer), Laurence Mason (Floyd 'D')

SUMMARY: Detroit comic book store clerk Clarence Worley meets a girl called Alabama in a cinema. They go out after the screening to discuss the film, are charmed by each other and end up having sex. Waking up, Clarence finds Alabama crying on his balcony in the freezing cold. She confesses to him that she didn't meet him by accident; she's actually a call girl hired by his employer Lance because he believed that Clarence needed to 'get laid'. Alabama is more upset than Clarence: he had one of the best evenings of his life, not simply the sex they had but also the time he spent watching the movie with her, talking to her and eating pie in the diner with her. He says that her revelation about her reasons for being there can't change that. She's upset because she thinks she really is in love with him and she's horrified she met him this way. He still doesn't care and they get married. Clarence goes to see Alabama's pimp, Drexl, ostensibly to get Alabama's possessions. An argument ensues and Clarence kills Drexl leaving with a bag that he thinks contains her clothes. On getting back home to Alabama he discovers that it, in fact, contains a huge stash – approximately a million dollars' worth – of uncut cocaine. They visit Clarence's father, an ex-cop, to tell him of their marriage and ask him for help in finding out whether the police department are likely to finger him for the crime. Husband and wife then leave for LA where they intend to sell the cocaine for a fifth of its value to a big shot movie producer. They are unaware that they are being followed by the Mafia, from whom Drexl stole the drugs in the first place, and that – coincidentally – an elaborate sting is being prepared by the LAPD to trap the producer they're intent on making a deal with. After a massive firefight in which they're only tangentially involved, Clarence and Alabama escape to Mexico with a suitcase full of untraceable drug money. Here they raise their son, whom they name Elvis after Clarence's hero, the King of Rock 'n' Roll.

DEVELOPMENT: Tarantino's screenplay was, like *Natural Born Killers* (and indeed *Reservoir Dogs*), written as a potential directorial debut for himself. *True Romance* was the first script that the budding writer actually completed, having spent his teens beginning, but never completing, various drafts of putative spec projects. Tarantino has since intimated that he has come to feel that all these abortive ideas came to nothing because he was writing more because he wanted to be a writer than because he had a story that he wanted, or needed, to tell. *True Romance* was, he quickly realised as he wrote it, that story that he needed – the one he wanted – to tell.

The previous screenplay of Tarantino's that had come the closest to being completed was a five-hundred-page unfinished draft entitled *The Open Road* from which some of the material that would form *True Romance* (and indeed later *Natural Born Killers*) was culled.

With *True Romance* Tarantino intended that he and Roger Avary[1] would form a limited partnership, get together a budget of around $1.2 million and shoot the film together. They had both been impressed by the Coen brothers' *Blood Simple* (1984) and the way the film had been put together using small investments from rich professionals, such as doctors and lawyers, who had no interest in motion picture production but interest in getting a decent return for a small investment in a short space of time.

---

[1] Roger Avary. Long-time pre-fame friend of Tarantino's. Co-writer *Pulp Fiction*, for which he won an Oscar. Writer/Director *Killing Zoe* (1994), *The Rules of Attraction* (2002) and *Glamorama* (2005).

After months of failing to get the project off the ground Tarantino abandoned the idea of making *True Romance* and began developing projects that could be realised even cheaper – writing *Natural Born Killers*, a screenplay he felt could be effectively produced for around half of *True Romance*'s imagined budget.

With *Natural Born Killers* now his first directorial feature of choice he began to look into the possibility of selling *True Romance*. Principally this was in order to finance *Natural Born Killers* as an independent production, although he has also since confessed that he would have sold *True Romance* for any amount of money offered to him, as the purchase of the script by anyone for any purpose would have validated him, and proved to himself that he was a professional writer.

Tarantino did eventually sell the script to low-rent exploitation filmmaker Samuel Hadida for an up-front payment of $13,000, a downpayment on a full fee of around $30,000. This was simultaneously the Writers Guild of America's minimum (and therefore the smallest sum the company could legally have paid Tarantino had he been a union member, which incidentally he wasn't) and also the most money the screenwriter had earned in his life up to that point. The producers attached Bill Lustig to the project as director. Tarantino was initially happy the man behind such films as *Maniac* (1980), *Vigilante* (1983) and the *Maniac Cop* trilogy (1988, 1990, 1993) would be shooting his script, but became concerned that Lustig would not be able to make the crossover between the straight-down-the-line exploitation filmmaking of the kind he'd previously been involved in and the more mainstream romantic drama that was *True Romance*. In this sense Tarantino had a point. Few directors have ever been truly successful in crossing over from the exploitation circuit to mainstream movie making. The most notable exceptions are probably Jonathan Demme and James Cameron, both of whom started out making films like *Crazy Mama* (1975) and *Piranha II: The Spawning* (1981) respectively and both of whom ultimately won

Academy Awards for their mainstream work. It's also true that Lustig is a static camera visceralist whose work, while often thrilling and high impact, has never really demonstrated depth of character or an ability to stay in the minds of its audience after viewing.

At about this time Tarantino was employed as an uncredited script doctor at a production company where one of his colleagues was a former protégé of Tony Scott's. Tarantino had always been a fan of Scott, comparing him favourably to his (generally perceived as more respectable) brother Ridley. It has always been Tarantino' s contention that the younger Scott was the 80s and early 90s equivalent of Douglas Sirk, in that both directors worked in unfashionable, intellectually unpopular genres and despite huge box-office returns and distinct visual styles of their own were therefore destined to be unappreciated in their own eras. Tarantino has even defended Scott's much-maligned Simpson/Bruckheimer produced, Tom Cruise/Nicole Kidman vehicle *Days of Thunder* (1990) on several occasions (despite the fact that it features two scenes in which Robert Duvall's character is reduced to praying to a car).

Thanks to their mutual contact Tarantino got to meet Scott on more than one occasion and eventually Scott was passed Tarantino's screenplays to read. By this time *Reservoir Dogs* had been written and, on reading it, Scott was so thrilled with the script that he suggested he could direct it. This could have been the big break that Tarantino had been working towards his whole life but he politely explained that he wanted to direct *Dogs* himself and that the money he was currently earning meant that he would soon be able to mount it as a small-scale independent film himself. Scott then read *True Romance* and *Natural Born Killers* and came to the conclusion that instead he would like to direct the former, which he liked even more than *Dogs*. Tarantino explained that the rights to the script had already been sold on, but that he couldn't imagine the producers not wanting a director of Scott's status to take on the picture should he so choose. A deal was duly struck for the film to be made with Scott as director.

This deal was made before *Reservoir Dogs* was shot and released. After that picture came out the producers contacted Tarantino and offered him the chance to direct the script of *True Romance* as his second film. Tony Scott volunteered to step up to a 'producer' role should Tarantino want to do this but the writer declined, explaining that he had written *True Romance* to be his directorial debut and that, while he was happy to see it made by someone else his own sophomore directorial project would be something else entirely (see **Pulp Fiction**).

SCREENPLAY: A viewer watching *True Romance* may conclude that it's the most traditional of Tarantino's screenplays. They'd be right, but they'd also be quite wrong. To the audience it appears that this boy-meets-girl tale is, structurally speaking, straightforwardly linear with a plot and a counter plot which develop in parallel to one another and ultimately intersect. It also has the only unequivocally 'happy' ending of any Tarantino screenplay pre-*Jackie Brown* and the only easily definable Tarantino avatar character in the whole of the writer's canon. The thing is that while the protagonist and the boy-meets-girl conceit are Tarantino's, the linear structure and the happy ending are contributions brought to the project by director Tony Scott.

Once Scott began making *True Romance* Tarantino made a decision to have minimal contact with the director during actual production. He never visited the film's set during actual shooting, although he and Scott did discuss the film in both pre- and post-production. Tarantino has since described the idea of writers becoming involved in films they've written but aren't going to direct in an almost binary manner: either the writer should be on set every day and be involved in every aspect of the production or he should not be involved at all. Evidently in this instance, he chose the latter over the former. Indeed the first time he saw the film was at the premiere. He brought virtually the entire cast of *Pulp Fiction* with him.

The script that Tarantino wrote is slightly different to the one that director Scott actually shot, although the changes that it went through could be considered to be substantially fewer than average for a Hollywood production.

The most significant change is that the screenplay as written has an 'answers first, questions later' structure akin to Tarantino's first two directorial features. Scott straightened the story out into a linear progression during production and, while he at one point made an abortive start at editing the finished material into the script order, was sufficiently confident in this decision to stick to it.

In the film as released the plot unfolds in strictly chronological sequence. It begins with Clarence, continues through his meeting with Alabama, their marriage, his murder of her former pimp and accidental theft of the suitcase of cocaine followed by the couple's rendezvous with Clarence's father, Cliff, and then Clarence and Alabama's adventures in Los Angeles. The screenplay shares the same opening scene with the finished movie (the 'I'd fuck Elvis' sequence) but instead moves, after a suggestion that this is where the title cards and credits should go, to Drexl's confrontation with Floyd and acquisition of the cocaine. This scene occurs around eighteen minutes into the film as released as opposed to around five as Tarantino intended. The script then moves to Alabama and Clarence visiting Clarence's father in order to ask him for help. Then Clarence phones Dick Ritchie to tell him he's coming to Los Angeles. Next there's the scene of Don Vincenzo questioning Cliff Worley and then the story follows Clarence and Alabama to Los Angeles. Only once they're there and Dick Ritchie asks Clarence how Alabama and he met does Clarence tell him, leading to flashbacks showing how they met, Clarence killing Drexl and the accidental theft of the cocaine.

What the re-ordering of the film into chronological sequence does is that it removes some of the script's subtleties. Had the film been in the same order as the script then the audience would be ignorant of Clarence's murder of Drexl until Cliff is told about it by Don Vincenzo and even then they would be unsure if the Don was telling the truth or not. There would not be absolute confirmation that Clarence has the drugs until Clarence himself begins to discuss his plans with Ritchie later. Tarantino's structure also allows the audience to spend quite a lot of time with Alabama and Clarence before learning that he worked in a comic book store for minimum wage, that she was a call girl and that he murdered her pimp. In the finished film the sheer charm of the performances and the fairytale gloss of Scott's shooting style mean that the facts about them, perhaps baldly off-putting in print, don't matter. But with a more straightforward shooting style they might have. They might have put the audience off the characters and that is presumably one of the reasons Tarantino constructed his story in such a manner. The audience get to know them before they know what they've done and consequently they're already on their side.

Another lost subtlety also concerns the release of information. As written the story starts with the audience knowing less about the world the characters inhabit than the characters do, with Clarence and Alabama in particular being ahead of the audience in terms of what they know about what has happened. After the scheduled flashbacks the audience is on an equal footing with the characters and then, as the plot moves on, the audience begins to see what happens to other characters who have no immediate connection with Clarence or Alabama, and suddenly knows more than the central characters. This motion from confusion to equality with the characters to being ahead of them is a pleasing structural conceit and while its loss is not necessarily to be mourned, it should certainly be appreciated.

Ultimately the only 'problem' with the re-ordered screenplay, and it's one that is going to be noticed only by the most needlessly contemplative cineaste, is that Dick Ritchie is introduced to the audience some forty minutes into the film and without having been previously mentioned by any other characters. This is unusual for a Hollywood movie, indeed for any movie, as the cutting away to a character never before seen or talked about in a location never before visited can pull the audience out of the mood that the picture has created up to this point. This does happen, to an extent, in the finished *True Romance*, but Michael Rapaport's performance is so goofily appealing and the audition for *The New TJ Hooker* scene so amusing that the audience is almost immediately sucked right back in.

The aforementioned Tarantino avatar character is Clarence Worley as played by Christian Slater. Clarence, as Tarantino did at the time of the script's creation, works for minimum wage in a video store (albeit one that also sells comic books). Clarence is a man as thoroughly mired in popular culture as Tarantino himself, with a bedroom full of videos of exploitation pictures and a love of comic books, foreign cinema and no set path through life.

Tarantino's screenplay works (mainly) via a combination of four complementary elements, all of which feed into one another. The first is the many sudden reversals between comedy and violence, the second is his consistent verbal inventiveness and the third (which is not quite the same as the second) is to write lengthy speeches for characters to expound in direct contravention of what are held to be the normal rules of filmic storytelling. The fourth is have characters say things which reflect on the experiences and personalities of other characters in a way which the character who is speaking cannot intend or understand, but which an attentive audience should pick up on.

These are, of course, consistent seams in Quentin Tarantino's work, but it's notable that they should be so fully developed in what was his first completed script.

An example of something which combines the first two equally can be seen in what was, in script terms, the second scene. Drexl interrupts the characters' banter about who is prepared to do what in the bedroom, and who would lie about what to whom, in order to start a massacre, or as the script puts it: 'Then in a blink, he points the shotgun at Floyd and BLOWS him away.' The script goes from comedy to quite shocking violence in just a few seconds.

A good example of the third element is the scene where Clarence confronts Drexl. Drexl gets a speech of 184 words in which he challenges Clarence's masculinity, questions his motives and mocks his ability to negotiate and then Clarence responds with another speech of 127 words taking on and rebutting every single one of Drexl's charges while relaying to Drexl information that Drexl clearly doesn't know in order to establish his power over him. Shortly afterwards Drexl attacks Clarence and, when Clarence retaliates, a massacre ensues. This illustrates two of the major functions of Tarantino's monologues. One is to reveal character in a manner which, while defiant of the then norms of Hollywood screenwriting, is a more accurate reflection of the way that Tarantino's generation (Generation X lest we forget, the pop-culture obsessed generation of Bret Easton Ellis and Douglas Copeland) actually talk. The second is to provide pause between those shocks and reversals, to delay, disorientate and calm down the audience in-between set pieces and, in effect, soften them up for the next big change of mood or plot revelation.

Examples of Tarantino's linguistic inventiveness, amusing constructions that he conjures to evoke ideas or mood include Clarence's dismissal of a certain kind of film as 'Safe geriatric coffee table dogshit'. This is brilliant precisely because it both means nothing and clearly evokes the kind of film Tarantino is trying to belittle. Equally poor quality cocaine is later dismissed as 'nose garbage', something else which gives an immediate impression of what the character means without having any obvious precedents. Clarence's announcement that when it comes to sugar in his coffee he's 'not satisfied until the spoon stands straight up' is brilliant because it teeters on the brink of being literally true while obviously being a comic exaggeration. It's an emblematic example of the line between reality and deliberately setting out to be entertainingly extreme that Tarantino's screenplays walk.

One of the very best scenes in the screenplay from the point of view of demonstrating these seams wrapping together is Alabama's confrontation with Virgil in the hotel room in LA. As this begins Virgil is waiting in the room for Alabama. She arrives and he immediately starts to coldly interrogate her. She, without pausing for breath, denies that she's Alabama, denies knowing anyone called Clarence, says that she's called Sandy and that her husband is a football player. She not only seems to convince Virgil, she also seems to charm him, he compliments her and seems to prepare to leave. Then, when her guard is down he attacks her. That's two reversals in as many minutes. The viewer moving from fearing for Alabama to delighting in her cheek and front to being shocked at the violence in what seems like no time at all. Then the scene almost stops, and Virgil gets one of Tarantino's in-depth, character-revealing monologues. In it he muses on his lot as a professional killer, and how the first murder you commit is always the most difficult. This not only increases audience understanding of Virgil and moves him out of the sphere of being the stereotypical 'dumb henchman', it also contains several examples of Tarantino's linguistic invention (i.e. 'It's gotten to the point now I'll [kill] just to watch their expression change') and the speech reflects on the other characters in the drama. The audience has already seen that the innocent Clarence found his first murder harder than his second and later that he's more than prepared to potentially commit a third. By the end of the scene Alabama herself will be forced to kill Virgil to save her own life (in another reversal) and, as the film goes on, the audience will also see her kill more and more often, it becoming easier every time.

CASTING: While writing his script Tarantino had visualised Joan Cusack as Alabama and Robert Carradine as Clarence. Due to the vast amount of time between the writing of the script's first draft (see **DEVELOPMENT**) both actors were arguably too old for the roles written with them in mind. As Alabama, Scott cast Patricia of the vast Arquette acting clan which includes her father Lewis and her sister Rosanna and brothers Richmond, Alexis and David. Born in April 1968, she grew up in a commune in Virginia. Her major debut was in *A Nightmare on Elm Street 3: Dream Warriors* (Chuck Russell, 1987), one of the least dull of the long-running series of generally not scary and unfunny murderous child-molester horror comedies. Scott didn't immediately think of Arquette for the role, but became convinced she was the only actress for it after seeing her award-winning performance as a mute epileptic in HBO's *Wildflower* (1991). *True Romance* stands as a career highlight for the actress along with David Lynch's criminally underrated *Lost Highway* (1997). It is actually her son, Enzo (b. 1989), who plays Clarence and Alabama's son Elvis at the end of the picture.

Christian Slater was cast as Clarence. Tarantino had written Clarence as the kind of young man who could conceivably be working in a dead-end job for a minimum wage while in his mid to late 20s. He felt it was imperative that the actor playing him both not be traditionally good looking and lack movie-star charisma otherwise the story wouldn't work. He must have therefore initially been surprised when the already rather famous pin-up Christian Slater was cast. Slater had played the young Tucker in Francis Ford Coppola's and George Lucas's *Tucker: The Man and His Dream* (1988) and starred in *Pump Up The Volume* (Allan Moyle, 1990), *Heathers* (Michael Lehman, 1989) and *Young Guns II: Blaze of Glory* (Geoff Murphy, 1990). However Slater is terrific in *True Romance*; unshaven, scruffy and geeky, he sublimates his movie star swagger beneath Clarence's personality and creates a character who is both believably a terminally single man slaving away for a minimum wage and someone Alabama could slip a napkin with 'You're so cool' written on it to. It's slightly disconcerting then to read Slater's own comments on the character some dozen years later: 'I didn't think he *was* very cool . . . I thought he was kind of a dorky guy who worked in a video/comic book store. I think she was writing that in more an ironic kind of way.'

Scott's picture takes an intelligent approach to casting the characters of Tarantino's script. Around the central pairing Scott's team cast an interesting variety of skilled character actors none of whom appear for a great deal of screen-time thanks to the episodic nature of much of the plot. While this results in a terrific cast list, it also results in the film seeming slightly discontinuous.

Clarence's father, Cliff Worley, is played by Dennis Hopper. The warm, avuncular, slightly confused Cliff is a real departure for Hopper who is best known for his monstrous portrayals of psychotics in films like *Blue Velvet* (David Lynch, 1986), *River's Edge* (Tim Hunter, 1987) alongside his iconic turn in the self-directed, self-penned *Easy Rider* (1969). Even Hopper's more personable turns, such as his Oscar-nominated performance in *Hoosiers* (David Anspaugh, 1986), had been as damaged men with a dark side that bubbles under their actions.

Watching Hopper's performance in the film is always a surprise. He's such a fine actor that *obviously* he can play the kind of character Cliff Worley is, he just so very rarely *does*. The contrast between Hopper's perceived persona and performance is unimaginably vast and Cliff is possibly the most recognisably real human being in the film, Hopper perhaps picking up on the reality behind lines that were written by Tarantino with his stepfather Curt in mind. Hopper, like Slater and Arquette but unlike the rest of the cast, accompanied Scott's unit on its journey to shoot exteriors in Detroit.

Born in 1963, Brad Pitt dropped out of college to pursue his acting dream in California. Lean years followed where he

TARANTINO True Romance

drove for strippers, transported appliances and dressed as a giant chicken to advertise fast food. At the time of casting he had just finished shooting *Kalifornia* (Dominic Sena, 1993) and initially read for the part of Clarence. Pitt didn't really like the script which he saw as too obviously the fantasy of one young guy and didn't really want to play Clarence. In the end he was never asked, but Scott did ask him to play the small role of Floyd, Dick Ritchie's room-mate. Pitt was charmed by the wit of the idea of playing a character whose easy, unknowing giving-up of information to the Mafia gets so many people killed. Although not much rated at the time as a performer Pitt quickly proved his worth to the production, improvising with Michael Rapaport around the concept of Floyd as 'the room-mate from Hell' adding the lines about 'cleaning products' and Floyd's easy consumption of Dick's beer. It was also Pitt's idea to make Floyd a stoner. As the character was permanently housebound and clearly itinerant he theorised there must be a reason for this and struck on the idea of the character being permanently stoned. He even provided the Bob Marley-style rainbow woollen hat that Floyd wears (having found it on the street in Hollywood) and christened the steaming bong that props provided for the centre of the room 'Russell' and addressed it as such on and off camera. Floyd's interrogation by the hoods is one of the movie's great moments, the sheer joy of the super-stoned Floyd treating his interrogation by the mob as if it's a hallucination of him being on a game show and giving little jogs of victory every time he gets a question 'right' is something to behold. Pitt's career has since gone into the stratosphere with an Oscar nomination for *Twelve Monkeys* (Terry Gilliam, 1995) and strong roles in great pictures such as *Se7en* (David Fincher, 1995), *Ocean's Eleven* (Steven Soderbergh, 2001) and *Fight Club* (David Fincher, 1999) as well as the lead in the odd less than successful film such as *Troy* (Wolfgang Petersen, 2004).

Val Kilmer, who had previously worked with Scott on *Top Gun* (1986), also read for the role of Clarence but, unlike Pitt, he was really keen to play it. Having settled on Slater, Scott rewarded Kilmer's enthusiasm with the role of 'Mentor', a role which is, in all but name, the ghost of Elvis Presley. Kilmer, a skilled mimic, is terrific as Elvis and evens performs some of the King's material for the soundtrack. Kilmer had previously starred in *Willow* (Ron Howard, 1988) and played Jim Morrison in Oliver Stone's *The Doors* (1991). He went on to play the dark knight detective in *Batman Forever* (Joel Schumacher, 1995) and was quoted by Batman creator Bob Kane, before his death, as his favourite of all the actors who had played Batman. Kilmer's career since has been misfires and failed blockbusters (such as *The Saint* (Philip Noyce, 1997) which managed to be both) which is nearly as frustrating for the actor's admirers as it must be for him.

Gary Oldman was hired by Scott while the actor was appearing in *Romeo is Bleeding* (Peter Medak, 1994) and arrived on the set for Scott's film to shoot at 5 a.m. having finished the previous film just four hours earlier. Oldman too added a great deal to his character during production, conceiving the idea that the character should be a one-eyed white Rasta with a hybrid Jamaican-East Coast accent. Another highly rated character actor Oldman had appeared with *Reservoir Dogs*'s Tim Roth in *Rosencrantz and Guildenstern are Dead* (Tom Stoppard, 1990) and played Lee Harvey Oswald in *JFK* (Oliver Stone, 1991), Dracula in *Bram Stoker's Dracula* (Francis Ford Coppola, 1992), Sid Vicious in *Sid and Nancy* (Alex Cox, 1986) and Joe Orton in *Prick Up Your Ears* (Stephen Frears, 1987). Since *True Romance*, Oldman has directed the multi-award winning, semi-autobiographical *Nil By Mouth* (1997) and appeared in supporting roles in quality mainstream films like *Harry Potter and the Prisoner of Azkaban* (Alfonso Cuaron, 2003), *Batman Begins* (Christopher Nolan, 2005) and *Hannibal* (Ridley Scott, 2001), as well as playing Stansfield in *Leon* (Luc Besson, 1994) and Ludwig van Beethoven in *Immortal Beloved* (Bernard Rose, 1994).

Christopher Walken was a former dancer who had won an Oscar for his performance in *The Deer Hunter* (Michael Cimino, 1978) following an astounding cameo in *Annie Hall* (Woody Allen, 1977) and gone on to an eclectic mix of roles including Max Zorin in the James Bond adventure *A View To A Kill* (John Glen, 1985) and the lead in *King of New York* (Abel Ferrara, 1990). Continuing *True Romance*'s connection with *Batman* movies, he played villain Max Shreck in *Batman Returns* (Tim Burton, 1992).

The cast of the film actually appears more impressive now than it was when it was released and it was impressive enough at the time. Two showy minor roles – Big Don and Virgil – are played by Samuel L Jackson and James Gandolfini respectively. Both were only bit-part players at the time, both have become major stars since: Jackson partially thanks to Tarantino's *Pulp Fiction* and Gandolfini as the multi-Emmy winning star of HBO's *The Sopranos* (1999–2006). Tom Sizemore, who plays one of the cops, is also better known now thanks to *Saving Private Ryan* (Steven Spielberg, 1998) and some well-publicised legal problems. Chris Penn (Nicky Dimes) appeared in *Reservoir Dogs*.

QUOTES:

Dick: 'I don't have a pot to piss in or a window to throw it out of.'

Clarence: 'One thing this last week has taught me is it's better to have a gun and not need it than to need a gun and not have it.'

Clarence: 'I ain't no fag, but Elvis he was prettier than most women. I always said that if I ever had to fuck a guy, if I absolutely had to – I'd fuck Elvis.'

Elvis: 'Killing him's the hard part. Getting away with it's the easy part . . . If you don't get caught at the scene with the smokin' gun in your hand, you got away with it.'

AUTOBIOGRAPHY: Tarantino has said the material between Clarence and Cliff Worley in *True Romance* is the most autobiographical scene he's ever written despite the fact that he's never even met his father. This absolutely makes sense in the context of a film in which the central character is a self-portrait even though none of the events of the screenplay actually occurred – or as the man himself put it 'none of this crap happened to me but it's very kinda autobiographical none the less'. It's very telling that the romance between Clarence and Alabama, which Tarantino has admitted he wrote at a time when he'd never had a 'proper girlfriend' himself, is something that is initiated by her rather than him. It perhaps indicates a desire on the writer's part, as channelled through the character, to be swept off of *his* feet. The revelation that Alabama didn't come across Clarence by accident but was hired to do so, makes her seduction of him more 'plausible' from the point of view of a man lacking sexual self-esteem, but her consequent falling in love with him could be seen to legitimise the adolescent complaint 'she'd like me if she only got to know me'. It's an interesting paradox, born out of Tarantino's own life experiences.

'I'D FUCK ELVIS': Val Kilmer's performance as the ghost of Elvis is a great pleasure of the film. Kilmer made a point of watching as many of Elvis's movies as he could and listened to the King's music almost constantly. Kilmer actually performs some of the Elvis records on the soundtrack while the Big Bopper's version of 'Chantilly Lace' is also used, as in *American Graffiti* (George Lucas, 1973), in order to avoid a clash with the Presley estate over use of the King's likeness and material. (This is also why the character is credited as 'Mentor' onscreen.) Ultimately Tarantino's pre-eminence in Hollywood led to him getting to know Lisa Marie Presley, Elvis's only child, and he actually watched the film with her on one occasion. What she made of a character obviously based on Tarantino himself expressing his desire to have sex with her late father has never been reported.

RECURRING ELEMENTS: Alabama is mentioned in
Reservoir Dogs and the plot climaxes in a Mexican
stand-off. Lee speaks of someone called Bonnie, an
off-screen character who is a colleague of his. It has been
intimated that this is the same Bonnie who appears in *Pulp
Fiction* (Jimmie's wife) and who is also mentioned in
Reservoir Dogs. Equally the audience is perhaps expected to
assume that Alabama's pimp, Drexl Spivey, is related to the
fence Marsellus Spivey who is also mentioned in *Reservoir
Dogs*. Drexl also mentions the actor Charles Bronson, who
is also namechecked in *Reservoir Dogs*. Mass-murderer
Charles Whitman is mentioned, as he is in the screenplay of
Natural Born Killers. On 1 August 1966 Whitman scaled the
inside of the University of Texas Tower in the state capital of
Austin and then, in a terrifying display of brutality,
proceeded to snipe people down from his vantage point with
a Scoped 6 mm rifle. He fired almost unimpeded for 96
minutes before being killed by law enforcement officials; he
killed fourteen people outright and wounded dozens, many
of whom later died from their injuries. On a lighter note,
Alabama has an affection for pie, like a lot of Tarantino
characters including Fabienne and Jules in *Pulp Fiction* and
Mickey in *Natural Born Killers*. Clarence Worley is, like
Eddie Cabot in *Reservoir Dogs*, a grown man who addresses
his father as 'Daddy' which is surely quite unusual.
Tarantino's work continues to be literally lavatorial with, as
before, gunplay taking place outside the bathroom while one
of the characters is in there. The actor Max Julien is
mentioned in the context of his appearance in *The Mack*
(Michael Campus, 1973). He later came in to read for the
part of Marsellus in *Pulp Fiction*. As in all of Tarantino's
'Tarantino-Universe' films there's a discussion of
cunnilingus. In *True Romance* it's between Big Don, Floyd
'D' and Drexl and concerns the fact that they find the
concept of performing it emasculating. Well, apart from Big
Don and they don't exactly put it in those terms. Drexl uses
the phrase 'from a diddled-eyed Joe to a damned-if-I-know'

which is also used by Holdaway in *Reservoir Dogs*. Clarence asks Eliot 'Why are you trying to fuck me?' during negotiations about the sale of the cocaine. He prefaces this with a long question about what he looks like. This same rhetorical trick is employed by Jules in *Pulp Fiction*. Don Vincenzo offers Cliff Worley a Chesterfield cigarette, Mr White does the same to Mr Pink in *Reservoir Dogs*. The topic of men being raped in prison is again broached, this time by the two LAPD officers as they threaten Elliot; Nice Guy Eddie, Joe and Vic discuss (well, actually, mock) institutionalised prison rape in *Reservoir Dogs*. Don Vincenzo ties Cliff to a chair and has him tortured. Mr Blonde does this to Marvin Nash (also a cop) in *Reservoir Dogs*. Clarence stares into the mirror and has an auto-conversation with himself, something that is a common feature of Tarantino movies. As in *Dogs* there's a character called Marvin.

RETRO REFERENCES?: Tarantino completed his first draft of *True Romance* reasonably quickly and has since noted that he went to the cinema to see the then newly released Norman Mailer's *Tough Guys Don't Dance* the day he finished it. If he went to see the picture the first day it was released then that pins the script as complete on 18 September 1987. If not then it was certainly before the end of the month. This incidental detail is important in one respect. The references in *True Romance* have been praised as being slightly retro. Alabama's favourite movie star is Burt Reynolds and her turn-ons include Mickey Rourke. These are so out of date by 1993 they're amusingly camp and mannered. In 1987 they're exactly contemporary. Burt Reynolds was one of America's biggest movie stars and Mickey Rourke had become a sex symbol thanks to the likes of *9½ Weeks* (Adrian Lyne, 1985). This long lead time between scripting and production might also be why the TV show Dick Ritchie is auditioning for *The New TJ Hooker* (a series that never actually existed) rather than *TJ Hooker* (which was in production in the mid-80s). *TJ Hooker* actually finished production in 1986 so maybe Tarantino was angling for a reunion TV movie, new season or revival almost straight away?

SPURIOUS INTERTEXTUALITY: Clarence is also the name of the main character in the abortive *My Best Friend's Birthday* (1984–7). The comic book that Clarence shows Alabama isn't *The Amazing Spider-Man* #1 as the dialogue in the scene leading up to it suggests. It's *Sgt Fury and His Howling Commandos* #18 (May 1965) written by Stan Lee and drawn by Dick Ayers (penciller), Chic Stone (inker). The cover is by Jack Kirby, Lee's longtime creative partner, and both the splash page and the final page appear to be by him also, although he isn't credited. You cannot now, and could not when *True Romance* came out, buy the comic for $4 in a back issue store although this may be another result of the length of time between the screenplay being written and being produced. Clarence mentions *Apocalypse Now* (Francis Ford Coppola, 1979) as being the best Vietnam war movie ever made. Second best is the fictional, Lee Donowitz produced, *Coming Home in a Body Bag*. Alabama and Clarence watch *A Better Tomorrow II* (John Woo, 1987) at one point. In the screenplay this was to be *Master of the Flying Guillotines* (Yu Wang, 1975) but Scott changed it, possibly as an acknowledgement to Woo's use of 'Mexican stand-off' scenes in his picture. *True Romance*, of course, ends in such a manner. It is worth mentioning that Tarantino, who is never shy about crediting, revealing and praising his influences, has stated on more than one occasion that when he first wrote the screenplay for *True Romance* he had never seen a John Woo film and that consequently he regards the Mexican stand-off climax as being as much his own as Woo's, them both having decided to use it independently of one another. Clarence's reference point for driving in a determined and cool manner is Steve McQueen in *Bullitt* (Peter Yates, 1968). The use of a spectral Elvis as a mentor figure for Clarence seems obviously indebted to the similar use of Humphrey Bogart in Woody Allen's *Play it Again, Sam* (Herbert Ross, 1972). The questions that Clarence asks Alabama in the diner are almost exactly, word for word, those in the questionnaire asked of centrefold playmates in *Playboy* magazine. Lee Donowitz mentions *Doctor Zhivago* (David Lean, 1965) as a film he really likes, in fact one he'd like to break off his conversation with Clarence to sit and watch. *Freejack* (Geoff Murphy, 1992), a Mick Jagger/Emilio Estevez SF pot-boiler nobody would break off a conversation with a pot plant to go and watch, is also seen in the background at one point. *The Good, The Bad and The Ugly* (Sergio Leone, 1966) and *Mad Max* (George Miller, 1979) are praised by Clarence as 'movies' in comparison to anaemic motion pictures that win numerous Academy Awards despite being 'unwatchable movies adapted from unreadable books'. It should also be pointed out that Alabama is so perfect for Clarence, and her connection with him so profound, that when she's confessing that of the things which Clarence likes and that she has said she likes too only *The Partridge Family* is revealed to be a lie. She even likes *Star Trek*.

THE VISTA: The film that Clarence is watching when he first meets Alabama is *The Street Fighter* (Shigehiro Ozawa, 1974) starring Sonny Chiba, which was the first film ever rated X for violence (rather than for sex) in the history of American film censorship. What he's actually attending is a triple bill screening of three Street Fighter movies which also includes *Return of the Street Fighter* (Shigehiro Ozawa, 1974) and *Sister of the Street Fighter* (Kazuhiko Yamaguchi, 1974). The scenes in the movie theatre were shot in the Vista, an old cinema on the corner of Hollywood Boulevard and Sunset Boulevard. The place has an interesting history, especially considering its location. Having been a prestigious locale it fell into disrepair and became a porn cinema, and then a rep cinema, before being renovated and becoming, once again, a first-run picture house. During production some friends of Tarantino's saw the marquee outside the cinema and actually tried to buy tickets for the screening, only to be told that it wasn't really on. They were disappointed, even more so when they realised that their hopes had been raised and then dashed by a film written by someone they knew.

TRUE ROMANCE?: The biggest change made to Tarantino's screenplay by Scott was the ending. As written, the script had Clarence die in a hail of bullets and Alabama leave alone trying to convince herself that she'd always felt that Clarence was 'an asshole' and that while he'd been a way out of her life on the streets, she'd never really loved him. When told that Scott planned to change the ending and allow Clarence to live and go off to live in Mexico with Alabama, raising their child called Elvis, Tarantino stated that he felt that the ending shouldn't be changed for commercial reasons, to make *True Romance* a more straightforward Hollywood movie with a happy ending and attendant greater appeal to mass audiences. Scott responded that his reasons for changing the ending weren't commercial but entirely human; that he had spent so much time with the characters that he wanted them to be happy, to win rather than lose. Tarantino conceded that the director's view was valid, finding it difficult to argue with the man who directed *Revenge* (1990) and Scott agreed to shoot both versions of the ending. Having finished production, and edited both together, Scott preferred his own ending over Tarantino's and it was duly used on the film as released.

Tarantino's ending, as shot by Scott, is problematic. For some reason it is difficult to 'read', with it being unclear to the audience whether Alabama is consoling herself in her grief by being as negative as possible about Clarence or whether she is revealed as a grand manipulator who used and discarded him and who really doesn't care that he's now dead because of her. This isn't the case on the page and Scott's footage of Tarantino's ending is an indication of the only place where the director's version of *True Romance* diverged so widely from what was written that it became untenable. Scott was, and is, right, as Tarantino later (entirely ungrudgingly) admitted.

Patricia Arquette plays Alabama as very much in love with Clarence and the audience can't and won't believe that she didn't love him, even if they are told by her herself. The audience also has come to like these characters so much, thanks to the performances and glossy romantic production, that they, like the director, desperately want them to be happy. Scott's ending is a better ending for the movie that he made. Tarantino's ending might have been a better ending for the movie he intended to make, but that film isn't the film that reached cinemas. Scott's film isn't a tragedy, it's a romantic fantasy.

The title of Tarantino's *True Romance* was an ironic joke. Tony Scott's is heartfelt. The former is perhaps slightly smarter, albeit in a deliberately 'hard' adolescent way.

This change of ending is, entirely appropriately, a perfect example of something that Alabama herself concludes right at the beginning of the film. Yes, when life is going badly one can claim that 'that's the way it goes' but it's equally valid to point out that 'every once in a while it goes *the other way* too'.

MUSICAL NOTES: Tarantino's screenplay contains, albeit only because he wrote it to direct himself, extensive notes on songs to be used on the soundtrack of the completed film. Tony Scott eschewed most of Tarantino's choices only retaining 'Itty Bitty Tear' as sung by Burl Ives (which is heard the first time the audience see Cliff Worley). Scott's film has a specially composed score – something generally not true of any of Tarantino's directorial features which all use stock music of various kinds. One piece of Hans Zimmer's[2] score is deliberately referential to *Musica Poetica*

---

[2] Hans Zimmer. Composer *Days of Thunder* (1990), *The Lion King* (1994) (for which he won an Oscar), *Gladiator* (2000), *Batman Begins* (2005), etc.

by Carl Orff and Gunild Keetman. This is taken from the
film *Badlands* (Terrence Malick, 1973) one of the key films
of the 1970s and an obvious influence on *True Romance*
(one that, to be fair, neither Tarantino nor Scott have ever
denied).

'PART EGGPLANT': Probably the most famous scene in
True Romance, and certainly the screenwriter's favourite, is
that in which Dennis Hopper's Cliff Worley is interrogated
by Christopher Walken's Don Vincenzo. The scene begins as
a straightforward asking-for-information by Vincenzo and
his hoods and ends in Cliff's murder. What passes between
those two points, however, is a fascinating combination of
shock dramatic reversals and tremendous acting.

After Cliff claims he has no idea where Clarence is
Vincenzo tells him that he can tell when someone is lying,
having spent a long time studying his father who was the
'world heavyweight champion of Sicilian liars'.

Cliff responds by telling Vincenzo, at some length, that his
reading of history texts has revealed to him that the reason
that Sicilians are ethnically different from other Italians is
due to the interbreeding of ethnic Africans and ethnic
Italians after the African Moors conquered Sicily. Vincenzo
laughs and even kisses Cliff on the cheek, and to the
audience it looks as if some mutual respect is building
between these two very different men based upon one's
appreciation of the other's courage. Don Vincenzo then
shoots Cliff three times in the head.

During the scene both men get to perform speeches so
long they really do qualify as monologues. Monologues are,
as noted earlier, not exactly unusual in Tarantino's work,
partially due – perhaps – to the declamative, declarative
nature of the writer's own speech patterns. Both actors rise
to the challenge of the long speeches tremendously,
especially Hopper. Hopper recalls the time spent shooting
the scene as a 'wonderful creative day' and notes how much
he enjoyed working with Walken. Both actors have denied

that they improvised around the scripts insisting only one exchange 'You are part eggplant' and 'You're a cantaloupe' was worked out by them. Indeed, Tarantino later commented that, watching the scene for the first time, he felt almost embarrassed that actors he admired so much, and whom he had been watching since childhood, had so rigorously and painstakingly learned every word, pause and hiccough of the pages and pages of dialogue he had written for them to say; learned it without smoothing out any of the occasional deliberate awkwardness or substituting synonyms for any of his chosen words.

Ironically Walken's best acting in the scene is entirely silent. Witness his quite extraordinary facial tic between Cliff's line 'Sicilians were spawned by niggers' and his response 'Excuse me?' Those few seconds are a real shuffle-back-the-disc-and-rewatch moment as Walken subtly flexes muscles in his face to suggest Don Vincenzo's lightning quick emotional journey from shock, to acceptance that Cliff isn't lying, to confusion, to becoming genuinely inquisitive.

The scene begins brutally, presenting Vincenzo as a stock hood and Cliff as a helpless victim before becoming, thanks to the speech about the Moors and the performance, tremendously funny and strangely affecting. The last shock (one of Tarantino's 'many reversals', see **SCREENPLAY**) is the murder of Cliff, which the audience feels more deeply than perhaps anything else in the movie.

While the punchline of the scene (when the one of Vincenzo's hoods who can speak English explains to the one who can't that 'He said Sicilians were spawned by niggers so Don Vincenzo killed him') is very funny, perhaps a large portion of the audience would prefer to see Clifford survive the film so touching is Hopper's performance.

CRITICAL REACTION: The *New Yorker* wasn't in the mood to praise the second produced screenplay by US cinema's wunderkind, calling the film 'slick, repellent' and reliant on 'formula', concluding – somewhat bizarrely – that neither writer nor director knew what they were doing – 'Tarantino and Scott are as much prisoners of pop fantasy as Arquette and Slater; they transform everything in their path into a cheap turn-on'. In the *New York Times* Janet Maslin chose to see the same film very differently – 'a vibrant, grisly, gleefully amoral road movie . . . sure to offend a good-sized segment of the movie-going population' she commented, perhaps thinking of other critics as well. Ms Maslin thought Arquette's performance full of 'surprising sweetness' and the film as a whole much 'surer' of itself and much funnier than similar recent films such as *Kalifornia*. She was also impressed with the variety of minor roles played by major stars commenting that 'each of the minor performers here is treated as a guest star, and allowed to make the most of his character's little idiosyncrasies'. On the whole, she considered *True Romance* 'a movie-mad fairy tale with a body count for modern times'. The *Chicago Sun-Times*'s Roger Ebert was also feeling positive – and indeed defensive of Tarantino, commenting that there were few objections to *True Romance* he had not 'thought of, and I dismiss them all with a wave of the hand'. The reason? 'This is the kind of movie that creates its own universe, and glories in it.' *True Romance* was a movie 'made with such energy, such high spirits, such an enchanting goofiness, that it's impossible to resist'. While praising Scott's handling, Ebert considered Tarantino the film's real author. In *Rolling Stone* the feeling was also positive. The film was 'savagely funny' and a 'thrill ride'. The magazine correctly judged that the 'blistering confrontation scene' between Hopper and Walken, thanks to both men being 'in peak form', would be 'talked about for years'. With Arquette and Slater a 'wildly comic and sexy pair of bruised romantics' the whole film was 'dynamite'.

THE NUMBERS: *True Romance*'s total US take was $12,281,500. It was released on 10 September 1993 in the

United States. With an estimated budget less than its US take it has to constitute a substantial profit success across the last ten years of international sales, VHS and DVD releases.

FINAL COMMENT: Scott's film is ludicrous, glossy, bug-eyed and flashy in a way that Tarantino's own never are. The performances are different from how you'd expect them to be in a Tarantino movie, with every actor seemingly occupying their own physical universe and psychological space rather than existing as part of a coherent framework of people who could realistically be in the same room as one another as they do in Tarantino's own films. Can you imagine Gary Oldman's Drexl talking to Walken's Don Vincenzo? They couldn't occupy the same screen any more than Mickey Mouse could convincingly share a scene with *Taxi Driver*'s (Martin Scorsese, 1976) Travis Bickle. This piecemeal feeling is, in part, created by the presence of heavyweight stars in little cameo roles, many of them isolated from the story's main action for much of their screen time and left to do their own thing. It gives the film the feeling of being some kind of vast collection of star turns. That said, there isn't a single performance in here – those star turns included – that isn't absolutely note perfect on its own terms and within its own frame of reference. Slater and, especially, Arquette steal the breath as the desperately in love, so uncool they're fabulously cool young lovers.

Scott's visual style – a lot of stationary camera set-ups with frequent, very fast cutting, stages flooded with smoke and diffused light and echoing with lots of big sound effects – is a million miles from Tarantino's but his more charming, less cohesive, less self-conscious but more straightforwardly slick, buddy-movie version of Tarantino-land works beautifully. Had Tarantino made this film himself it might have been non-linear and have earned its ending of purest tragedy but it wouldn't have been a tenth as lovable as the film Tony Scott made. For a lot of people, the writer of this book included, that would be too high a price to pay.

TARANTINO True Romance

Sleep With Me (1994)

Tarantino's lengthy cameo as a character named Sid in this Meg Tilly and Eric Stoltz starring rom com sees him deliver a monologue on the 'hidden' homosexual subtext of *Top Gun* (Tony Scott, 1986), the 'shades, guys, planes' blockbuster which propelled Tom Cruise to the forefront of his generation of film stars. *Top Gun* is, of course, so butch it's unfeasibly camp but Tarantino's brilliantly enunciated demonstration of why *Top Gun* is *really* about a never-mentioned sexual relationship between Cruise's Maverick and Anthony Edwards's Goose elucidates the point with terrifying clarity. While obviously reminiscent of his on-screen deconstruction of Madonna's record 'Like A Virgin' in *Reservoir Dogs* the monologue is, in part, actually the work of Tarantino's friend Roger Avary. Although seemingly intended to be slyly subversive and shockingly funny, Tarantino's and Avary's analysis of the film is so compelling that it has entered pop culture and become, essentially, the dominant reading of the film's basic self – although it is worth pointing out that some of the 'quotes' that Tarantino says come from *Top Gun*'s dialogue are, in fact, subtly altered in order to make the 'truth' of the reading more immediately obvious and amusing.

Crimson Tide

Tarantino provided some 'script doctoring' input into this 1995 Tony Scott-directed, Jerry Bruckheimer-produced submarine action drama at the director's request. This was mostly to improve the dialogue (a 'script doctor' is someone who provides script additions to a film's screenplay for financial remuneration but no credit). A few lines in the film, such as a seemingly endless discussion of the comic book superhero the Silver Surfer, undeniably bear Tarantino's stamp (indeed a poster of the Silver Surfer, former herald to Galactacus, appears in Tarantino's *Reservoir Dogs*) but they don't lift the movie above the level of 'ordinary'. Tarantino's influence is felt in other ways though, such as with a character named 'Vossler', an obvious reference to his pre-fame colleague Rand Vossler, the one-time putative director of the original *Natural Born Killers* screenplay.

Natural Born Killers (1994)

Original Screenplay by Quentin Tarantino

SUMMARY: Mickey and Mallory Knox, a pair of husband and wife serial killers, who cut a dance of death across America murdering forty-eight people in less than three weeks, are in prison. They are to be moved to a state-run mental institution for the criminally insane thanks to trumped up charges claiming them as mentally deficient; which they aren't. Thanks to the industry that has grown around their notoriety, shock-journalist Wayne Gale wants to make a follow-up to his TV documentary about them. He interviews Mickey for this, eventually becoming dragged into Mickey's (ultimately successful) attempt to flee incarceration, rescue his wife and set out on the road again. Despite convincing himself that he has forged a bond with the couple, Wayne is killed by them after they escape the state's custody. They leave his camera behind as a record of what they've been doing, knowing that someone will collect it and use the footage to fuel America's obsession with them.

DEVELOPMENT: Quentin Tarantino wrote his second screenplay *Natural Born Killers* at the end of the 1980s as a potential directorial feature which could be made for less than $1million. He eventually abandoned it, and wrote (and subsequently succeeded in directing) *Reservoir Dogs* instead. After the success of *Reservoir Dogs*, Tarantino was asked by Rand Vossler, who controlled the rights, whether he wanted to direct the screenplay for *Natural Born Killers* as his second directorial feature, but he declined. Vossler then sold them on to Jane Hamsher and Don Murphy who offered the screenplay to various production companies and eventually Oliver Stone became involved in the project. Stone initiated a rewrite, undertaken by David Veloz while Stone was busy directing *Heaven and Earth* (1993). Veloz had graduated from the University of California's film school in 1991. Since working on *Natural Born Killers*, Veloz has written and directed *Permanent Midnight*, starring Ben Stiller as a heroin-addicted comedy writer, and scripted *Behind Enemy Lines* (John Moore, 2001), a military thriller starring Owen Wilson and Gene Hackman. A second rewrite of *Natural Born Killers* was then undertaken by Stone himself in collaboration with Richard Rutowski. Rutowski was Stone's former assistant and later became his regular producer. He'd also played 'Death' in Stone's *The Doors* (1991). It was this rewrite that added the idea of the internalised demons and the Native American element, and this version that Stone cast and based his directed film upon. Tarantino requested that his 'written by' credit be replaced with a 'story by' one, and was quoted as saying 'I really didn't want anyone to think I'd written some of the stuff that was in there!'

SCREENPLAY: Despite Oliver Stone's objections, Tarantino's original screenplay was published by Faber & Faber in the UK in the mid 1990s. What the book contains is a highly imaginative, if slightly shapeless, script that doesn't attempt to understand the Mickey and Mallory characters (in the manner that Stone's rewrite would) and instead concentrates on exploring the media circus that surrounds them. They are unknown and unknowable, not because they are (as Mickey claims) 'not human', but because the viewer is never allowed close enough to them to be sure of the truth about them. This is clearly deliberate on screenwriter Tarantino's part – he keeps the characters at a distance precisely because they are the focus of the media maelstrom that his script is really about. This fairly straightforward conceit is designed to make the audience question how much they know about real people who are surrounded by such a media frenzy. Dramatically it's what German poet and theatrical practitioner Bertolt Brecht called *verifrehndung* (untranslatable but essentially 'alienation technique'), dividing the audience from the characters in a manner conducive to making the audience concentrate on the issues.

If that sounds like a stretch for Tarantino's pop appreciation of culture it's worth noting that, as well as being massively influential on most branches of drama, Brecht moved to Hollywood and scripted pictures like *Hangmen Also Die!* (Fritz Lang, 1943) and wrote the lyrics to 'Mack the Knife'.

While the structure of the *Natural Born Killers* screenplay is not entirely linear, it is basically so. It makes use of many brief flashbacks often, and unusually, from the characters' points of view (such as when Mickey interrogates Grace in the courtroom) although occasionally not (to show the murder of Mallory's parents). (Had they been filmed as intended, they would have cut away briefly before returning to the 'present time' action, for example, in 'The Bonnie Situation' section of *Pulp Fiction*, where the audience sees a hypothetical moment of Bonnie coming home to find gangsters and a corpse in her living room.)

The structural unorthodoxy that sits at the centre of the screenplay concerns the episode of *American Maniacs*, the fictional TV series presented by the character Wayne Gale, which concentrates on Mickey and Mallory's crimes. The second quarter of the screenplay is given over entirely to a relation of this, as yet, unfinished instalment of that TV series. Had the screenplay Tarantino wrote been produced, the section would have formed a good 30 per cent or so of the finished feature. This is effectively one huge flashback, although it is one experienced by all the characters simultaneously with the audience.

There are other structural tricks in the script: one is to disrupt the potential film's audience by having the TV crew's camera stop working just as it appears Mickey is about to explain why he and Mallory do what they do.

The screenplay reads as a satirical black comedy rather than a thriller with blackly comic elements, and the key element of a redemptive character curve or defining redemptive moment is absent from the script entirely. Wayne Gale is also perhaps Tarantino the screenwriter's only entirely unappealing character (although the rewritten version of Richie Gecko could give him a run for his money). He is spectacularly obnoxious, a grotesque carnival parody of the very worst aspects of all newsmen and is simultaneously completely unreal and entirely convincing. Even Mickey and Mallory appeal to the audience more than Gale; they are, at least, in love with one another and the distance Tarantino puts between the audience and them means that we hold on for the possibility that there is some framework within which we can understand them (though there isn't). Gale is played in Stone's film by Robert Downey Jr, as good an actor as has ever worked in Hollywood, and it would have been interesting to see him work his way through Tarantino's version of the character; it would also have been interesting to see how Tarantino the director would have handled the Knoxes leaving Gale bleeding to death in the sand next to his camera.

In terms of the dialogue, there are few of Tarantino's standard rhetorical monologues (perhaps because the topic is further outside his own experience?) than in *True Romance*, but Wayne Gale gets to deliver what seems a largely insincere speech on the unfairnesses of the penal system. There is also Mickey's lengthy courtroom argument (he defends himself and Mallory) which argues that, as one of the men he killed was a highly trained martial artist whose hands were weapons, he was rendered armed and dangerous merely by holding out his hands, to kill him was, in a sense, self-defence. It's smart rhetorical trickery, but seems slightly out of character for Mickey, a rare case of the author's own cleverness inappropriately leaking through to his characters.

The script also contains many notes for the director on how to shoot various scenes, specifying types of film or camera lenses to be used and whether the film should be processed in black and white or colour. Tarantino has noted that if he were writing scripts for others to direct he wouldn't do this, but *Natural Born Killers* was intended as a self-directed project and thus the notes are more *aides-mémoires* than instructions. What is useful about these notes in this case is that it enables a reader to gain a good idea of what the film would have been like technically even while mourning the fact it was never shot and having no idea what inventive camera set-ups Tarantino would have come up with.

To read *Natural Born Killers* is not to see an unmade movie in your head; the script is, though, a very clear planning document for the movie Tarantino wanted to make. Stone's film is not looked at in any detail here. This is largely because, while it is an interesting and at times impressive film, Tarantino has gone to great lengths to distance himself from it and has publicly worried that people will think he wrote what ended up on screen. It's not a Tarantino film in any real sense and has no place other than as trivia in a look at his career.

QUOTES:
Mickey: 'You say "Why?" I say "Why not?"'

Dr Reingold: 'Mickey and Mallory know the difference between right and wrong. They just don't give a damn.'

Wayne Gale: 'You don't mind if I call you a serial killer, do you?'

Movie Mickey: 'Time to get naked and boogie!'

McClusky: These two rat shits are a walking reminder of just how fucked up our system really is.'

RECURRING ELEMENTS: Names that appear both in *Natural Born Killers* and other Tarantino scripts include: Scagnetti (a policeman here, a parole officer in *Reservoir Dogs*); Spivey (a hostage here, a pimp in *True Romance* and an off-screen fence in *Reservoir Dogs*); and Newendyke (Tim Roth's character in *Reservoir Dogs* is Freddie Newendyke/Mr Orange, while in *Natural Born Killers* it's the name of an unseen hostage). As in *Reservoir Dogs* there is a policeman called Nash. Mickey obsesses over Mallory's bare feet while incarcerated. The script features, though doesn't end with, a Mexican stand-off. The screenplay indicates that sound effects can be used off-screen to suggest a vast chase involving helicopters but which can be staged for a lot less money. Tarantino eventually used this technique in *Reservoir Dogs*.

SPURIOUS INTERTEXTUALITY: The ending of *Butch Cassidy and the Sundance Kid* (George Roy Hill, 1969) is mentioned, as is *El Dorado* (Howard Hawks, 1966). Bruce Lee is invoked as part of Mickey's 'self-defence' speech in court. Mickey asks someone to 'Riddle me this!', the catchphrase of The Riddler in DC's *Batman* comics. Mickey is thrilled that his episode of *American Maniacs* got 'a larger Nielsen share' than the one about Ted Bundy, but is equally pleased that he didn't beat the episode about Charles Manson, as he wouldn't want to beat the King. Chat-show master David Letterman is also mentioned. At one point the script's stage directions intimate that dialogue is to be delivered at fast-talking 'His Girl Friday pace', referring to the 1940 Cary Grant comedy a fantastic movie Tarantino has often mentioned as an inspiration. The *American Maniacs* production team's list of great journalist coups includes Elton John confessing his bi-sexuality to *Rolling Stone*, the coverage of the Hindenberg disaster, Truffaut talking about Hitchcock, the Watergate scandal, David Frost interviewing Richard Nixon, and Raymond Burr witnessing Godzilla destroying Tokyo. This last example is, obviously, fictional and from the movies *Kaijû no Gojira* aka *Godzilla, King of the Monsters*, made in 1956 and directed by Ishirô Honda and Terry O Morse and *Gojira* aka *Godzilla 1985*, made in 1984 and directed by Koji Hashimoto and R J Kizer.

Two fictional movies, which don't exist outside Tarantino's own work, are also featured: *Thrill Killers* is the biopic made of Mickey and Mallory's crime spree; and

Conquering Huns of Neptune is a 'Burr Brothers' exploitation flick said to have inspired them (it so inspired them, they let its directors live when the Burrs accidentally got involved in one of Mickey and Mallory's massacres).

MUSICAL NOTES: Both Mickey and Mallory mutter and sing songs; tunes they like include Johnny Cash's 'Ring of Fire' (actually written by his wife June Carter and Merle Kilgore, incidentally), 'Love Grows Where My Rosemary Goes' (by Edison Lighthouse, as later mentioned in *Reservoir Dogs*) and 'He's a Rebel' (written by Gene Pitney, produced by Phil Spector and recorded by The Crystals). Mickey also knows 'Leader of the Pack' (written by Ellie Greenwich, recorded by the Shangri-Las) and 'Town Without Pity' (another Pitney composition) as well as Burt Bacharach's 'I Only Want To Be With You' and 'Needles and Pins' (penned by Jack Nitzsche and Sonny Bono and released by The Searchers).

This may seem like a random collection of the records Tarantino likes, but each one plugs into the script's main themes, concentrating on the steadfastness of Mickey and Mallory's love for one another, their status as outsiders, the pain they cause others, the pain caused to them, the pain they cause to themselves and the crushing nature of the media storm around them. A nice, accidental prefiguring of future Tarantino projects is apparent from the inclusion of 'Long Time Woman' as sung by Pam Grier, which would eventually feature (alongside Pam herself) in *Jackie Brown*.

FINAL COMMENT: Quentin Tarantino has written some brilliant screenplays. Oliver Stone has directed some brilliant films. Neither the screenplay Tarantino wrote for *Natural Born Killers* nor the film Stone made is an example of either of those. That Tarantino's pre-fame screenplay was reworked by a similarly strong-willed and idiosyncratic director is nothing more than a rather odd coincidence. It could just have easily ended up as a cheap exploitation flick, directed in a very standard manner and marketed with Tarantino's name foremost. It would probably have been a much less confused, though no less controversial, production if it had. The screenplay is, like *True Romance*, Tarantino's attempt to add to the grand genre of road movies; it's also bleaker, nastier and less sympathetic

Pulp Fiction (1994)

Miramax Films Presents
A Band Apart and Jersey Films Production
A Film by Quentin Tarantino
Pulp Fiction
Casting by Ronnie Yeskei, CSA, Gary M Zuckerbrod, CSA
Music Supervisor: Karyn Rachtman
Costume Designer: Betsy Heimann
Production Designer: David Wasco
Editor: Sally Menke
Director of Photography: Andrzej Seluka
Co-executive Producers: Bob Weinstein, Harvey Weinstein,
Richard N Gladstein
Executive Producers: Danny DeVito, Michael Shamberg,
Stacey Sher
Stories by Quentin Tarantino and Roger Avary
Produced by Lawrence Bender
Written and Directed by Quentin Tarantino

TAGLINES: 'Girls like me don't make invitations like this to just anyone.'

'You won't know the facts until you've seen the fiction.'

'I don't smile for pictures.'

'Just because you are a character doesn't mean you have character.'

CAST (IN ORDER OF APPEARANCE): Tim Roth (Pumpkin), Amanda Plummer (Honey Bunny), Laura Lovelace (Waitress), John Travolta (Vincent Vega), Samuel L Jackson (Jules Winnfield), Phil LaMarr (Marvin), Frank Whaley (Brett), Burr Steers (Roger), Bruce Willis (Butch Coolidge), Ving Rhames (Marsellus Wallace), Paul Calderon (Paul), Bronagh Gallagher (Trudi), Rosanna Arquette (Jody), Eric Stoltz (Lance), Uma Thurman (Mia), Jerome Patrick Hoban (Ed Sullivan), Michael Gilden (Phillip Morris Page),

Gary Shorelle (Ricky Nelson), Susan Griffiths (Marilyn
Monroe), Eric Clark (James Dean), Joseph Pilato (Dean
Martin), Brad Parker (Jerry Lewis), Steve Buscemi (Buddy
Holly), Lorelei Leslie (Mamie van Doren), Emil Sitka ('Hold
Hands You Lovebirds'), Brenda Hillhouse (Butch's mother),
Christopher Walken (Captain Koons), Chandler Lindauer
(Young Butch), Sy Sher (Klondike), Robert Ruth
(Sportscaster #1), Rich Turner (Sportscaster #2), Angela
Jones (Esmarelda Villalobos), Don Blakely (Wilson's
Trainer), Carl Allen (Dead Floyd Wilson), Maria de
Medeiros (Fabienne), Karen Maruyama (Gawker #1), Kathy
Griffin (Herself), Venessia Valentino (Pedestrian/Bonnie),
Linda Kaye (Shot Woman), Duane Whitaker (Maynard),
Peter Greene (Zed), Stephen Hibbert (The Gimp), Alexis
Arquette (Man #4), Quentin Tarantino (Jimmie), Harvey
Keitel (The Wolf), Julia Sweeney (Raquel), Lawrence Bender
(Long-Hair Yuppie Scum)

SUMMARY (IN CHRONOLOGICAL ORDER): After
having collected a valuable briefcase containing an
unspecified desirable commodity from some wayward
associates, hitman Vincent Vega and his partner Jules
Winnfield have to clear up after a corpse when Vincent
accidentally kills a fellow employee of gangster Marsellus
Wallace while he's riding in their car. After being helped out
of this tight spot by a 'problem solver' known as 'The Wolf'
they go for breakfast, where Jules foils a robbery and
announces that he's giving up his life of crime although he
agrees to accompany Vincent back to Marsellus's base of
operations in order to deliver the briefcase. As they arrive
Vincent has a brief conversation with Butch Coolidge, a
fighter who is being paid by Marsellus to take a dive. That
night Vincent has to take Mrs Mia Wallace out for dinner
while Marsellus is not in town; she overdoses on his heroin
thinking it to be cocaine, and he fights to save her life. She
goes home and they promise to never talk of the evening's
events. Despite being paid off, Butch Coolidge refuses to

take a dive in the ring, and inadvertently kills his opponent in the process of winning the boxing match which he has bet heavily on himself to win knowing that the information about the fight being fixed has permeated LA gambling circles. The next morning, while fleeing the state, he kills Vincent – who has been sent after him – and is later captured, along with Marsellus who, thanks to Jules's resignation, is also pursuing him himself, by a pair of rednecks who plan to rape and murder both of them. Butch escapes, and then returns and rescues Wallace, unable to leave even him to that fate. A grateful Marsellus cancels out the contract on Butch and relieves him of his debt on the condition he leaves Los Angeles and never comes back.

DEVELOPMENT: In March 1992, having been given script development money by Tristar to write his next picture, Quentin Tarantino hired an apartment in Amsterdam and began to work on material he had come up with alongside his pre-fame friend Roger Avary, planning to develop it into a projected 'portmanteau' picture. The basic idea for *Pulp Fiction* had occurred to Tarantino years before, hence Avary's involvement in its genesis, but he later said that the concept of how to write the script effectively only occurred to him while cutting *Reservoir Dogs* alongside his film editor Sally Menke. Unusually for Tarantino he didn't begin work immediately upon being seized by the idea and instead he ruminated on the script for months before renting his Amsterdam apartment and setting to work. He found that the script changed shape as he wrote it, becoming more personal and less generic as it unfolded. One of its central characters, Vincent Vega, acquired a recent trip to Europe as part of his backstory so that Tarantino could get the character to vocalise material that had occurred to him during this period of living outside of the United States for the first time.

The idea of a film containing several interconnected stories, perhaps linked with a framing sequence, had mostly

been used for cheap horror movies in the past, but had lately
garnered some critical respect with *New York Stories*
(Woody Allen, Francis Ford Coppola, Martin Scorsese,
1989). Tarantino took as his model *Black Sabbath* (Mario
Bava, 1963), an Italian horror film, and used the format to
work in material reminiscent of the kind of story that had
appeared in the magazine *Black Mask*. (Operating between
1921 and 1951 *Black Mask* was a crime fiction magazine
notable in that characters like Perry Mason, Sam Spade and
Philip Marlowe all made their first appearances within its
pages). He later admitted that this aspect of *Pulp Fiction*
largely became lost in the writing: 'I just finished the script
and it's not really like that at all.' He's partially right, for
while that element isn't as prevalent as his intentions might
suggest (so much so that the script's subtitle 'Three stories
. . . about one story' doesn't appear onscreen), it is an
important part of the film's appeal.

Having completed his screenplay, for which he was to be
paid $1 million by Tristar, Tarantino handed it into the
studio. They blinked, baulking at the perceived levels of
violence and profanity. The document Tarantino sent them
also had 'Last Draft' written on the front and was quite
clearly what he intended to film, 'what I'm prepared to
make', he said later. 'They were scared of it,' he also
commented. 'And they didn't think it was going to be
funny.' Tristar packed up on the project and Tarantino was
'very disillusioned', having previously felt that Tristar, a
company run by Michael Medavoy who had insisted on
running Orion Pictures as though it were an independent
company throughout the 1980s, would be able to offer him
the support he needed to get the film made his way.
Fortunately Miramax, the company run by the brothers
Harvey and Bob Weinstein stepped in to fund the picture,
giving Tarantino the independent 'studio' that he used as his
base for filmmaking until the Weinsteins departed the
company in early 2005.

SCREENPLAY: *Pulp Fiction*'s structure isn't as fantastically complicated as that of *Reservoir Dogs* or the later *Kill Bill* but it is richer than either. This is because not only is it out of order, it also contains what one might call key 'moments' which reflect on other scenes in the script. For example, on a clearly crass, but also quite clever, level Jules's intonation in the prologue that 'Marsellus Wallace doesn't like to be fucked by anybody except Mrs Wallace' has a completely different resonance with the audience when seen again as part of 'The Bonnie Situation' because in a scene that we're shown before this (but which takes place chronologically after it) the audience has seen Marsellus being sexually assaulted by another man. The dividing up of the screenplay into these sections also allows the film to contain three sections each of which end with a kind of redemption. This not only confirms (as *Jackie Brown* and *Kill Bill* would later prove beyond doubt) that it is redemption that most interests Tarantino dramatically but also allows the most significant of the three redemptions (Jules's) to occur at the end of the movie even though it takes place in the middle of the story. Equally, it should be remembered that, as in *Reservoir Dogs*, Tarantino is partially playing with structure for the sheer pleasure of it; to demonstrate that non-chronological movies can be made, made well, and be easily understood. As Tarantino has said in interviews more times than you can count, it's not that he doesn't like linear structure, it's just that he wants it acknowledged that it isn't the only way to make a movie – 'It's not like I'm on this major crusade against linear narrative ... what I am against is saying it's the only game in town.'

Pulp Fiction basically comes in six sections:

1. Prologue 1: In the diner
2. Prologue 2: Vincent and Jules's Hit
3. 'Vincent Vega and Marsellus Wallace's Wife'
4. 'The Gold Watch'
5. 'The Bonnie Situation'
6. Epilogue: In the diner

This is the order the pieces occur in the finished film. Chronologically they occur 2, 5, 1, 6, 3, 4. This isn't actually 100 per cent accurate because 1 and 6 actually take place simultaneously and 4 begins with an establishing scene set some twenty years before, but it's basically correct. It's also possible, although not certain, that the night on which Butch throws the fight is the same night on which Mia and Vincent go to Jack Rabbit Slims, in which case some elements of the end of 3 and the beginning of 4 would overlap. A version of the film cut together to represent the events in the order in which they happen might be more 'correct' but it would be less satisfying dramatically. Even leaving aside the enormously pleasing symmetry of the film ending more or less exactly where it began – a device probably borrowed from *Once Upon A Time in America* (Sergio Leone, 1984), a film which also contributes the shot of Vincent's beatific smile while in a heroin haze – the rearrangement places the story pieces in their most aesthetically pleasing order. It also assists in the creation of the impression – partially accurate – that this is a collection of short stories rather than a single narrative.

The prologue is a fascinating piece. We begin in a diner, as in *Reservoir Dogs*. Tim Roth is there, as in *Reservoir Dogs*. But this time he's using his real accent, rather than pretending to be American. This time he's sitting with a woman, and there are no speaking female characters in *Reservoir Dogs* at all. These two, obviously lovers, are having a conversation about different kinds of robberies and the pressures of a criminal lifestyle that obviously echoes *Reservoir Dogs*. The very point of their discussion – that robbing banks involves too much planning, too many armed people and too little likelihood of success to be worthwhile – could almost be a reaction to the events of *Reservoir Dogs*. And then they start to rob the diner. In the space of just a few seconds the audience has observed a rapid combination of things they'd expect from a Tarantino picture having seen *Dogs*, combined with a commentary on it and reversals of those expectations. Suddenly after this, the viewer is catapulted into the electrifyingly fast pace of the theme tune (specified in the script) which is as memorable as, but very different from, the slow, cool, expressive music used to open Tarantino's earlier film. This is another example of the first few moments of this film simultaneously confounding and playing along with the audience's expectations.

The use of language in the prologue is very precise. Honey Bunny's use of the word 'execute' is absolutely key. She says the neutral, even moralistic, 'execute' rather than the pejorative 'murder' or the straightforward 'kill'. She's hiding her own willingness to kill in order to gain money by theft behind a cloak of self-righteous language. The American state 'executes' people for capital crimes. It's a *punishment*. Honey Bunny's choice of words indicates that she sees the killings she is 'forced' to commit in the course of her life of crime in the same self-justifying framework. This is particularly important as it introduces us to the thematic concern over Jules's monologue (see **EZEKIEL 25:17**) which he insists is a direct quotation from the Bible, and which also gives his actions a pseudo-justified framework. What the audience doesn't know yet, thanks to the structure, is that Jules (who we haven't even encountered yet, thanks again to the structure) is in this diner himself and that it will be him who resolves the crisis that Honey Bunny and Pumpkin have created. (Another example of this moral relativism in the film concerns Vincent Vega's attitudes. Vincent is a heroin-shooting, multiple-murdering pig-ignorant career criminal; but he's one who thinks it's morally wrong for someone to damage someone else's car for fun and is slightly disgusted by people with piercings. Tarantino the writer tries hard to present people who have views, opinions and their own moral universes which, while very different from the audience's, are obviously both real and feel right to them.)

After this we cut into the second sequence which is actually chronologically the first and more properly part of the fifth, leaving the audience suspended with regard to what happened in the diner after we left it. On first viewing some viewers may, due to the portmanteau nature of the plot, assume that it's actually a non sequiter.

The next scene is Vincent and Jules in Vincent's car, talking about Amsterdam, from where Vincent has recently returned. Again the use of language is deceptively precise; Vincent Vega has spent three years in Europe but he has, judging by his comments, spent all of his time there eating in McDonald's, drinking beer and getting stoned. He's up on the finer points of Dutch law in relation to the selling, buying, possession and carrying of hash-weed but he can't speak a word of any language other than English. He's ignorant despite the pride he takes in his meagre knowledge and, a few moments later, Jules has to explain the concept of a television pilot to him. Like a lot of wannabe snobs he takes a misplaced pride in the fact that he doesn't watch television. Vincent is, and this has escaped a lot of people's notice, a genuinely culturally illiterate character, perhaps Tarantino's first. We know from the script he likes heroin, Elvis and hamburgers, but he lacks the depth and breadth of knowledge of trivia demonstrated by characters like Clarence Worley or Alabama Whitman in *True Romance* or even his brother Vic in *Reservoir Dogs*. (Even when, later in the picture, Vincent pulls out his one piece of pop-culture knowledge that it's Mamie Van Doren not Marilyn Monroe the script acknowledges that this is merely him having one of very few 'moments'.)

It's also worth noting that Vincent and Jules's banter is, in time-honoured Tarantino tradition, designed to sooth the audience after the sudden explosion of violence at the end of the diner scene and to lull them into a false sense of security before what is to come. Jules's and Vincent's following scene in the apartment contains much the same kind of banter, but this time there's a palpable undercurrent of menace. Jules's sudden shout of 'I don't remember asking you a goddamned thing!' is a very small example of the kind of reversal Tarantino excels at. It's actually quite frightening as the audience suddenly gets a feeling for what this man (who has started to come across as funny) is capable of. Just a few moments later, after another dampening down in comic rhetoric – more chat about burgers and the metric system – the audience *sees* what he's capable of as Jules shoots an unarmed man dead to make a point. Jules and Vincent begin firing in unison shortly afterwards and suddenly there's a caption card as the audience is moved to another place, another time and the first of the film's three stories 'proper' which is entitled 'Vincent Vega and Marsellus Wallace's Wife'. In the script the prologue ended a little later, with Bret charging out of the bathroom and firing his gun at Vincent and Jules. Tarantino obviously chose to end the section earlier in the editing, eschewing making a cliffhanger out of if and how Jules and Vincent survive, perhaps so that their 'miraculous' survival in the film's third story 'proper' didn't seem to be a cop out or to avoid viewers asking themselves, while watching 'The Gold Watch', if and how Vincent could die twice.

More than either of the two stories to follow 'Vincent Vega and Marsellus Wallace's Wife' feels like a short film – one that works on its own terms and at a pace slightly removed from the rest of the picture. This is partially a recognition of the story's place as a secret between the characters who go through it (as is established at its end) but is also Tarantino the director trying out something that Tarantino the writer has previously played with a little – the drama dominated by a female character.

In this Vincent, who we have already encountered, takes the fabulous Mrs Wallace out 'not on a date' but in order to amuse her while her husband is out of town. Mia Wallace has already been built up in the second prologue, along with her equally as yet unseen husband, through Jules's and Vincent's conversation about Marsellus having a man crippled for giving her a foot massage. What is especially remarkable is that despite all this build up Tarantino's screenplay (and direction, see **KEY SHOTS**) manages to force the audience to forget the implicit threat that hangs over Vincent's head should he either fail to entertain Mrs Wallace or, and this is perhaps more likely, entertain her too much. Their banter is written and played as flirtatious, with nicknames ('Cowgirl') banded around, and an obvious rapport developing between them, leading up to their dance. Also worth pointing out here is Tarantino making subversive use of a cliché. 'Powder my nose' is usually a euphemism for going to the lavatory. Here it's a punning (and much more accurate, come to think of it) euphemism for snorting cocaine,

'Why do we feel it's necessary to yak about bullshit in order to be comfortable?' asks Mia a few minutes later. This is why she connects with Vincent. She isn't ignorant, but she'd rather not talk about cultural nonsense out of choice. This is Tarantino again commenting on his own perceived techniques and filmmaking persona. A few minutes later Vincent's ignorance is further emphasised by his confused reaction to Mia's declaration that her pilot was 'My Fifteen Minutes' – clearly a reference to Andy Warhol's statement that in the future everyone would be famous for fifteen minutes – which goes way over his head.

The audience is lulled into a sense that the rest of the film, or at least the rest of this story, is going to be as idly dreamy and vaguely romantic. The violence of the two prologues seems so long ago. As Vincent debates with himself in the mirror, Mia dances to 'Girl, You'll Be A Woman Soon'. It's an interesting choice of music for the script to make. Whatever the songwriter's original intentions it's a record which carries within it the implication that the singer is about to have sex with the implicitly virginal person to whom he is singing the song; or that he would were she old enough to be 'available'. (This is, while at the very least faintly unpleasant, not particularly rare territory for pop music, think of, for example, Abba's 'Does Your Mother Know').

While no member of the audience would map this scenario onto the Vincent–Mia relationship as it has evolved over the story we've been watching – or assume that Mrs Wallace is virgo intacto come to that – the general sense of the record conveys the idea of Mia as someone who Vincent must repress his obvious desire for. It's awkward and difficult and funny and strangely touching; and then Mia accidentally overdoses by snorting Vincent's heroin believing it to be cocaine.

This classic Tarantino reversal of tone leaves Vincent in a terrible situation. If she dies, he's dead himself. Vincent, of course, takes Mia to his drug dealer, Lance. Dialogue makes clear the horror that Vincent feels at his situation and his unashamed bullying of Lance into taking Mia into his house by invoking Marsellus is quietly nasty. He's basically threatening Lance with death, but then he is being refused entry to the home of someone who earlier told him '*Mi casa, es cu casa.*' It is, and this has generally gone uncommented upon, Lance's fault as much as anyone else's that Mia is in this state. It's Lance who ran out of the right kind of carrier for Vincent's heroin and gave it to him in a cocaine baggie instead. As Lance and Vincent try desperately to revive Mia, the scene descends into a sort of black farce, with Lance's wife desperate to get what she thinks is a corpse out of her home while Vincent and Lance argue over who should do what and why. Again the injured professional pride of someone who has had their own moral universe trampled on arises. Lance has never administered an adrenaline shot to the heart because, he claims, none of his friends would be stupid enough to mess up 'getting high' to this extent.

'This ain't no fuckin' joke man!' bellows Vincent as he tries to make things right, except of course it is. It's very funny indeed even though it really shouldn't be.

The second story begins in another, entirely different, vein of black comedy. The audience is pushed back decades to a time not long after the Vietnam War. A boy who simply wants to watch cartoons is being lectured about a gold watch. Captain Koons's speech to the pre-teen Butch Coolidge is classic Tarantino writing; in it, Koons explains how this watch was worn by the boy's father, grandfather and great-grandfather when they fought in the Vietnam War, Second World War and First World War, respectively. Koons initially takes time to fill in this family context of the timepiece in exhausting detail: he knows when the watch was made, who it was made by, where it was bought, where it was stored between wars, the names of all its previous owners and all sorts of other details. This sheer level of information is initially intimidating to the audience; as it clearly is to Butch. It also convinces us, absolutely, that it's all true. The litany of deaths and the invocation of so many wars and sacrifices fill the scene with eerie verisimilitude; this means that when the scene becomes strange and less comfortable – as Koons describes how he hid the watch 'up my ass' after Butch's father died of dysentery – the audience really doesn't know how to react. The level of detail previously used to establish Butch's lineage is now used to portray a grotesque, incomprehensible comic hell. Koons's words are solemn, ludicrous, heartfelt, grim and hilarious all at once. The scene is at the same time comically scatological and deeply moving. It's never the same experience watching this scene, no matter how many times you see it. Mainstream American culture finds the mocking of the military unconscionable to the point of perhaps being actually treasonous and this scene walks the line between serious and ridiculous, acceptable and unacceptable with remarkable skill.

Yet there is still more going on here; the shape of the scene's dramatic motion, from the noble to the domestic to the brutal to the debased is also the dramatic motion of the rest of 'The Gold Watch' itself. After this scene, 'The Gold Watch' goes from Butch's refusal to throw a fight to his homely interactions with his lover Fabienne to his confrontation with Marsellus to the horrible goings-on in the basement with Zed and the Gimp. As the 'Beaumont' plot would later be in the *Jackie Brown* script, this scene is the shape of 'The Gold Watch' in microcosm. In addition to this it sets up to the audience, as well as to Butch, that he is a man in a long line of self-sacrificing heroes. This means not only that the audience anticipates his later heroism but that the audience would be disappointed if it did not come about and thus doubly rejoice when it does. Just as the Coen brothers' *The Big Lebowski* (1998) goes out of its way to place its central 'Dude' character into a lineage of American heroes that includes the gumshoe and the cowboy, this scene makes sure we know that Butch is – or should be – a soldier.

As is so often the case with Tarantino, the words in the scene are picked precisely, even perfectly, to achieve this. Koons twice calls the young Butch 'little man' forcing responsibility upon him, denying him childhood as a separate state to adulthood, making it merely a precursor. The small, but smaller. He also tells him he's 'sure heard a bunch about you'. Even before getting onto the tale of the watch he is loading expectation and responsibility onto Butch's shoulders. It works – the next few scenes make clear that receiving the gold watch was the most important moment in Butch's life; the memory of Captain Koons is one he carried with him at every moment. The very next scene reveals to the audience that they have seen it as he has dreamed of it, moments before he goes out to do the single most dangerous thing he has ever done – fighting to win in a fight he has been paid to throw.

Audiences also might like to consider the not unappealing notion that, given that Koons insists that if *he* had died and Major Coolidge had survived he'd be 'talking to my son Jim right now', there's the implication that Koons himself had a watch or some other precious item that Coolidge would have had to store in his anus. The idea that this seemingly unique story is nothing of the sort is oddly likeable.

The adult Butch wakes from a dream about Captain Koons and the audience realises that the boy being talked to is the same man we saw taking instructions to throw a boxing match from Marsellus Wallace near the beginning of 'Vincent Vega and Marsellus Wallace's Wife'. In that scene there is some interesting ambiguity in the dialogue (as well as the camera set-up – see **KEY SHOTS**) as Butch takes his orders; Butch answers Marsellus's questions with deliberately evasive phrases that seek to imply that he is going to do what Marsellus tells him without stating it. 'It certainly appears so,' he says and later, 'I have no problem with that Mr Wallace.' Marsellus though, understands this and insists that Butch repeat the line 'In the fifth my ass goes down.' What Marsellus misses is that this isn't specific enough; Butch can go down in the fifth round and get up afterwards to win the fight, after all.

Before 'The Gold Watch' can return to its central subject matter it needs to get the plot out of the way first. Butch's journey away from the boxing ring is in a taxi driven by a surreally lascivious woman who is excited by Butch's apparel and thrilled by the news on the radio that the man he beat in the boxing ring has just died. There's some more well-chosen words as she denies that her interest in the machismo of boxing and the brutality of death makes her odd; it's just 'a subject I have much interest in'. Butch doesn't actually shrug and sarcastically retort 'sure, because that's not weird at all, right?' but Bruce Willis's face manages to achieve the same effect anyway.

After meeting with Fabienne and discovering that she has left his watch behind, Butch has to go back to his apartment for it; despite the danger to himself he has to do this because he owes it to three generations of Coolidges and to Captain Koons. There's more surprising writing by Tarantino before this though. Initially there's the marvellous domesticity of Butch's relationship with Fabienne, where the two of them natter about what it's best to have for breakfast and what's on television. This is interesting because the 'banter' aspect of their conversations is highly reminiscent of the conversations between the Reservoir Dogs, yet that had been held to be entirely 'masculine' by many commentators on the release of that film. Here it works as the style for conversations between not only a man and a woman but a man and a woman who are very clearly in love. Fabienne also gets a little Tarantino monologue of her own as she explains to Butch how she wishes she had a pot belly. Not only is it refreshing for a female character on film to speculate that she's too thin, the scene also confirms beyond doubt that this style of dialogue can work entirely outside the context of quipping gangsters. Also interesting is the scripted manner in which Butch becomes so angry upon being told by Fabienne that she's left his watch behind that he physically attacks the furniture. Both Fabienne and the audience are frightened that he will attack her. We think we have the measure of Butch; to see him commit wife battering would violate our understanding of, and sympathy for, him. The audience understands his horror at losing his most valuable possession, but couldn't contemplate sympathising with him if he crossed that line. Instead, he calms down, only to freak out again when in the car on his own as he drives away. This seemingly incidental set of moments adds greatly to Butch's character, both reinforcing his ambiguity and reassuring the audience.

Butch arrives in his apartment where initially he meets no trouble. So easy is his acquisition of his prize watch that he becomes cocky, wanders into the kitchen and begins to make himself breakfast (this has, in fact, been set up already as Fabienne has gone for breakfast without him). Butch opens a cupboard and takes out a box of Pop Tarts. He then takes out two Pop Tarts and puts them in the toaster. He sees something that is out of shot and then he hears the lavatory flush. Vincent emerges, and Butch kills him with his own gun before fleeing.

After Butch encounters Marsellus in the street and the two fight only to accidentally fall into the clutches of two redneck rapist gun-store owners, the tone of the piece takes a sharp turn. If 'Vincent Vega and Marsellus Wallace's Wife' was a twisted romantic comedy with a shock ending and 'The Bonnie Situation' will be (or was, it's already happened, we just haven't seen it) a kind of screwball comedy with elements of the silent comic short, 'The Gold Watch' now twists into a kind of Tobe Hooper pastiche exploitation horror with hillbilly rapist murderers, and abasement in dungeon basements.

Butch manages to escape but, as he's about to leave, he realises that he can't leave anybody to die like that. He begins rooting around the pawnshop for a weapon. He picks up a variety of weapons, including a chainsaw, before settling on the one he needs for his rescue of Marsellus: a samurai sword. This is pure symbolism of which the character is necessarily unaware; he takes the sword for practical reasons, it's a silent weapon that doesn't need to be revved like a chainsaw or cocked like a gun. It's infinitely more deadly than a baseball bat. Yet his carrying it symbolically places him into a longer line of heroes than even his actual ancestors; it makes him a samurai, the weapon ennobles him just as he's about to do something noble. His reward is his freedom, yes, but also the knowledge that he has done, and can do, the right thing. If Butch had left Marsellus to die then he would still have been free, but he wouldn't have had that important self-knowledge. To not throw a boxing match but to fight on and prove that you are the better fighter may *seem* like a noble act but its nobility is detracted by the money Butch has made betting on himself and is pretty much dispelled by the fact that he (unintentionally) killed his opponent in the ring. Saving Marsellus enables Butch to prove to himself that he's a good person. He too is redeemed.

'The Bonnie Situation' is the final one of the main triptych of stories. It is the most straightforwardly comic. In it, Vincent accidentally kills a man in the back of his and Jules's car and the two of them, with assistance from Jules's friend Jimmie and a fixer known as 'The Wolf', have to clear it up. There are elements of silent comedy, the Three Stooges and Laurel and Hardy, in the physical panic and fretting wordplay here but it isn't particularly complex compared to the other two sections. It begins with some interesting dialogue, though, as Jules becomes offended by Vincent's refusal to accept that their escaping death is a miracle and – and this is very telling – by Vincent's casual blasphemies despite being a man who, a few minutes earlier, was willing to misquote the Bible in order to scare people. This use of language, of what people do and don't find offensive in speech based on their experiences and backgrounds is an important topic in relation to 'The Bonnie Situation' for while, as I said, 'The Bonnie Situation' isn't the complex section of *Pulp Fiction* dramatically, it has, over the years, proven the most controversial.

This is because of the huge amount of uses of the word 'nigger' in it, particularly by white characters. It is easy to dismiss the uses of the N-word by white characters in *Reservoir Dogs* as dialogue confirming the prejudices of bad people. In (the rest of) *Pulp Fiction* (as well as 'The Bonnie Situation) it isn't as easy as that. The relatively large number of black characters, the frequency of its utterance (often by sympathetic characters) and the many contexts in which it's used make making sense of the use of this often justly taboo word difficult.

'I went to an all-black school' Tarantino once claimed, seemingly oblivious to the fact that he's (largely) Caucasian himself. What is certainly true is that he grew up in a poor, multi-racial part of Los Angeles where a sizeable portion of the community he lived in was non-Caucasian and where a lot of the ambient culture was dominated by art created by, or for consumption by, African-Americans.

On another occasion Tarantino tried to explain it thus: 'I don't know if I want to be black. I have an affinity for black culture; it has nothing to do with my pigmentation. I just grew up around a lot of black guys, and there were black influences inside my household. My mother used to date black men.'

These reasons, excuses to some, provide background to Tarantino's dramatic use of the N-word, but it's not the whole story. While the below isn't necessarily a reflection of my own views it's clearly the logic that the script operates under. The basic answer is that Tarantino sees himself, and his work, as essentially post-racist (although he's never used that term himself). That's a bold claim, and one that needs some further examination, but it's essentially true.

There are words ('bastard' is a good example) which are essentially offensive to many but which have completely transcended their actual meaning (in this case 'illegitimate') and become terms which can be used both negatively and positively depending on the context. There are other words (the best example is 'cunt') that are exactly the same except that one section of society (in this case, women) is generally more offended by it than another because the word's literal meaning (although it has been largely transcended in this instance also) has more to do with them than it does with other sections of society (i.e. men). 'Nigger' is, for Quentin Tarantino, one of these words. Growing up where he did, around the people he did, he saw the word used in a variety of contexts and clearly came to feel, or always felt, that it had transcended its original American usage as a derogatory term used by whites against blacks in exactly the same way that the far less controversial 'boy' (when used to describe an adult) has. Some people disagree with this instinctive diagnosis, but it's clearly the way that Tarantino uses the N-word in his screenplays. There are multiple contexts for its use, and these contexts, and the way it's used, reflect on the characters who use it, not the writer who wrote the words for the characters to say. (To use an extreme example, nobody would assume that someone who wrote a film in which a Nazi passionately defended his ideology was a Nazi themselves.)

What complicates this variety of definitions further are the distinct but complementary concepts of desensitisation and reclamation. In the 1960s Jewish comedian Lenny Bruce (who knew a fair few things about prejudice himself) once included the word 'nigger' forty times in a single routine because he believed that if you repeated a word often enough it would lose its power to make children cry. The great black stand-up comedian Richard Pryor spent decades doing the same thing. That's desensitisation. Reclamation is, in its simplest form, the use of the N-word by black people to describe other black people affectionately so that the word loses its perjorative meaning completely. The best examples are in hip-hop, including the massively influential act *Niggers With Attitude* and the lyrics of the acts spun off from them, or produced by former members. (This actually opens up the interesting side issue that the next heavily black-culture-influenced white American to take America by storm, Marshall Mathers aka Eminem, has publicly stated time and again that he refuses to say 'Nigger' in any context whatsoever seeing the word, despite its reclamation through the art form he's part of, as not his to use.)

The N-word is used in a variety of contexts in *Pulp Fiction*: not all of them positive, not all of them negative. When Jules or Marsellus Wallace uses the N-word it's clearly meant to be in this reclaimed sense. Marsellus even uses it to describe Vincent (who is white). When Lance uses it to Vincent to denigrate people who don't know as much about drugs as he does it's clearly because he *is* a racist and ignorance and being black are, in his mind, equivalent things. That Vincent is in both scenes just makes the whole thing a bit more difficult to decipher, probably deliberately so.

This finally brings us back to extensive use of the word 'nigger' in 'The Bonnie Situation'. Jimmie, who is white and played by Tarantino himself, uses the word many, many times and often to Jules, who does not react at all. The audience knows from before Jimmie appears that he is friends with Jules.

What is less often noticed is that Jimmie's wife, Bonnie, the person who they're clearing up for, is herself black (she appears in a cutaway). Does this mean that the script, and by extension Jules and Bonnie, sees Jimmie as black by proxy, or at the very least not racist by proxy? I think it does. I think that as far as the script's concerned Jimmie's use of racial epithets carries no more force than Jules's or Marsellus's. That's quite a difficult concept to grasp in a film which contains actual racists.

Samuel L Jackson, who plays in all of Jimmie's scenes, and who has become a close friend of Tarantino's, has certainly implied that he sees Tarantino himself that way. 'He has an affinity for black culture. And he likes to write black characters. He's like my daughters' little white hip-hop friends. They're basically black kids with white skin.'

Jackson has also publicly defended Tarantino on other occasions; after the release of *Jackie Brown* a reporter from *Black Diaspora* magazine verbally attacked Samuel L Jackson at a press junket for being part of *Pulp Fiction* and *Jackie Brown* when they used the N-word so much. 'Why are you so offended?' Jackson demanded of her, arguing that in both films the term was used as a term of endearment as often as it was used in a derogatory manner. On discovering that she was from Trinidad, and that there nobody used 'that word', he virtually bellowed at her, 'I grew up in Tennessee, where I heard that word yelled at me from off of buses ... believe me, if I'm not offended by it, why should you be?'

Tarantino has argued that his characters have to be true to who they are, and speak as they would, ('I'm creating the characters. And I can honestly tell you that where I'm coming from, I'm not lying: the characters are true to themselves') and provided the counter argument that to deny him the right to write black characters is itself racist; which is quite a heavy discussion to arise out of a largely comic piece.

After the conclusion of this 'Bonnie Situation' Vincent and Jules go to a diner for breakfast, and the audience slowly realises that this is the same diner, and at the same time as the robbery in the first prologue. Here Jules's redemption is completed by an extraordinary act (see **VIOLENCE?**).

Samuel L Jackon's performance of his character's final speech is the key to Jules and the whole movie. What Jules understands after his life is spared either by a fluke or by an act of God (depending on how you want to see it) is that he wants to be 'good' and that the life he has led before now has not been out of choice. As he quotes his own misquoted biblical phrasings he deconstructs it for the benefit of himself, Pumpkin and the audience. 'I never really questioned what it meant,' he says, thinking it was just some cold-blooded thing to say before committing a murder. He rejects the interpretation that he is the righteous man, Pumpkin is the evil man and the gun is the shepherd protecting him and the interpretation that 'you're the righteous man and I'm the shepherd and it's the world that's evil and selfish'. He knows he's not intellectually dishonest enough to accept either of those even if he'd like them to be true, however, '. . . that shit ain't the truth. The truth is you're the weak. And I'm the tyranny of evil men. But I'm tryin'. I'm tryin' real hard to be a shepherd.'

There's nothing to add to that.

CASTING: John Travolta had been the biggest movie star in the world thanks to roles in *Saturday Night Fever* (John Badham, 1977) and *Grease* (Randal Kleiser, 1978) but he had fallen slowly, yet spectacularly, from favour. By 1993 he had reached the point where he was appearing in the excruciating series of *Look Who's Talking* 'comedies' with Kirstie Alley. *Pulp Fiction* put Travolta back on the top of the Hollywood heap, winning him several awards and an Oscar nomination. He made the film for a salary of $100,000, below his fee even for that time, and despite reservations about playing a heroin user. Travolta relished working with Tarantino saying 'He lets you put all the icing on the cake. For Vincent, I could mock up the hair, the accent, the walk, the talk.' It's the performance of his career; a very skilful demonstration of a short-tempered, none-to-bright man with an abundance of pride, a man who moves warily and slowly, incapable of doing anything other than the grunt gangster work he does, and needing all of his concentration to simply stay alive. While Tarantino wrote the screenplay before Travolta was cast no one would deny the fact that it's Travolta winning the Jack Rabbitslim's twist contest that adds extra context to the scene. It's not only that the man can obviously dance better than any guy you've ever met, seeing Travolta dance invites the audience to compare Vincent Vega with Travolta's earlier roles, and see in the pudgy, opiate-addled Vincent Vega the decline of the generation that was young at the end of the 70s.

Morehouse College, Atlanta, graduate Samuel L Jackson had auditioned for *Reservoir Dogs* and appeared in a small role in *True Romance*. An experienced stage and television actor, and former drug addict, he had beaten his problems to become a respected industry staple. Pre-*Pulp* roles include in *Jurassic Park* (Steven Spielberg, 1993) and a cameo in *Goodfellas* (Martin Scorsese, 1990) although he was best known for his role in Spike Lee's masterful *Jungle Fever* (1991).

Bruce Willis had come to public attention as wisecracking David Addison in the alarmingly self-aware TV series *Moonlighting* (1985–9) before breaking into movie leading roles with the romantic comedy *Blind Date* (Blake Edwards, 1987) and action comedy thriller *Die Hard* (John McTiernan, 1988). Superstar status seemed inevitable, but *Pulp Fiction* came at a point where Willis was actually failing to move into more serious roles and better movies than his recent projects, such as the execrable *Death Becomes Her* (Robert Zemeckis, 1992). *Pulp Fiction* came out in the same year as Willis's appearances in the far less impressive *North* (Rob Reiner, 1994) and the downright awful *Color of Night* (Richard Rush, 1994). It's an extraordinarily strong performance from Willis (he claimed the script was 'like Shakespeare'), full of ambiguity, pain and repressed violence, and it anticipates his strongest, later career, roles in *Twelve Monkeys* (Terry Gilliam, 1995), *The Sixth Sense* (M Night Shyamalan, 1999) and *Unbreakable* (M Night Shyamalan, 2000). Uma Thurman was immediately noticeable in *Henry and June* (Philip Kaufman, 1990) and *Dangerous Liaisons* (Stephen Frears, 1988) and played the planet Venus in *The Adventures of Baron Munchausen* (Terry Gilliam, 1988). 'Quentin is a great collaborator,' she said of her director. 'He is extremely clear about what he wants, but he's not close minded; he's no bully.' Tarantino was utterly enamoured of his leading lady; they became fast friends and he would later call her his 'muse'. He had no doubts about casting Thurman saying 'I talked to damn near every actress in Hollywood about the Mia role with the idea that when I met Mia I'd know it. Uma came to dinner and I knew within minutes that she was Mia.'

The smaller roles are filled out with people playing impressively against type. Amanda Plummer (Honey Bunny) is a pathetic, snivelling coward and Rosanna Arquette's performance as Jody is deeply irritating in exactly the way it's meant to be – a triumph for an actress who clearly doesn't care whether or not her character is liked by the audience. Tim Roth (Pumpkin) gets to use his real accent in a Tarantino film while Harvey Keitel (see **Reservoir Dogs**) plays the clean, in control and utterly cool Winston Wolf – a part utterly unlike any he'd been strongly associated with.

QUOTES:

Fabienne: 'It's unfortunate that what we find pleasing to the eye and what we find pleasing to the touch are seldom the same.'

Fabienne: 'Tulip is much better than Mongoloid.'

Jules: 'I was just sitting here drinking my coffee, eating my muffin, playing the incident in my head, when I had what alcoholics refer to as a "moment of clarity".'

Marsellus Wallace: 'Pride only hurts. It never helps.'

Jules: 'Cops tend to notice shit like you driving around a car that's drenched in blood.'

Jimmie: 'It's not the coffee in my kitchen, it's the dead nigger in my garage.'

Jules: 'Damn this morning air's some chilly shit.'

The Wolf: 'Because you *are* a character doesn't mean you *have* character.'

Jules: 'He's about as European as English Bob.'

Jules: 'If the answers frighten you Vincent, you should stop asking scary questions.'

Vincent: 'All right, it was a miracle. Can we go now?'

KEY SHOTS: Tarantino's virtuoso and versatile camera style uses the (probably Godard-inspired) technique of parody and subverting film conventions in order to draw attention to them. Mia Wallace's drawing a square (well, actually a rectangle) on the screen as she calls Vincent a 'square' and the use of deliberate bad back projection (aka 'process shots') to show the streets behind characters as they drive along in a car has been noted often. What is less remarked upon is the constant shifts in how the camera is used, always tailored to the essential drama of the scene being shot but segued into the style of the preceding scene in such a way that there is little or no 'jolting' from one scene to another. It's the work of a master manipulator of his audience. Early in the film there's a long tracking shot (over two and a half minutes) during which Vincent and Jules discuss massaging Mia Wallace's feet. Either side of this long tracking shot the conversation is shot in two-shots and in wide shots, emphasising the two men's closeness and the ease with which they work together (compare this with the conversation they have after Jules's 'moment of clarity' which is shot in profile, the two men do not get into the same shot, because they're no longer close). After the two decide not to enter the room just yet, the camera, which has stayed on them constantly, refuses to follow them as they move away from the door and indulge in small talk. It's as if the camera is seeking to remind the characters that the door – the job – not the conversation, should be their focus.

When Vincent arrives at Lance's house begging for help with the overdosed Mia the scene is shot with a handheld camera and using merely 'available light' (rather than filmic light sources) which gives the scene the verisimilitude and pace of documentary footage. Later in the same scene the camera is unwilling to enter the room in which Lance is searching for his medical black book; this adds to the audience's fear that he won't find it, as we can't see him looking and don't know how likely he is to acquire it. It also means viewers don't get to look at the dying Mia for a long time adding to the tension. A similar technique is used with completely different results in Butch's girlfriend's apartment. Here having the camera lurk outside the bathroom in which she and Butch are getting ready for bed cunningly implies intimacy. The viewer feels as if they're eavesdropping through the door of the bathroom, penetrating a private world.

The camera initiates a slow, slow creeping into close-up as Butch realises that he doesn't have his watch, and asks his girlfriend if she's left it behind, a very subtle way of cranking up, almost imperceptibly, the tension in what is, in dialogue terms, an ordinary domestic scene.

The scene in which Christopher Walken cameos as Captain Koons giving the young Butch the abovementioned watch isn't, as many recall it to be, one long take of Walken delivering the monologue. The camera actually cuts back and forth from Walken to the child several times. It is also handheld throughout, and begins – after a close-up of the television on which young Butch is watching cartoons – with a point-of-view shot (from Butch's perspective) into which Koons walks. It's reminiscent of several moments in *The Deer Hunter* (Michael Cimino, 1978) for which Walken won an Oscar for his performance as another Vietnam-era serviceman. Walken performed the monologue three times, and the three, fairly long, close-ups of him reciting sections of it, all come from different takes. Pleasingly, given the film's time shifting narrative, this scene, chronologically the first thing that happens in the film, was the last piece of the picture shot.

Earlier in the film, but later in the narative, when Butch, now an adult, is being lectured by Marsellus Wallace on how he should throw his fight, his face is horizontally bisected into areas of light and dark, reflecting his choice between right and wrong. The background around him is almost entirely red, reflecting equally on Marsellus's perhaps demonic nature.

Red is also used in the dizzyingly unpleasant sequence in which Vincent shoots up heroin. Slow, painful, mechanical, shot in close-ups with a black background so sinister that the scene almost becomes abstract, it's dreadful in the little used sense of 'filled with dread'. The blood that fills the syringe is red, as is the light on Vincent's face as he smiles (an assured reference to the final shot of *Once Upon A Time In America* (Sergio Leone, 1984). If anyone seeing this scene thinks it's glorifying drug use, they don't have eyes. The horrific sight of Mia dribbling, with blood pouring out of her right nostril a short while later, should surely be enough to convince any doubters. The lingering close-up on her bloodied, drool-smeared face is enough to give anyone The Fear. Uma Thurman's commitment in this scene can't be praised enough.

Another nice use of the camera is that Vincent's gun is out of shot in Butch's apartment; the audience sees it after Butch does, the camera following him to pick it up after he's discovered it but before we have. Again it's Tarantino teasing us slowly, revealing the information he thinks we need to have.

One remarkably clever use of a set up is in the pawn shop, where there is a neon sign for Killian's Red beer. Some of the letters aren't lit up, the sign thus says 'Kill Ed'. When Butch escapes on Zed's motorcycle, he looks at the rapist's key ring, a huge metal letter 'Z'. Z plus the sign equals 'Kill Zed' which is what he's just done. The motorcycle has 'Grace' painted on it, which is what Butch has earned by his unselfishness.

RECURRING ELEMENTS: Pumpkin and Honey Bunny are a Mickey and Mallory type couple (*Natural Born Killers*).Vincent Vega is the brother of *Reservoir Dogs*'s Mr Blonde, who is Vic Vega. Honey Bunny uses the word 'execute' as a euphemism for the murders she commits during her life of crime; Seth Gecko does the same thing in *From Dusk Till Dawn*. Tarantino gets the trunk shot out of the way in the eighth minute. Again, the topic of cunnilingus comes up. Interestingly Samuel L Jackson brings it up as he does in *True Romance*. Jimmie's wife Bonnie is mentioned in *Reservoir Dogs* in which (albeit in a cut scene) the term 'Bonnie Situation' is also used. Bonnie is, as a glamorous black nurse, obviously a character based partially on the central figure of *Coffy* (Jack Hill, 1973) played by Pam Grier who appears in *Jackie Brown* and is also mentioned in *Reservoir Dogs*. The idea of banks being insured and that therefore it almost being the staff's and customers' duty not to resist robbers is brought up by Pumpkin and Honey Bunny, having previously been a point of discussion between Mr Orange and Mr White in *Reservoir Dogs*. Uma Thurman's Mia Wallace is the first female Tarantino character to swan around in bare feet. As in *Reservoir Dogs* Tarantino pulls the 'diagetic music joke' where a piece of music the audience thinks they can hear and the characters can't turns out to be audible to the characters too. Vincent has an auto-conversation with himself in the mirror as happens with Mr Orange in *Dogs*. The phrase 'deadliest women in the world' to describe an Uma Thurman character is virtually the basis of *Kill Bill – Vol. 1*. Fabienne says that 'anytime of the day is a good time for pie'; not a line reuse but a recurrence of female Tarantino characters (Mallory in *Natural Born Killers*, Alabama in *True Romance*) being partial to pastry. Vincent misses the beginning of the coffee shop robbery and is also later killed because of his habit of reading in the lavatory. Lots of characters in Tarantino films (like Clarence at the end of *True Romance*) miss out on the beginnings of things due to being in the lavatory. It's a nice example of Tarantino's use of 'real life' chaos in genre situations in order to add texture and seeming reality (how many other films can you remember people going to the lavatory in?).

SPURIOUS INTERTEXTUALITY: Vincent (Travolta) calls Mia (Thurman) 'Cowgirl' and in return she calls him 'Cowboy'. Thurman was in *Even Cowgirls Get the Blues* (Gus Van Sant, 1994) while Travolta was in *Urban Cowboy* (James Bridges, 1980). Coincidence? Unlikely in Tarantino world. The shop in which Marsellus and Butch are tortured is named Mason-Dixon. Mason-Dixon were stenographers who mapped the route of a railroad in the early nineteenth century. The route of the line became known as the boundary (though it wasn't exact) between the states that permitted the owning of human slaves and those that didn't both before and during the American Civil War. Here this information is used to clue the audience into the fact that these people are rednecks, straight out of *Deliverance* (John Boorman, 1972) and *The Texas Chainsaw Massacre* (Tobe Hooper, 1974) in fact. Mia's haircut is that of Louise Brooks in G W Pabst's *Pandora's Box* (1928). The moment where Butch, waiting at the crossroads in his car, has his path crossed by Marsellus Wallace is a direct borrowing of the moment in *Psycho* (Alfred Hitchcock, 1960) where Marion Crane (Janet Leigh) sees her boss walk in front of her car while she is fleeing from him having stolen $40,000. Tarantino is, incidentally, an outspoken defender of the remake of *Psycho* (Gus Van Sant, 1998) and good for him. Although never mentioned it's fair to assume that Jules is named after the great black actor Paul Winfield. Jules's habit of reciting pieces of the Bible is reminiscent of the Robert Mitchum character's habit of doing just that in *Night of The*

Hunter (Charles Laughton, 1955). It's also indebted to the homilies delivered by Sonny Chiba in his *Shadow Warriors* TV series (see **Kill Bill – Vol. 1**). The fighter Butch is meant to lose to is Floyd Wilson, the same fighter who is fighting an opponent paid to take a dive in *On The Waterfront* (Elia Kazan, 1954). To add an extra layer the billboard for the fight shows Butch and Floyd's surnames in huge letters – Wilson vs Coolidge. Both Wilson and Coolidge were American presidents: Woodrow Wilson (4 March 1913–4 March 1921) and Calvin Coolidge (3 August 1923–4 March 1929) – albeit two who never actually 'fought,' i.e. contested the same presidential election. The other two fighters named on the billboard are Vossler and Martinez, two friends of Tarantino's from his days in the video rental trade. Jules being friends with Jimmie is probably a nod to François Truffaut's *Jules et Jim* (1962). The Wolf dresses almost exactly like Vito Corleone in early scenes in *The Godfather* (Francis Ford Coppola, 1972) even down to the pencil moustache and hair. The opening exchange between Jules and Vincent about what the French call quarter-pounders is achingly reminiscent of a Mark Twain penned conversation between Jim and Huckleberry Finn about why the French don't speak English. Jules refers to *The Guns of Navarone* (J Lee Thompson, 1961) and *Superfly* (Gordon Parks, 1972) while Mr Wolf jokes about 'Lash LaRue'. LaRue was the eponymous 'Man With The Steel Whip' in the 1937 movie serial which, as I'm sure Tarantino knows, was the primary model for the *Indiana Jones* series. Jules also refers to the pig Arnold featured in the TV series *Green Acres* (1965–71). Film director Douglas Sirk, the king of 50s melodrama, is mentioned, as are Jerry Lewis and Dean Martin and black radio comedy duo Amos and Andy (who were, scandalously, played by white actors).

CRITICAL REACTION: As publicised by Richard Corliss in the October 1994 issue of *Time, Pulp Fiction* once caused a viewer to collapse with a seizure (during a screening in

New York City's Lincoln Centre); this is just about the most
extreme reaction you can imagine but it's also just one end
of the vast sliding scale of reactions to Tarantino's second
film proper. As with anything which seems to arrive on a
wave of hyperbole, there were many naysayers, including
some people obviously merely reacting against what they
perceived as received wisdom, but reviews were generally,
overwhelmingly positive. Janet Maslin, writing in the *New
York Times* of 23 September 1994 admitted that she had
found the level of excitement surrounding the movie
'suspect' but that having seen the picture the 'proof is on the
screen'. 'You don't . . . enter a theatre to see *Pulp Fiction*,
you go down a rabbit hole,' she opined, calling the film a
'stunning vision of destiny, choice and spiritual possibility'
which was 'surprisingly tender'. In *Time* Richard Corliss
immediately grasped the film's importance: 'It towers over
the year's other movies . . . it dares Hollywood films to be
this smart about going this far. If good directors accept
Tarantino's implicit challenge, the movie theater could again
be a great place to live in.' It was nominated for seven
Oscars including Best Picture, Best Actor (John Travolta),
Best Supporting Actor (Samuel L Jackson), Best Supporting
Actress (Uma Thurman), Best Film Editing (Sally Menke)
and Best Screenplay (Quentin Tarantino and Roger Avary)
of which only the last was converted into an actual statue on
the night. The film received many other awards of which the
most significant was, of course, the Palm D'Or from the
Cannes Film Festival. 'Best Picture' and 'Best Director'
awards came from the Los Angeles, New York and National
Board of Review Critics' Circles and the film won four
Independent Spirit Awards, including Best Picture.

PULP TIME: *Pulp Fiction* is a pun. The film pulps fiction; it
takes as many separate elements as it can and crushes them
into one circular mass which begins where it ends and ends
where it begins. It also pulps *time*. That's why the plot is
non-linear to the point whereby some ordinary moviegoers

have claimed it doesn't make sense; why so many of the clocks in the picture are set to the same time (4.20); why The Wolf is at a cocktail party which is clearly being held in the evening when called by Jules and Vincent in the morning (and he can't be in a different time zone, he arrives to visit them in minutes); and why almost all of the picture takes place on the same day and before breakfast. It's also why the film ends where it began – in the diner with Pumpkin and Honey Bunny. That's why Lance is eating a brand of cereal which hasn't been made since 1983 and why Mia Wallace has only a record player and a reel-to-reel tape machine rather than a CD player and a tape deck. That's why Vincent can go to a retro 50s diner and meet someone (Butch) who is later seen treating a 1940s taxi cab as if it's a contemporary object. That's why Butch watches a television set that is both visibly a very old-fashioned model and clearly very new. There are many other examples of this temporal twisting in the film.

THE BRIEFCASE: Too much time and effort has been devoted to the MacGuffin of what is in the briefcase that Jules and Vincent are sent to retrieve; but as that's what the MacGuffin is meant to do I suppose one can't complain too much. Most people's favourite theory is that it contains Marsellus Wallace's soul, which he has sold to the Devil (hence the glowing light and the fact that the combination is 666). Also seen to back this up is the plaster on Marsellus Wallace's neck. Apparently mythologically speaking it is possible to extract someone's soul through the back of their neck, though no exponent of this theory has ever identified which myths state this. Other, less eccentric, explanations include that it's a suitcase full of gold, or of stolen Academy Award statues or that it contains a gold lamé suit that once belonged to Elvis. Of course, it doesn't really matter, it's designed so that each audience member 'fills in the blank' themselves, and it works.

VIOLENCE?: Roger Ebert said that it took him three viewings to realise that *Pulp Fiction* was nowhere near as violent as he thought it was, that indeed a quick calculation showed that more lives were saved than taken in the course of its drama (the body count, onscreen and off, is nine, by the way). However, there's more to it than the admirable Mr Ebert took time to adumbrate. Even more so than *Reservoir Dogs* (which boasts only nine onscreen deaths, but much talking about gunplay and fisticuffs), *Pulp Fiction* is characterised not by actual violence but by characters' communications with each other using language which is evocative of, or directly about, violence. These are violent people and while we rarely see them be violent, we always know that they can be. *Pulp Fiction* is like a calm, near empty street in a nevertheless rough part of town. This *impression* of violence without *actual* violence is one of the film's oddest, yet most impressive, achievements. It just *isn't* a violent movie. Another thing it also certainly isn't is, despite what some contemporary reviewers implied, is an action movie of any kind. There's very little violence onscreen and nothing that could be described as an action sequence. When Jules kills the men hiding the briefcase the camera is on him, not them. The same is true when Vincent accidentally kills Marvin. When Butch cuts Maynard open with his samurai sword he does it facing the camera and with Maynard facing him, so that the audience doesn't see the blood or even the blow from the blade.

The film also tries to emphasise that one should not trust violence, violent means or weapons. More weapons either fail to work or work in the 'wrong' way in the film than function in the manner their owners' intend. The gun that misses Jules probably simply misfires, the gun that kills Vincent is used by its intended target on its owner, the gun that accidentally kills Marvin in the backseat also misfires for no discernible reason, leaving a man dead and two others to clean up, literally and metaphorically. Guns are eschewed in the pawn shop sequences and, in the coffee shop, Jules doesn't simply use his gun to prevent a massacre, he also refuses to kill using it (see below).

Pulp Fiction could be argued to be a very straightforwardly moral (even moralising) piece. All the characters are gangsters, yes, but Jules and Butch are redeemed and Vincent is punished – not for his crimes but for specifically eschewing the redemption which is offered to him and which Jules takes. Butch puts his life on the line for an enemy because it is morally the right thing to do ('Jingi', see **Reservoir Dogs**, again) and Jules not only saves the lives of countless people in the coffee shop for the same reason, he also refuses to simply kill Honey Bunny and Pumpkin when he has the chance. This would be the simple way to achieve the desired effect of saving the innocents in the diner – trade the lives of the two criminals for the dozens of customers. But this new reformed Jules isn't cold enough to be that utilitarian. He has to save Pumpkin and Honey Bunny too. The trade he makes is not to trade a small number of lives of the guilty for the larger number of lives of the innocents (the standard method of resolving conflict in adventure fiction), by killing the robbers to save the robbed. No, he gives the robbers the money they want, including his own, while threatening *them* with a gun. He gives up his possessions, at risk to himself, in order to try to provide for Pumpkin and Honey Bunny something of the life-changing moment of revelation he experienced in the apartment. He takes an unnecessary risk in order to save someone whom he doesn't know and who doesn't want to be saved because it's morally right. Can you think of a more straightforward definition of heroism?

THE NUMBERS: *Pulp Fiction* cost about $8 million. It came out on 14 October 1994 in the US and took $9.3 million by the end of that weekend. It's eventual United States gross would be nearly $108 million and it took £10.7 million in the UK, with a final worldwide gross of around $213 million. *Pulp Fiction* also shipped 715,000 rental VHS copies in its first week; then a record.

EZEKIEL 25:17: Immediately before performing a hit, Jules recites what he calls Ezekiel 25:17. This isn't actually what it is – Ezekiel 25:17 actually states: 'And I will execute great vengeance upon them with furious rebukes; and they shall know that I am the Lord, when I shall lay my vengeance upon them.' Here's what Jules says, adding bits from the 23rd Psalm and his own rhetoric: 'The path of the righteous man is beset on all sides with the iniquities of the selfish and the tyranny of evil men. Blessed is he who in the name of charity and goodwill shepherds the weak through the valley of darkness, for he is truly his brother's keeper and the finder of lost children. And I will strike down upon those with great vengeance and with furious anger those who attempt to poison and destroy my brothers. And you will know that my name is the Lord when I lay my vengeance upon thee.'

FINAL COMMENT: 'Trying to forget anything as intriguing as this would be an exercise in futility.' Deceptively intelligent, consistently stylish (yet resolutely unglamorous, a difficult amalgam to pull off), utterly involving and morally complex, this is a film which is not only the best work in the career of everyone involved, it's also very likely to remain so. It's probably the best film of the 1990s (certainly of the first half of that decade). It's a hallmark of truly great films that, when you rewatch them, they are always better than you expect them to be – even if you're expecting them to be the best film you've ever seen. It's a quality that *Nosferatu* (FW Murnau, 1922), *The Godfather* (Francis Ford Coppola, 1972) and maybe three dozen other films in the history of the motion picture share. It's a heady boast, but that's the company *Pulp Fiction* is, and should be considered to be, in.

The Vega Brothers

One Tarantino project that has been long rumoured, and has his fans champing at the bit, is *The Vega Brothers*. This would, obviously, involve the pairing of Michael Madsen's Vic Vega (from *Reservoir Dogs*) with John Travolta's Vincent Vega (from *Pulp Fiction*), with possibly even an appearance from Virgil Vega (James Gandolfini in *True Romance*). Tarantino has never talked publicly about the project in anything but the vaguest terms, saying that he'd like to see those actors play those characters again and that he thinks audiences would too. Of course, the stumbling block one runs into in envisioning a project like this is that both (indeed, all three) characters are dead, having been killed off in their respective films. A 'prequel', while desirable on some level, would run into the additional problem that all the actors are noticeably, if not actually dramatically, older than they were when they played their characters' deaths. One suggestion, much mooted by speculators, is that either Madsen or Travolta would actually play the father of the three Vegas seen thus far and the other actor would play *his* brother, a neat way of using the character archetypes, actors and names without violating the continuity of the previous films. Of course, Tarantino could simply ignore the characters' deaths and make the film anyway, but that seems unlikely, given his approach to the fidelity of his internal fictional universe. In 2004 Tarantino suggested to reporters that he had worked out a way to make the film at some point, a solution to his problems that avoided the idea of the actors aging, but he was not about to tell them what it was. The wait continues.

Palme D'Or

Certainly the biggest filmic honour that has been bestowed on Tarantino is *Pulp Fiction*'s winning of the Golden Palm at the 1994 Cannes Film Festival. Tarantino is rarely seen in public without some kind of ironic detachment but the recording of him accepting perhaps film's most prestigious prize saw him genuinely overawed by the experience. 'I never expect to win anything,' he muttered and then deadpanned, 'I don't make the kind of movies that bring people together.' As jury president Clint Eastwood read out Tarantino's winning of the prize, Tarantino was heckled, loudly, obnoxiously and in French by a portion of the audience, but that didn't seem to spoil the experience for him to any great extent.

Ten years later Tarantino would return to Cannes as the jury president, fulfilling a lifelong ambition. His jury would controversially give the Golden Palm to Michael Moore's documentary *Fahrenheit 9/11*, a concentrated attack on the administration of President George W Bush and its response to the 11 September 2001 attacks on New York and Washington. Tarantino insisted that the film's success wasn't due to politics and that it had won because 'it was the best film we saw'.

Director for Hire?

Most film directors, including those regarded as deeply personal filmmakers like Terry Gilliam or Tim Burton and even big names like Steven Spielberg, generally work-for-hire, coming on to projects developed by studios, screenwriters or even other directors in order to shoot them. Tarantino has never done this, making him . . . George Lucas excepted . . . perhaps the only director with blockbuster box-office clout (defining as a blockbuster a film that makes more than $100 million) who has never done so. This does not mean, however, that no one has ever asked him to.

In the years immediately after *Pulp Fiction* Tarantino was offered a number of projects on such a basis until it became clear he wasn't going to accept any of the offerings. He was asked if he wanted to direct *Men in Black*, based upon the comic series, but he was not interested enough to even read the script. (Barry Sonnenfeld eventually shot the film.) Writer Ed Solomon's fast-paced, sharp-talking screenplay would actually have been a good match for Tarantino, although the suggestion that Tarantino direct may have been made for other, duller reasons: the Men in Black do, with their black suits, ties and shades, resemble the Reservoir Dogs more than a little.

Tarantino was also, and this seems bizarre in retrospect, offered *Speed* to direct. Given that until *Kill Bill – Vol. 1* he didn't consider himself to have made, or even be capable of making, an 'action movie,' this is perhaps an indication of how far some industry perceptions of the man and the filmmaker vary from the essential truth. *That* film was eventually made by Jan de Bont; the only real links between it and *Men in Black* are that both are pretty good in their own ways and that both have *appalling* sequels. Again the differences between them, however, illustrate the difficulty Hollywood was having in understanding the nature of Tarantino's talent.

Tarantino later told the *New York Times* that had he been offered *Hero*, the David Peoples script which was eventually shot by British director Stephen Frears as *Accidental Hero*; he *would* have taken that on as a project, because he liked the script so much, but felt the movie as shot and released was lacking. (He would have cast John Travolta rather than Dustin Hoffman in the lead.) 'The movie is hitting its head on the ceiling of [Frears'] talent, but the script wants to go to the moon.'

ER – 'Motherhood' (1995)

Created by Michael Crichton
Theme by James Newton Howard
Music by Marty Davich
Producer: Paul Manning
Co-executive Producer: Lydia Woodward
Executive Producers: Michael Crichton and John Wells
Produced by Christopher Chulcak
Written by Lydia Woodward
Directed by Quentin Tarantino
Copyright © 1995 Warner Bros Television
Constant Productions
Amblin Television
Production = 456623
Episode 1.25
Transmitted: 11 May 1995 (NBC)

REGULAR CAST: Anthony Edwards (Dr Mark Greene), George Clooney (Dr Doug Ross), Sherry Stringfield (Dr Susan Lewis), Noah Wyle (John Carter III), Julianna Margulies (Carol Hathaway), Eriq La Salle (Dr Peter Benton)

GUEST STARS: Abraham Benrubi (Jerry), Deezer D (Malik), Khandi Alexander (Jackie), Christine Harnos (Jean Greene), Andrea Parker (Linda Farrell), Valerie Perrine (Cookie Lewis), CCH Pounder (Dr Angela Hicks), Gloria Reuben (Jeanie Boulet), Beah Richards (Mrs Benton)

GUEST STARRING: Patrick Collins (Dr Netzley), Elizabeth Norment (Mrs Sandburg), Marion Yue (Dr Sandra Li)

CO-STARRING: Ellen Crawford (Lydia Wright), Yvetter Freeman (Haleh), Vanessa Marquez (Goldman), Angel Aviles (Ramos), Laura Ceron (Marquez), Kelly Coleman (Nina), Ali Glazer (Kaitlin Sandburg), Kathy Griffin (Dolores Minky), Brenda Hillhouse (Mrs Schaffer), Angela

Jones (Michelle), Tamal Jones (Joanie), Aymara De Llano (Joanie Lafferty), Seidy Lopez (Guitterez), Jonathan Neal (Jeffrey), Christopher Richardson (Jesse), Marc Dakota Robinson (Steven), Joe Sachs (EMT), Viola Kates Stimpson (Ethyl), Abraham Verduzco (Plamer), Emily Wagner (Pickman), Lee R Sellars (Chopper EMT)

DEVELOPMENT: *ER*, one of the longest-running, most successful and highest-quality drama series in the history of American network television began life as a film script written by popular novelist Michael Crichton. Crichton's draft concerns the actions of the staff of the Emergency Room of a busy Chicago hospital over the course of exactly twenty-four hours. The screenplay ended with the suicide of troubled nurse Carol Hathaway. Director/producer Steven Spielberg read the screenplay and formulated an intention to direct a film based on it. However during discussions about the project Crichton and Spielberg became involved, almost by accident, in another project entirely. Spielberg asked what Crichton was currently working on, and the novelist explained that he was researching a novel about genetically recreated dinosaurs. Together they made *Jurassic Park* (1993) and *ER* went on the back burner, before being abandoned more or less entirely. Abandoned that was until Crichton's screenplay, no longer a project Spielberg wanted for himself, became a TV movie-cum-pilot for a television series, which Spielberg was then attached to as a name/nominal executive producer. The *ER* pilot episode does not have a separate title of its own – as is often the case with pilot episodes – but is sometimes referred to by the latterly applied title '24 Hours'. The series was picked up for prime time and debuted on NBC in late 1994. A decision was made to retain the character of Carol Hathaway for the series with the first episode of the proper series detailing how she survived the self-administered overdose she'd been expected not to at the end of the pilot film.

PREVIOUSLY ON *ER:* Dr Susan Lewis's itinerant, drug-dependent sister Chloe is pregnant and living with Susan because she has no money and nowhere else to go. Nurse Carol Hathaway is planning to marry Tagge, an ambulance driver, while working alongside her former lover Dr Doug Ross. Ross still holds a torch for Carol but considers that part of their relationship to be over. Something of a ladies' man, one with demons and a drink problem, he is also a committed – and at times inspirational – doctor with a rare gift for paediatric medicine. He is trying to settle down with a single mother with whom he has a good relationship.

SCREENPLAY: An executive producer/writer on the series, Lydia Woodward had previously worked on *China Beach* (1989) and *Hooperman* (1983). She has written many episodes of *ER* and went on to work on *Citizen Baines* (2001) and *Presido Med* (2002). It is difficult to ascertain how much, if any, rewriting was done by Quentin Tarantino during the process of making the episode. A few lines of dialogue in the episode ('Mother's Day. I had no idea it could be so dangerous', 'You're good, I knew you when you were bad' and Doug's marvellous non sequitur: 'There's a horse in my parking space') seem to be more in Tarantino's style than Woodward's, although any suggestion that they originate with the director rather than the screenwriter is pure speculation. Equally, while Carter's labelling of the stars he sees out of the window as 'Curly, Larry and Mo' after the Three Stooges seems to be exactly the kind of thing Tarantino would do (go through the man's interviews and see how often he mentions the Three Stooges – it borders on constantly) there's no evidence at all that it was he who did it in this instance. It is possible that the script's dialogue was partially penned knowing the identity of the director, and that this almost subliminal stylistic shift is a result of that. Certainly, much of the verbiage is more flippant than one would associate with *ER* at this point in its run.

Something that is certainly present are many moments in the episode where a scene as scripted is clearly improvised around in order to create intriguing 'stage business' for the actors and audience. For example: Doug is conversing with his girlfriend while standing in front of a hospital curtain. The scene is carefully shot and played so that the audience doesn't notice that it *is* a curtain; the audience concentrates on the action in the foreground and a conversation that refers to one of the series' ongoing plots. Just as the conversation reaches what should be its climax a nurse pulls back a screen and loudly demands to know if Doug is coming back in, asking him to walk back into one of the episode's non-sequitur subplots – in this case one about a group of flatulent boys. It's a really very funny moment which does seem to have initially been scripted as a simple relaying of information.

QUOTES:
Susan: 'How'd you get through it?'
Jennifer: 'Drugs.'

Doug: 'So you bowed to the reverend's wishes?'
Mark: 'I try not to look at it that way.'

KEY SHOTS: *ER* is, ordinarily, one of the most impressively shot series on television anyway. Its regular directors include the multiple Emmy-award-winners Thomas Schlamme, John Wells and Jack Orman. However, Tarantino's episode is more noticeably directed than the series often is; which is to say it contains many flourishes, idiosyncrasies and numerous shots that could be considered outside of normal television grammar. They seem to betray the fact the director is almost certain that he won't ever do this again, and he can therefore use every idea he's ever had about directing hospital drama. It also needs to be remembered that as Tarantino only ever worked on one *ER* episode he did not find himself in the position – which serial television directors often do – of editing one episode while shooting another and prepping a third and also that, unlike virtually everyone else ever to direct for the series, he had no other producing, writing or acting commitments on other instalments of the series. All this, of course, should not be used to denigrate his achievement in creating such an arrestingly shot 44 minutes of drama, but merely to put his episode in its proper context.

One thing Tarantino's episode is very firmly not is self-indulgent. Susan and Carol walking down a corridor, almost strutting, wearing sunglasses and then turning to the left replicates one of the most recognisable shots in *Pulp Fiction*, but this is the only moment of the kind of self-reflexive pandering that one might associate with a theatrical director of Tarantino's character working on one episode of a TV series.

In the first scene a handheld camera follows Susan Lewis around her apartment as she panics while trying to find her keys and prepare her sister for her journey to hospital. The scene uses two cameras: one that hurries and scurries backwards and forwards around Susan replicating her physical actions with camera motion (Tarantino does a similar thing, albeit comically and with less success, in his section of *Four Rooms*); the other is trained on Chloe and replicates her *lack* of motion with its own. The scene then cuts between the two cameras at intervals. This is hugely effective as it creates a sense of urgency, and allows the audience to see the profound character differences (education, sensitivity, understanding) between these two physically similar sisters in a scene which also has a plot point.

Tarantino's shooting of a conversation that Doug and Carol have effectively gets across their alienation from each other even though the conversation is largely work-based and could have been played entirely straight. In the scene, which takes place in a drug dispensary, the camera looks down a deep, long, narow room. Doug is in the room looking to the side and checking through drugs as he talks to

Carol who is in the far back of the shot, visible only through a dispensary window. Although they converse freely they don't look at one another and the physical space between them is used. At the end of the scene Doug walks out of the boxy room he's in – exiting to the left and going out of shot in the process. He then has to walk back into shot to stand next to her. It's a really striking physical representation of how far apart they are, and how far Doug has to go to connect with her even over the most trivial, or at least non-personal, things.

Tarantino also introduces numerous recurring physical motifs in the episode which are separate to the camerawork. The audience inevitably has to conclude that these were his innovations as no other *ER* episode contains such a plethora of physical gags or pieces of irrelevant 'business'. Indeed Tarantino has said that much of his approach to film is to introduce the awkwardness of real life into genre situations (his demonstrative example being that no one who ever steals a car while being pursued in a film ever discovers that it's a manual/stick-shift car and they only know how to drive an automatic) and much of what transpires in this episode smacks of that approach.

For example, several characters (Carter, Susan, Mark) pour coffee over themselves and/or spill milk on the floor. Susan even does so in the manner of the old silent movie joke of checking a wristwatch while having a cup in her hand. Another recurrent physical motif is of people falling over in comic ways. Right at the beginning of the episode Carter falls off his chair in surprise as Susan and Chloe come in. The scene is shot from the front, so he physically disappears behind the desk – and out of the audience's view as he does so. This also happens later in the episode when the older and littler of the two little old ladies that Carter is sent to treat collapses sideways off a bed. She's just about recognisable as a human being in the shot before she collapses: a huge black shadow almost filling the screen, with the audience able to see a sliver of recognisable setting to her right. Then she disappears revealing the astonished Carter to the audience. It is really very funny.

Tarantino also takes an unusual approach to that mainstay of *ER*'s storytelling – surgery in the trauma room. The series normally uses a fluid, handheld or Steadicam, approach to shooting scenes in surgery. The camera bounces around the actors remaining at roughly shoulder height. There are few cuts and those that are there are barely noticeable as the filming cuts to another camera doing very similar things to the one it's cut away from. Tarantino eschews this completely, instead choosing to cut from the actors to a number of extreme close-ups of the grim realities of surgery. The audience gets a creeping close-up on the surgical bone cutter and another on it going into the patient. There are other close-ups of hands and fingers working in studied, bloodied frenzy and close-ups on the wheels of clamps and restraints moving as the clamps are put in place or pulled away. It's literally and figuratively visceral.

Watching the episode the audience senses a textual sympathy with the children and parents who are brought in; less so with the gunshot victims, the gangbangers and those who have OD'd. This is unusual for the series, which often empathises with the most unlikely people and has had leading characters who have remained consistently unsympathetic while being compelling. (Peter Benton is the best example, but the later creations of Robert Romano (Paul McCrane) and Kerry Weaver (Laura Innes) are almost equally good.) Tarantino tries to push his audience into not empathising with some of the patients by not showing their faces when they are brought in (a version of what he does during the surgery scenes). He instead emphasises the reactions of the other, regular, characters to the events occurring around them. The name, face and life of the boy who comes in foaming at the mouth from a drug overdose seem to be irrelevant to Tarantino. The audience doesn't see the boy's face at all except in indistinct mid-shot. What matters is the effect it has on Chloe. The camera remains close on her face throughout the sequence, registering her reactions and her panic.

There are also lots of 'luxury' shots, odd little moments of inventiveness that – while they do have a visual frisson – don't necessarily tie in to the episode's bigger themes or scenes. These include a dramatic pan in a sideways arc from a shot of Carol on the phone – she's been talking for a while and the audience has come to assume that she is alone in the room. As the camera moves away from her, the audience sees that Mark and Susan are standing there silently observing her. She knows they are there. This not only forces us to reassess the visual set-up of the scene but also the context in which Carol said what she said. She had company and was aware that people could hear her. It changes the context of her words. Carol then leaves the scene and the camera does a little shuffle forwards and then bounces back as she exits, almost as if it's trying to decide for the viewer whether to follow her or stay with Susan and Mark.

In another inventive moment, the camera stares through a vast magnifying glass device that Doug uses to look into someone's eye. The audience doesn't find out what it is or what it does or what the person Doug is treating has wrong with them, but they can enjoy the visual distortion all the same.

Another example is when Carol and Susan go and hide on the hospital's roof to sunbathe during a particularly hectic moment of their shift. The camera is low down, at roof/floor level so creating a looming presence out of the barely recognisable Susan and Carol who, with clothes rolled to expose as much flesh to the sun as possible, lie flat out on sunbeds.

One very clever camera moment, which does have a story point, is when Peter Benton runs out of surgery to answer a phone call that concerns his ailing mother. The camera doesn't follow Peter out of the operating theatre; neither does it cut to a new camera set up outside. Instead Peter dashes out of surgery and out of shot, only to come back into shot to the left of the frame, barely visible through the window of the trauma room. The camera begins to travel towards him, as if it knows the audience is more interested in Peter's life than the operation being performed on a guest character. Peter then runs away out of shot before the camera has really got close to him, so it pulls back and returns to the matter at hand: the patient on the table. This deliberate, faux-indecision is a masterstroke on the director's part. It really ratchets up the tension for the viewer.

Later in the episode Doug and Mark play baseball, a common occurrence in this series, but it's done with a single stationary camera and an unnaturalistically lit set. We don't see the actors' faces as they talk, a partial reflection of how difficult it now is for these two characters to communicate. This is similar to how Susan and Chloe's mother is first presented when she finally appears after being talked about extensively in previous episodes. She appears in the hospital and the character about whom we've heard so much is invisible, her face hidden behind the flowers and balloons that she has brought to the hospital for the birth of her first grandchild. While her face isn't at all present, her voice, grating and hectoring, is and we understand on a greater level Susan's resentment of her mother's uniquely oppressive blend of absence, laziness and unheeded, unneeded, insistent criticism.

MUSICAL NOTES: 'Blackbird' (Lennon/McCartney) is, as pointed out more than once in the episode, a track from the Beatles' 1968 album *The Beatles*; more often referred to these days as *The White Album* because of its plain white sleeve. (The album was actually going to be called *A Doll's House* until rather late in the day; the August 1968 release of Family's album *Music From A Doll's House* nixed that idea and it seems that none of the Fab Four could come up with an alternative title at this late stage.) McCartney wrote 'Blackbird' without any input from Lennon while the Beatles were studying at the Maharishi Yogi's Rishikesh retreat in the spring of 1968. (Many, if not most, of their co-credited songs were, by this point, entirely individual compositions; the credit remained for contractual reasons and because both men considered themselves to have 'a gentleman's agreement' over credits.) Composed on an acoustic guitar (there was no electricity at the Maharishi's retreat) that had had its E strings dropped to a D, the chords of the melody are carried principally on the second and fourth strings. The track was recorded on 11 June 1968 with McCartney himself the sole instrumentalist and vocalist.

Although McCartney has always intimated that the song's lyrics should principally be taken literally (and they were inspired by a real event, that of being woken by a blackbird singing at night) they also have a metaphorical quality seeming to represent a figurative 'awakening on a deeper level' to quote the late Ian MacDonald, author of *Revolution in the Head*, the definitive book on the Beatles' music.

The lyrics have also been taken by numerous American commentators (including, somewhat unfortunately, Charles Manson) to specifically refer to the struggle for civil rights in America. Given the content of the episode the choice of song could not be more appropriate. Awakenings are covered by Susan's realisation of familial love, Doug's realisation of what he's capable of, Carter's realisation of what it is to be a doctor and Carol's slow realisation that she shouldn't really be marrying Tagge. (In the next episode she calls the marriage off.)

Even the most contentious reading of the song's meaning fits naturally into the portions of the episode which concern themselves with the brilliant Peter Benton, the black surgeon who is also an unknowing beneficiary of the Affirmative Action plan. A man who is fundamentally incapable of admitting when he is wrong, or that there is anything of which he isn't personally capable, 'Motherhood' allows us a glimpse at Peter at his most vulnerable after the death of his mother. His inability to leave her bedside or wash and dress the body combines with his profound pain that for all his skills as a doctor he could do nothing to help his mother. The use of the blackbird helps the audience reflect on the extraordinary struggles of the first generation of African-Americans to be fully enfranchised and what Peter's mother must have sacrificed for him and what he has gone through to get where he is.

AVAILABILITY: If you're a Tarantino completist, or maybe belatedly want to get into one of the best television series ever produced in English, 'Motherhood' is available on DVD in both the UK and US but only as part of the whole 'ER Complete First Season'. An individual disc release seems phenomenally unlikely after all this time.

FINAL COMMENT: When Susan Lewis, holding her niece in her arms, tells Carter 'I've delivered so many babies, and I never realised how little they are . . .' she's verbally representing the clash between the private and professional worlds of the doctors that ER the series is about. It's the same contrast that Peter finally understands when he ruminates on his mother's death at the end of the episode. Told by a woman at the nursing home that his mother died before he could get there, Peter barely hears her when, with equally sincere (but equally insincere seeming) grace, she tells him this using exactly the same words (the basic advised text for doctors informing of a bereavement), which he used earlier in the episode to tell a woman that her son had died. 'I've said those words I don't know how many times,' he mutters later, bitterly and desperately. Tarantino's absolute mastery of tone as a filmmaker is superbly demonstrated by this scene, which is brimful of real emotion and contains deeply affecting work from Eriq La Salle as Peter Benton. It's the pay-off for an instalment that has been, while impressive – even showy – a bit more of a cartoon than ER normally would be. It should make anyone dismiss the idea that Tarantino is perhaps incapable of graduating to directing straightforward drama free of the operatic tone and outside the crime-thriller milieu in which virtually all of his work sits.

It's also very telling that Tarantino, who has often referred to his work as representing a clash between genre conventions and the awkward messiness of real life, chose to direct an episode of *ER*. His episode articulates the clash between the conventions of hospital drama and the messiness of real existence very well while also illustrating the professional and personal clash experienced by the series's characters. It's a terrific blend of director and material and 'Motherhood' is satisfying as, and obviously part of, both *ER* the long-running series and Tarantino's own directorial canon. It represents an interesting and effective meshing of one man's very distinctive way of making films with mainstream TV conventions and the restrictions of public broadcasting standards.

Killing Zoe (1994)

Tarantino was executive producer of this feature, written and directed by his pre-fame friend and former fellow video store clerk Roger Avary. Eric Stoltz stars as Zed, a safebreaker who travels to Paris to rob a bank in the company of some old friends. The bank is the only one in the city which is open on the Bastille Day national holiday and the situation quickly dissolves into a bloody siege, which – coincidentally – also involves a call girl who Zed slept with the previous night. Set in Paris but shot in Los Angeles, *Killing Zoe* is an entertaining but ultimately unsatisfying feature which pales in comparison with Tarantino's own work. It is fair to say that Avary's film isn't, as was suggested at the time, a Tarantino pastiche, though it didn't help that, on the film's release, Tarantino's name was displayed more prominently on the posters than Avary's. The two men's creative styles are similar due to their long association. Avary's later *The Rules of Attraction* is a mini-masterpiece, somehow adapting a book many thought unadaptable. It's a far better indication of his clearly considerable talents.

Four Rooms (1995)

Miramax Films present
A Band Apart
A Film by Allison Anders, Alexandre Rockwell,
Robert Rodriguez, Quentin Tarantino
Four Rooms
Costume Designers: Susan L Bertram, Mary Claire Hannan
Music by Combustible Edison
Music produced by Mark Mothersbaugh
Production Designer: Gary Fruktoff
Editors: Margie Goodspeed, Elene Maganini, Sally Menke,
Robert Rodriguez
Directors of Photography: Rodrigo Garcia, Guillermo
Navarro, Phil Parmet, Andrzej Sekula
Co-producers: Paul Hellerman, Heidi Vogel, Scott Lambert
Executive Producer: Alexandre Rockwell
Executive Producer: Quentin Tarantino
Steadicam Operator: Bob Gorelick
Written by Allison Anders, Alexandre Rockwell,
Robert Rodriguez, Quentin Tarantino
Produced by Lawrence Bender

TAGLINE: 'Twelve outrageous guests. Four scandalous requests. And one lone bellhop, in his first day on the job, who's in for the wildest New Year's Eve of his life.

CAST: Tim Roth (Ted the Bellhop), Sammi Davis (Jezebel), Amanda De Cadenet (Diana), Valeria Golino (Athena), Madonna (Elspeth), Ione Skye (Eva), Lili Taylor (Raven), Alicia Witt (Kiva), Jennifer Beals (Angela), David Proval (Sigfried), Antonio Banderas (Man), Lana McKissack (Sarah), Patricia Vonne (Corpse), Tamlyn Tomita (Wife), Danny Verduzco (Juancho), Salma Hayek (TV Dancing Girl), Bruce Willis (Leo), Paul Calderon (Norman), Quentin Tarantino (Chester Rush), Lawrence Bender (Long Hair Yuppie Scum), Kathy Griffin (Betty), Quinn Thomas Kellerman (Baby Bellhop), Marc Lawrence (Sam the Bellhop), Unruly Julie McClean (Left Redhead), Laura Rush

Right The purest of the *Reservoir Dogs*? Mr White (Harvey Keitel).

Left 'Are you gonna bark all day little doggie, or are you going to bite?' Mr Blonde/Vic Vega (Michael Madsen); a career defining performance and one of *the* roles of 90s American film.

The crime magazine cover pastiche poster for *Pulp Fiction*.

Above 'You're so cool.' Clarence (Christian Slater) and Alabama (Patricia Arquette) embark on a *True Romance*.

Left The crime magazine cover pastiche poster for *Pulp Fiction*.

Top right Riding away with Grace? Butch (Bruce Willis) redeemed and ready for a new life. *Pulp Fiction*.

Bottom right Bloody Work. Vincent Vega (John Travolta) and Jules (Samuel L Jackson) clear up after themselves. *Pulp Fiction*.

Top left 'Menacing Couldn't-Give-A-Fuck Ted!' Chester (Tarantino) explains his game plan to Ted (Tim Roth). *Four Rooms.*

Bottom left 'A bastard, but not a fucking bastard.' Seth Gecko (George Clooney) and his brother Richie (Quentin Tarantino). *From Dusk Till Dawn.*

Right The *Jackie Brown* poster. Note the *Foxy Brown* pastiche logo.

Below 'What happened to your ass? You used to be beautiful.' Ordell (Samuel L Jackson) and Louis (Robert De Niro). *Jackie Brown.*

Left The Bride (Uma Thurman) dressed as Bruce Lee in *Game of Death* faces an army of people dressed as Bruce Lee in *The Green Hornet*. *Kill Bill: Vol. 1.*

Below 'Silly Caucasian girl likes to play with samurai swords.' O-Ren Ishii (Lucy Liu) in *Kill Bill: Vol. 1.*

Left Beatrix Kiddo aka Black Mamba aka The Bride aka 'Mommy' (Uma Thurman). *Kill Bill: Vol 1.*

Right A man who doesn't understand Superman. Bill (David Carradine) in *Kill Bill: Vol. 2.*

Left Pei Mai (Gordon Liu), *Kill Bill: Vol. 2.*

Left Thurman and Tarantino on the set of *Kill Bill: Vol. 1.*

Below Quentin Tarantino on location for *Pulp Fiction*

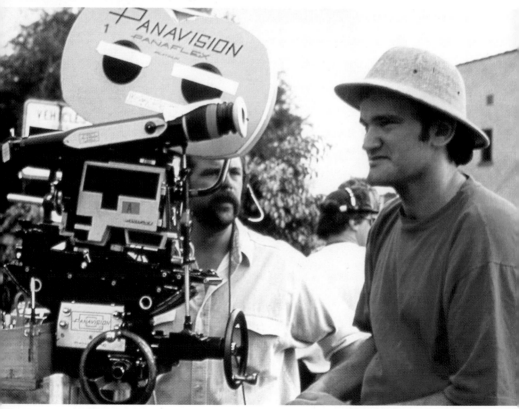

(Right Redhead), Paul Skemp (Real Theodore), Marisa
Tomei (Margaret)

SUMMARY: New Year's Eve. Ted the Bellhop's first, and
ultimately last, night in his new job sees him called by a
coven of witches to provide the missing ingredient for their
potion, trapped by a role-playing couple and caught up in
the escapades of two naughty children before being called to
the penthouse suite by film director Chester Rush.

DEVELOPMENT: Tarantino had previously declared his
love of 'portmanteau films' or films made up of several
interlinked stories and has indeed argued that, in a sense,
Pulp Fiction was one. It should really have surprised no one
when he announced that his new project, *Five Rooms*,
would be another. However it wouldn't simply have two
(collaborating) writers as *Pulp Fiction* had, it would have no
less than five separate writers/directors each of whom would
bring their own usual collaborators (in terms of
actors/editors/cinematographers) with them to create
roughly a fifth of the picture. Each filmmaker's piece would
be linked to the others' only by location (they would all take
place in the same hotel on the same night) and – in principle
– one recurring minor character, the hotel's new bellboy.
The project, as conceived, was basically the exact mid-point
between *New York Stories* (1989) and horror portmanteaus
like *The House That Dripped Blood* (Peter Duffell, 1970).
The former saw Francis Ford Coppola, Martin Scorsese and
Woody Allen each direct a short piece about the city where
most of their work had been set. The latter saw a police
inspector investigating a number of horrific deaths that take
place in the same house over a number of months and years.
Each 'case' had a different cast with the policeman reading
up on each murder *ex post facto*. This is distinct from, say,
Tales From The Crypt (Freddie Francis, 1972) in that, in
both this film and the films modelled on it, all the central
characters appear together in a framing story. In *The House*

That Dripped Blood and *Four Rooms* only one major character carries across all of the pieces (although in *Four Rooms* Angela also appears in more than one).

In many ways it could have seemed like an ideal new project for Tarantino. It spared him the difficult process of following up a film as nearly universally admired as *Pulp Fiction* was. It enabled him to use his production credentials and celebrity to get the work of his generation of filmmakers – many from 'The Class of '92' (see '**That Sundance**') – accessed and hopefully appreciated by the mass audience that had embraced him. These filmmakers were to be Richard Linklater, Allison Anders, Alexandre Rockwell and Robert Rodriguez. As individually diverse as people as they are distinct as artists, they were all known for low-budget, personal work. Linklater dropped out of the project early on and it metamorphosed into *Four Rooms*. This departure left Tarantino with three fellow directors.

ALLISON ANDERS: Anders was born in 1954 and grew up in Ashland, in rural Kentucky. Her early life was a difficult period. Her father abandoned the family when she was five years old and she was later a victim of violent domestic abuse – including an incident when her stepfather threatened her with a gun – and suffered a mental breakdown at fifteen. She spent some time hitch-hiking and has stated she's used these experiences in creating her small-scale personal films with young female leads. She travelled to London, became a mother for the first time and on her return to the United States enrolled in UCLA's film school, supporting herself and her family by working as a waitress. She was awarded the Nicholas Fellowship by the Academy of Motion Picture Arts and Sciences and also won the Samuel Goldwyn Award for a screenplay she penned. While studying, she wrote to director Wim Wenders – whose work she admired – and, after seeing her super-8 mm film-school work, he offered her a position as an assistant on his film *Paris, Texas* (1984). After graduation Anders made *Border Radio* with two other former UCLA students but it was *Gas Food Lodging* (1992), a personalised adaptation of Richard Peck's novel, which was feted at the 1992 Cannes Film Festival and won her the New York Film Critics' Circle Award for Best Director. Anders's later films include *Mi Vida Loca* (which opened at the 1993 Cannes Festival), a romance about girl gangs in the Echo Park neighbourhood of LA where Anders then lived, and the wonderful *Grace of My Heart* (1996) which starred Illeana Douglas as a 'Tin Pan Alley' type songwriter who longed to have a recording career of her own. Anders has also directed episodes of HBO's TV series *Sex and the City*, a perhaps counter-intuitive but ultimately effective marriage of mainstream television and Anders's skill for telling stories about strong women in difficult and demanding circumstances.

ROBERT RODRIGUEZ: Now a household name due to his *Spy Kids* (2001–03) trilogy of children's pictures, Robert Rodriquez was one of a family of ten children raised in Austin, Texas. He resolved to be a filmmaker upon first seeing John Carpenter's *Escape From New York* (1981) and, amongst other more orthodox methods of earning money, agreed to be a guinea pig for medical experiments in order to raise the budget for his first independently made feature-length film. This was the successful *El Mariachi* (1993), which has consistently been quoted as costing $7,000 to produce. Quentin Tarantino, who has called Rodriguez 'my brother' in public, appeared in Rodriguez's *El Mariachi* sequel/remake *Desperado* (1995) and the two collaborated on a film of Tarantino's pre-fame screenplay *From Dusk Till Dawn* (1996). A far less low-key filmmaker than Anders or Rockwell with a résumé which rests on action-adventure cinema (2004's *Once Upon A Time in Mexico*), SF teen flicks (1998's *The Faculty*) as well as the aforementioned children's films, Rodriguez's style contains directorial propensities for action, deliberate 'cool' and much broad comedy. His status as a respected figure partially comes from his 'jack-of-all-trades' versatility, being a writer/editor/director/production designer/effects designer/sound designer/composer/musician/producer who can also, incidentally, act. His current project is an adaptation of Frank Miller's comic book series *Sin City* co-directed with the author himself although given the ferocious speed at which Rodriguez works he will probably have made three more films by the time this book is published. He is, like Allison Anders, an enthusiastic proponent of digital filmmaking, valuing the advantages it offers to small-scale productions and those who enjoy guerrilla shooting as well as its editing advantages.

ALEXANDRE ROCKWELL: Rockwell's *In The Soup* (1992) won the Grand Jury prize at Sundance the year that *Reservoir Dogs* was exhibited. Descended from the Russian animator Alexandre Alexeieff, he studied at the Cinematique Français. His CV is slim but impressive, principally comprising *Hero* (1984), *Sons* (1989) and the ensemble comedy *13 Moons* (2003). An old-fashioned independent filmmaker who makes exemplary creative use of silence, Rockwell frequently collaborates with Steve Buscemi and Sam Rockwell. He is not related to the latter.

QUOTES:

Chester: 'First off, there is nothing homosexual about what we want you to do.'

Chester: 'I didn't like champagne until I had Cristal and now I *love* it . . . it's Cristal, everything else is piss.'

Chester: 'When the hell has America ever been fair? We might be right every once in a while but we're very rarely *fair*.'

Chester: 'I'm not a frog and you're not a bunny. So let's not jump ahead.'

Leo: 'What does punctuality have to do with love? Can you explain that to me?'

Chester: 'Like my old granddaddy used to always say, the less a man makes declarative statements the less apt he is to look foolish in retrospect.'

SCREENPLAY: Tarantino's section of *Four Rooms* was written by him on his own although a great deal of the dialogue seems extemporised. At the very least there's obviously a great deal of ad-libbing. 'The Man from Hollywood' lasts for approximately 21 minutes. In it Ted the Bellhop enters the penthouse to deliver a bewildering list of items ordered from room service and meets a small group of people. The group includes Chester, a big-time movie director, celebrating his opening weekend and his friend, Leo, whose marriage appears to be breaking down because he's had too much to drink and can't drive back to see his wife. Chester's friend, Norman, has bet Chester that he can light his Zippo ten times in a row without pausing. If Norman succeeds he wins Chester's prized vintage car; if Chester wins he gets to cut off one of Norman's fingers.

It has been said that this instalment is an adaptation of the Roald Dahl short story 'The Man from the South'. It isn't. Not quite. Instead it is a short comedy about a group of people who consciously attempt to recreate things that happened in that short story. Which isn't really the same thing at all. Throughout the episode Chester repeatedly invokes what he says is an episode of the *Alfred Hitchcock Presents* series (1955–62) entitled 'The Man From Rio' which he says starred Peter Lorre and Steve McQueen. What he's actually talking about is indeed an episode of *Alfred Hitchcock Presents* but it's actually called 'Man from the South' and *it* is an adaptation of the Dahl story. It does, as Chester insists, concern a man who makes a bet concerning the number of times he can light a Zippo, putting his finger up against the opportunity to win a new car. What the episode/story is about, and this is something that Chester misses but Tarantino couldn't have, is the insanity of betting for irreversible stakes. (You could, in fact, claim the story itself is an adaptation of the Middle English poem *Sir Gawain and the Green Knight* in which a mysterious figure forces people to wager their own heads, which gives an indication of the thoroughly well-worn nature of the central conceit Tarantino is using.) 'Man from the South' was, for reference, the fifteenth episode of *Alfred Hitchock Presents'* fifth season on air and it was first aired on 3 January 1960.

CASTING: The cast of 'The Man from Hollywood' was chosen by Tarantino himself and consisted almost entirely of old collaborators of his. Presumably this was because the quick shoot required people that Tarantino was familiar with. Bruce Willis (Leo) had been in Tarantino's *Pulp Fiction*. He isn't credited for his role as Leo but, rather amusingly, his hairdresser *is* credited at the end of the film. Tim Roth (Ted) had appeared in *Reservoir Dogs* and *Pulp Fiction*. Paul Calderon (Norman) had also been in *Pulp Fiction*, and Kathy Griffin (Betty) had appeared in *Pulp Fiction* and Tarantino's episode of *ER*. She also had a memorable role in *Seinfeld* as one of Jerry's short-term girlfriends (in 'The Doll', 22 February 1996, and again in 'The Cartoon', 29 January 1998), memorable firstly for her assertion that she was 'Wacko!' (when she was actually very dull) and secondly for coming back later for revenge. Jennifer Beals (Angela) had starred in *Flashdance* (Adrian Lyne, 1983) aged nineteen but her career momentum collapsed after the disastrous *The Bride* (Franc Roddam, 1985), a sort of rock-pop version of *Bride of Frankenstein* (James Whale, 1935) starring Sting. Her career since is an odd mix of independent films and TV movies. She was most effective on screen in *Devil in a Blue Dress* (Carl Franklin, 1995) (as the daughter of a black father and a white mother 'passing for white' in the days of racial segregation in the US), *In the Soup* (1992) for then-husband Alexandre

Rockwell and in *The Last Days of Disco* (Whit Stillman, 1998). Hers is easily the best and most engaging performance in *Four Rooms* yet she's had one of the least noticeable careers of its participants or had until her casting in TV's controversial *The L Word* (2004–) saw her become a recognised mainstream TV Actress.

Marisa Tomei won an Oscar for *My Cousin Vinny* (Jonathan Lynn, 1992) and appeared in *Welcome to Sarajevo* (Michael Winterbottom, 1997) and *In the Bedroom* (Todd Field, 2001). All three are testaments to her immense versatility – as indeed is her stoner cameo in *Four Rooms*. She later worked with Tarantino in an off-Broadway production of *Wait Until Dark* (1997).

KEY SHOTS: Although it is a silly, inconsequential piece, 'The Man from Hollywood' does contain some interesting shots and demonstrates Tarantino's skills at visual storytelling.

The prologue to 'The Man from Hollywood' was also shot by Tarantino even though it arguably does not constitute part of 'The Man from Hollywood' itself. The swinging, panning camera movement of Ted's desperate phone call to Betty makes it very obviously shot by Tarantino. The contrast with the camera's absolute stationary, anterior, almost sulking presence on the other end of the phone as Margaret deadpan drawls away, and the excited Ted in fluent stoner-speak, is the funniest aspect of the whole film.

It consists of a series of very long takes mostly, if not entirely, shot by Bob Gorelick's Steadicam. When Ted first enters the penthouse suite said Steadicam dodges around Ted in order to acquaint the audience with the occupants of the penthouse. It then continues to bob and spiral through Chester's rants about Cristal and his explanation of his love of Jerry Lewis and then on into his onanistic exclamations about the success of his own movie. This whole sequence is one take, ending with Norman lighting Angela's cigarette. The sequence is about six minutes, ten seconds long and very nearly breaks down on a couple of occasions due to actors' stumbles but it's still technically impressive. The three-shot that follows, though – a mugging Tarantino, Roth and Calderon – is probably the ugliest camera set-up in Tarantino's career.

It's worth noting that the camera follows Tarantino's Chester around once the character has been introduced, making sure our attention is almost always on this particular random mood-swinging psycho.

The shot of the camera looking out of the door at Bruce Willis is very like one in the video version of *Reservoir Dogs*.

On the positive side, the whole piece is beautifully lit from above and there are some meticulous compositions in here – pause the DVD at 73.05 and look at the precisely placed yellow hat with its red and blue stripes on a green glass table and the three cushions in exactly the same shade of blue, green and orange as the contents of the table, the blue carpet and the striking orange drapes.

The most striking shot, though, is the crane shot which begins above the table looking directly down from the ceiling and then swings in a huge arc into a close-up of Norman's hand holding the Zippo lighter. That shot alone makes *Four Rooms* worthwhile.

At the end of the piece the camera stays in the suite and lets Ted leave with his money as the credits roll and the characters left behind mug and scramble around the stationary camera in the panic of trying to get Norman to an emergency room. It's as if the camera has lost interest now Ted's fate has been decided.

RECURRING ELEMENTS: The (initially rather engaging) title sequence, animated in what appears to be a nod to the Pink Panther series of films, begins when the 'A Band Apart' logo of Tarantino's production company (which features a graphic showing the leads of *Reservoir Dogs*) shows Tim Roth's 'Mr Orange' unzipping (shedding) his character from *Reservoir Dogs* and becoming the bellhop character for *Four*

Rooms. Angela is barefoot all the way through 'The Man from Hollywood'. Not the first, nor the last, barefooted female character to quietly dominate a Tarantino piece. Tarantino's fictional brand of cigarettes 'Red Apple' are seen just before Ted rings Betty – they're near the switchboard. The 1964 Chevy Chevelle ('fucking beautiful car') is the same as Jules's car from *Pulp Fiction* and the car that Mr Orange and Mr White steal from the woman Mr Orange murders in *Reservoir Dogs*. Tarantino, as Chester, says, 'What the fuck was I saying?' during 'The Man from Hollywood'. His character, Mr Brown, says exactly the same thing in the first scene of *Reservoir Dogs*. Also as in *Dogs* there's a scene involving mutilation and a Zippo lighter.

SPURIOUS INTERTEXTUALITY: The set for the penthouse is eerily reminiscent in size, colour and shape of the red room that serves as the white lodge/black lodge from David Lynch's *Twin Peaks* TV series. Leo references John Wayne Bobbit who, famously, had his penis cut off by his wife when she discovered his infidelities. When Ted enters the penthouse Norman starts shouting 'Bellboy!' over and over again in an obvious direct reference to Phil Daniels's fit of rage at Sting's Bellboy character at the end of *Quadrophenia* (Franc Roddam, 1979). Although it isn't in Tarantino's section but in Rodriguez's, it's worth mentioning that the cartoon on TV in 'The Misbehavers' is the same cartoon Ritchie watches in Tarantino's and Rodriguez's *From Dusk Till Dawn*. Tarantino's Chester also mentions *The Bellboy* (Jerry Lewis, 1960) with Jerry Lewis and explains that he holds it to be 'one of Jerry's better movies'. In it, Jerry Lewis gives a silent performance as the eponymous hotel employee. Chester is incensed that Jerry Lewis gets more respect for his film work from European critics and audiences than from Americans. Producer Lawrence Bender who is visibly asleep on the sofa behind Margaret (Marisa Tomei) in the prologue is credited, as he was on *Pulp Fiction*, as 'Long Hair Yuppy Scum'.

THE LIST: These are the items Ted the Bellhop has to bring to the penthouse for the use of Chester and company: a block of wood, three nails, a ball of twine, a bucket of ice, a doughnut, a club sandwich, a hatchet 'as sharp as the devil himself'.

CHESTER'S FILMS: *The Wacky Detective* is the film of Chester's that is being celebrated by those in the penthouse. It took $72.1 million in the United States. This actually sounds like a small amount for a truly successful blockbuster three-day weekend these days but, had it been true, it would compare well with the opening weekends for *Jurassic Park* (Steven Spielberg, 1993) or *Independence Day* (Roland Emmerich, 1996), the two biggest blockbusters of the day. Chester Rush's new film is said to be *The Dog Catcher*.

CRITICAL REACTION: Few films can have been as consistently badly reviewed as *Four Rooms* was on initial release. Tarantino fan Roger Ebert of the *Chicago Sun-Times* wrote that the film looked 'carelessly prepared' and opined that, while Tarantino had 'the right idea in choosing to satirise himself' he unfortunately 'does not seem to understand why he is funny'. The *Washington Post* was absolutely crushing, suggesting that 'physical restraint would be the only reason why the average moviegoer wouldn't walk out on this stupefying attempt to create a kind of art-house Jerry Lewis movie'. In the *New York Times* Janet Maslin was equally scathing conceding that while the cast list was impressive 'you wouldn't want to see any of these people in a traffic accident, and you won't want to see them here'. In the *New Yorker* the writer punningly pointed out that it was a case of '*Four Rooms* . . . all empty'. The humour was 'sophomoric and repetitive' and the cast gave 'self-parodying performances' that were 'among the worst of their careers'. His conclusion? 'This movie is a collection of vanity projects directed by a bunch of people who were told they were cool once too often. They could all use a good slap at the box office.' It was a critical, rather than a commercial, slap that this not exactly expensive anyway film received. It is worth pointing out that all the above reviews, and indeed most others, hold that Rodriguez's section of *Four Rooms* is the best. This author absolutely disputes that. Tarantino's is the best of a bad bunch, with Rockwell's a reasonable second. Rodriguez's is ghastly. For example, Antonio Banderas isn't – as some people insist – giving a parody of his usual performance, he's giving the same performance he always does while the image of the dead, rotting hooker in the cut open mattress being vomited onto by Roth is pointlessly unpleasant, achieving nothing and blandly unamusing to boot.

THE NUMBERS: Released on 26 December 1995 *Four Rooms'* total US take was in the region of $4.3 million; based upon the initial investment of around $4 million that's an excellent immediate return. Even taking into account costs not included in the budget and the cinemas' take of that, *Four Rooms* must have made money via home markets and TV rights but it unquestionably did damage to the reputations of the four writers/directors involved and helped create momentum for a Tarantino backlash which concentrated on the man's acting appearances, celebrity and social ubiquity rather than his films.

FINAL COMMENT: Rather like watching someone else have a party those responsible for 'The Man From Hollywood' should have remembered that while they were all having fun, the audience might want to have some too. Roth tries very hard to create a screwball comedy atmosphere through his performance. Too hard in fact and his delivery and body language quickly become very irritating. It's the worst performance of his otherwise generally distinguished career. Of the actors only Jennifer Beals escapes with real credit, with Willis almost seeming somnambulistic and Tarantino himself giving a performance which, while quite entertaining to watch, doesn't really constitute the creation of a character. It's more a playing with of the director's own perceived public persona as filtered through the archetype of the out-of-control Hollywood egomaniac. 'The Man from Hollywood' is frantic and funny, even if it is self-indulgent and histrionic. If it didn't have A-list Hollywood talent in it, if it wasn't directed by someone who had just won the Palme D'Or and was regarded as the great white hope of American independent cinema 'The Man from Hollywood' would be regarded as an indulgent, occasionally funny piece that stands out as the most entertaining section of *Four Rooms*. Unfortunately, it does have A-list Hollywood talent in it and is directed by someone regarded as the great white hope of American independent cinema. As such it's a frivolous disappointment, albeit the least disappointing part of a film that is neither interestingly diverse nor satisfyingly coherent. It's also the polar opposite of *Pulp Fiction* in that it conspicuously fails to demonstrate the talents of virtually all of those involved.

Acting

It is interesting that acting is the only area of film production in which Tarantino has any formal training, yet it is the one area that critics have generally been unanimously negative about him indulging in. Indeed, Tarantino has often been repeatedly mocked for his acting aspirations, although it's worth pointing out that the first review of any of Tarantino's films to mention his acting was Roger Ebert's critique of *Reservoir Dogs* in which the venerable reviewer admitted to finding him 'interesting' as an actor, reasoning he could play 'crazy villains' very well.

Tarantino, in a later interview with Ebert, described acting as 'one of my palettes' and stated that he would not give up on his desire to appear in both his own films and other people's just because some critics disliked his doing so. Tarantino has also stated, and here he has a point, that his celebrity status gets in the way of his being taken seriously as an actor. It's not that there's anything in particular wrong with his acting, it's that his public persona is too large and it gets in the way of people being able to see the performance.

This is certainly a valid argument. If a few moments is taken to consider Tarantino's performances in *Pulp Fiction* and *From Dusk Till Dawn*, there really aren't many useful points of comparison. One character is an everyman, the other is a monster; one is quick talking, the other is a sinister, mumbling freak. They have generally very different body languages and speaking styles. Tarantino is never going to be a great actor, but he's right that he's been harshly treated by commentators.

As well as his own movies, Tarantino has appeared in a number of others, including several that are not discussed in detail in this book. In *The Coriolos Effect* (Louis Venosta, 1994) he has a voice-over cameo, while in Alexandre Rockwell's 1994 indie *Somebody to Love* he plays the smallish role of the bartender. He is an asylum attendant in *Eddie Presley* (Jeff Burr, 1993) and does a turn in Robert Rodriguez's 1995 remake of/sequel to *El Mariachi*, *Desperado*.

He starred in the dreary bank heist comedy/thriller *Destiny Turns on the Radio* (Jack Baran, 1995) with Jim Belushi, Dylan McDermott and James LeGros and cameoed as 'QT' in *Girl 6* (Spike Lee, 1996), a comedy-satire on Hollywood manners and methods. After *Jackie Brown* (in which he played the uncredited role of Jackie's answering machine) Tarantino scaled back his acting work, possibly as a response to criticism of his Broadway turn (see Wait Until Dark). He did, however, take the time to play the blind, sinister deacon in Adam Sandler – starring devil comedy *Little Nicky* (Steven Brill, 2000) opposite his friend Harvey Keitel as Satan.

He is also to play Comanche in *Hell Ride* (2006), a film directed by Larry Bishop, a writer/director/actor who had appeared in *Vol. 2*.

From Dusk Till Dawn (1996)

Miramax Films presents
A Band Apart
In Association With
Los Hooligans Productions
A Robert Rodriguez Film
Casting By Johanna Ray, CSA & Elaine J Huzzar
Special Make-up Effects by Kurtzman, Nicotero &
Berger EFX Group, Inc.
Music by Graeme Revell
Costume Designer: Graciela Mazon
Production Designer: Cecilia Montiel
Director of Photography: Guillermo Navarro
Co-producers: Elizabeth Havellan, Paul Hellerman,
Robert Kurtzman, John Eposito
Executive Producers: Lawrence Bender, Robert Rodriguez,
Quentin Tarantino
Story by Robert Kurtzman
Screenplay by Quentin Tarantino
Edited and Directed by Robert Rodriguez

TAGLINES: 'Vampires. No Interviews.'

'The Showdown is on.'

'One night is all that stands between them and freedom. But it's going to be a hell of a night'.

'How Far can Too Far go?'

'From Quentin Tarantino. From Robert Rodriguez. From Dusk Till Dawn.'

CAST: Harvey Keitel (Jacob Fuller), George Clooney (Seth Gecko), Quentin Tarantino (Richard Gecko), Juliette Lewis (Kate Fuller), Ernest Liu (Scott Fuller), Salma Hayek (Santanico Pandemonium), Cheech Marin (Border Guard/Chet Pussy/Carlos), Danny Trejo (Razor Charlie), Tom Savini (Sex Machine), Fred Williamson (Frost), Michael Parks (Texas Ranger Earl McGraw), Brenda

Hillhouse (Hostage Gloria), John Saxon (FBI Agent Stanley Chase), Marc Lawrence (Old Timer Motel Owner), Kelly Preston (Newscaster Kelly Houge), John Hawkes (Pete Bottoms), Tito Larriva (Titty Twister Guitarist & Vocalist), Peter Atanasoff (Titty Twister Saxophonist), Johnny 'Vatos' Hernandez (Titty Twister Drummer), Aimee Graham (Blonde Hostage), Heidi McNeal (Red-headed Hostage), Ernest M Garcia (Big Emilio), Gregory Nicotero (Sex Machine's Buddy), Cristos (Danny), Mike Moroff (Manny), Michelle Berube (Bar Dancer), Neena Bidasha (Bar Dancer), Veena Bidasha (Bar Dancer), Ungela Brockman (Bar Dancer), Madison Clark (Bar Dancer), María Díaz (Bar Dancer), Rosalia Hayakawa (Bar Dancer), Janine Jordae (Bar Dancer), Jacque Lawson (Bar Dancer), Houston Leigh (Bar Dancer), Janie Liszewski (Bar Dancer), Tia Texada (Bar Dancer), Jon Fidele (Monster), Michael McKay (Monster), Jake McKinnon (Monster), Josh Patton (Monster), Walter Phelan (Monster), Wayne Toth (Monster), Henrik von Ryzin (Monster)

SUMMARY: Brothers Richard and Seth Gecko attempt to flee Texas for El Ray, Mexico, where they will be able to trade a 30 per cent stake of their loot from a bank job for safety and security in a 'community' of escaped cons and criminals. In order to cross the Mexican border they kidnap a family consisting of a widowed father and his son and daughter and hold them hostage in their motor home, forcing them to play-act at the border in order to secure passage out of the United States.

Once in Mexico they go to a bar called the Titty Twister where a bar fight develops and they are set upon by a gang of vampires. With the help of some other non-vampiric patrons they fight their way out to safety albeit at the cost of the lives of Richie, the father and son of the family and the rest of the denizens of the bar. Seth departs for El Ray having struck his deal with the criminal gang, leaving daughter Kate to find her way back to America on her own.

DEVELOPMENT: Described by its author as a 'full-on, lurid exploitation-movie experience' the script for the film that became *From Dusk Till Dawn* was based upon a storyline by Robert Kurtzman, a make-up artist and special-effects man whose credits include *Goldmember* (Jay Roach, 2002), *Hulk* (Ang Lee, 2003) and *Army of Darkness* (Sam Raimi, 1993). Tarantino's screenplay, worked from Kurtzman's treatment, was written as early as 1990; the two had come into contact via Scott Spiegel, a filmmaker and old school friend of Sam Raimi and Bruce Campbell who had met Tarantino via another mutual acquaintance. Spiegel suggested Quentin as a screenwriter for Kurtzman's proposed project. Having read *True Romance* and *Natural Born Killers*, Tarantino was paid $1,500 in script development money and was told to write the screenplay so that the action of the film would offer opportunities to showcase the skills of those working for the Kurtzman (part-owned), Nicotero and Berger EFX Group, Inc. It was Tarantino's first paid writing job. The script would, however, languish unmade and shortly afterwards Tarantino found himself in a position to make *Reservoir Dogs* with producer Lawrence Bender.

In 1992 Tarantino first met fellow director Robert Rodriguez at the Toronto Film Festival where Rodriguez was exhibiting *El Mariachi* (1993). The two hit it off, forming an instant bond which has endured to this day. Rodriguez later said that meeting Tarantino made him 'wish I'd have had someone like that in high school with me. It would have made it so much easier.'

The relationship can be considered analogous to the professional/private partnership of George Lucas and Steven Spielberg which began in very similar circumstances within a different generation of young independent filmmakers. Whereas Lucas and Spielberg usually describe one another in public as 'my best friend' the Tarantino/Rodriguez relationship has been defined by both of them as explicitly fraternal, with each referring to the other as 'my brother' on more than one public occasion. Interestingly Rodriguez is one of, literally, a dozen siblings whereas Tarantino is an only child.

At the time of their first encounter one of the pair's many discussions about movies led to Rodriguez opining that he'd really like to make a horror film set in Mexico. Tarantino, recalling the unmade *From Dusk Till Dawn*, mentioned that he'd actually written an unproduced horror film set in Mexico and that the rights for it lay with the make-up production company who'd commissioned it. The idea of a joint project appealed to both men so Rodriguez asked if he could read the script. He liked it and then asked if it were possible to direct it. Tarantino was pleased with the idea, and offered to perform another rewrite on the script in order to make it ready for production.

Rodriguez's production of Tarantino's script was shot between June and August 1995 around the Texas–Mexico border. Rodriguez took the opportunity to include a Tarantino homage shot: when the opening credits finish and the Geckos retrieve their hostage, the audience look from the woman's point of view from inside the trunk of the car up at the Geckos. This angle is something of a trademark of Tarantino's, and features in all of his pictures. Generally though, Rodriguez's visual style is very different: his camera is more mobile than Tarantino's generally is, and he uses much shorter takes and quicker cuts. He also uses straightforward reaction shots, which Tarantino tends to avoid. Far more violence actually takes place on screen, with attendant increases in the amount of visible blood, than is the case in Tarantino's first three directorial features.

SCREENPLAY: Despite Kurtzman's status as the story's originator, the script as written comes across as pure Tarantino. It's brimful of references, quick-talking, has crime at the centre of its plot and is ultimately a story about a kind of redemption.

Unlike the bulk of Tarantino's screenplays, *From Dusk Till Dawn* has a straightforward linear structure in which the events of the story occur to the characters in the same order that the audience witnesses them. The structural conceit it does contain, however, is what might be termed a 'dogleg'. For the first seventy or so pages *From Dusk Till Dawn* seems to be a combination of crime drama and road movie which details how a pair of on-the-run criminal brothers kidnap a family headed by a preacher who has lost his faith in God and use them and their vehicle to successfully flee the United States for Mexico.

However, after arriving in Mexico the brothers and their hostages head to a bar where, on page eighty of the script, they are attacked by vampires who they have to defend themselves against at the cost of the lives of most of their party. While it would be a mistake to term the film 'two movies in one' what the script and the film made of it do is shift genre around two thirds of the way through. The picture changes from being a hard crime thriller into being an action/horror movie.

As the script switches genres, it also changes in terms of what its genre assumptions are, what is physically, emotionally and tonally possible within the film's own logic changes. It isn't just a sharp change in plotline (such as that accomplished, with great skill, in Alfred Hitchcock's 1960 masterpiece *Psycho*), it's a genuine change from being one kind of film to another.

Seth undergoes a radical shift in belief (if not in persona) because when confronted by the absolute evil of the vampires he is forced to believe in the absolute good of (an implicitly Judaeo-Christian) God as well because he is convinced that there must be a counteractive force in the universe to conflict with the evil he's seen with his own eyes. This is the kind of thing that happens in horror movies, not in gangland thrillers. Jacob Fuller rediscovering his own lapsed faith for the same reasons is the same type of character motion and originates in the same kind of film – even if it is expressed ('mean motherfucking servant of God') in a uniquely Tarantino manner.

Equally, all the external references to what is and isn't physically possible shift; despite Seth's worries that this may not be the case, the ways to kill vampires that the characters remember from horror films they've seen, work in the real world they inhabit because their real world now shares the logic of that fiction. Pieces of wood bound together will suffice as a crucifix and sunlight is deadly to vampires. Vampires also have the ability to pass the 'infection' of being such a creature on. (Although *From Dusk*'s vampires actually resemble classic movie zombies in their behaviour, their incoherent savagery and the way they turn their victims into vampires with a single bite, most vampire-related fiction suggests that vampirism is passed on not when a vampire bites a human, but when a human is invited to drink a vampire's own blood.)

The two new characters who are introduced to assist Seth, Jacob and family against the vampires, Frost and Sex Machine, are a leather-clad biker and a hard-as-nails Vietnam veteran respectively; the kind of characters who populate action–horror–exploitation movies, not the archetypes of crime fiction.

After the characters survive their ordeal and the story is over, the threads left dangling from the previous section of the story – Richie's crime, Seth's robberies, the pursuit of the Gecko brothers by United States law enforcement – no longer matter. Kate doesn't blame Seth for her father's and brother's death, even though they wouldn't even have been in the Titty Twister were it not for Seth, because she is indebted to him for helping her survive the ordeal. This is horror-movie logic – the disparate group brought together in adversity by facing truly monstrous opposition.

Throughout the screenplay Tarantino's standard reversions and inversions, introduction of violence and comedy into situations where they aren't expected, furious referentiality and inventive use of verbal constructions discussed in relation to previous films are all present.

For example, the opening scene doesn't begin in a way which is remotely suggestive of the bloodbath it becomes. As it starts, the audience doesn't even know that Seth and Richie, who will become the film's main characters, are present in the room. There's a whole extra text operating behind the opening conversation that a first-time viewer cannot possibly appreciate. The quite staggering violence is as unexpected as is the literally explosive end of the scene.

Examples of Tarantino's verbal inventiveness include 'he doesn't know rat shit from Rice Crispies', the brilliantly nonsensical, yet evocative, 'one long goddamn hot noodle shit ass fucking day every inch of the way' and Seth's description of himself and his brother as 'Real mean motor scooters'. As in all Tarantino scripts characters declaim at one another for half a page or even longer, often expositing at enormous length on a particular subject. Again, as always, the combination of wit, references and the dialogue's easy rhythm means that this simply doesn't matter.

Just because the screenplay is full of epic amounts of profanity, crude jokes and loaded with violence doesn't mean that it lacks subtlety. It just means that it isn't obviously subtle, but then if it were obviously subtle then perhaps it wouldn't so much be 'subtle' as in a state of pleading with its audience to see it as deep. *From Dusk Till Dawn* doesn't wear its complexities on its sleeve, but it is smarter, more thematically intelligent and deeper than it appears. There are small subtleties, such as Scott Fuller's belief that he knows what a hostage situation is like because he watches 'reality TV shows' (indicating the nature of the film as a piece which only references other entertainment pieces) and Jacob Fuller's lie to the border guards that he's taking his son 'to see his first bullfight', an ingratiating faking of an interest in something within Mexican culture but outside mainstream American culture.

More important though, is the ambiguity at the centre of the film's lead. Seth Gecko is actually quite an interesting and complex character. There is no doubt that he is an unpleasant person who has committed terrible crimes out of pure selfishness. He's killed in the pursuit of easy wealth and, like Honey Bunny in *Pulp Fiction*, uses 'execute' almost euphemistically as a sort of cover for the fact that he's a cold-blooded murderer. Yet Seth is manifestly a better person than Richie is. It may be small consolation to the families of those he's killed but Seth considers himself 'a professional thief' – a term that is also a source of some pride for *Reservoir Dogs*'s Mr Pink – and, also like Mr Pink, he insists that he doesn't kill people that he doesn't have to. He's appalled that Richie is a rapist, not simply morally appalled but also physically revolted to the extent that he wants to be sick. Seth is – and this is important – also appalled by Richie's random acts of violence as well as his sex crimes. As Richie's older brother, he feels that not only is he responsible for Richie in the here and now, but that he may have been in some way responsible for Richie becoming the depraved, vicious person he is, because he chose a life of crime and Richie always looked up to him.

Seth is also capable of admitting that he's made a mistake (such as after Jacob berates him for being 'such a fucking loser that you can't tell when you've won'), not something that is generally true of Tarantino's career criminal characters.

Another interesting moment in the script that reflects on Seth is when he questions Scott and Jacob Fuller about their relationship:

> **Seth:** So, what's the deal with you two, you a couple of fags?
> **Jacob:** He's my son.
> **Seth:** Yeah, how'd that happen? You don't look Japanese.
> **Jacob:** Neither does he. He looks Chinese.
> **Seth:** Oh, well, excuse me all to hell.

This exchange is interesting for three reasons. Firstly, it draws attention to the Hollywood motion picture habit of assuming that people from ethnically Asian countries look sufficiently alike for them to be interchangeable for film casting purposes. Secondly, as originally written in the script, Jacob corrects Seth with 'Vietnamese' not 'Chinese'. The casting of Ernest Liu made this small change necessary; although the fact that it was made at all indicates that to make this point was part of the reason for the scene. Thirdly, the scene also makes very clear a difference between Seth and Jacob. The idea of the kind of selflessness that Jacob exhibited in this adoption is – at this point – completely beyond Seth's comprehension.

Later on, after Richie's death, Seth is incapable of seeing that Jacob and Kate are genuinely sorry that Richie has died. Not because they liked him but because they, as recent victims of bereavement themselves, can empathetically connect with his pain. 'Bullshit!' Seth hollers when they express sympathy and goes on to explain his belief that Kate and Jacob would feed him to the vampires given half the chance. 'Then why didn't I?' asks Jacob and Seth is shocked that he doesn't know the answer.

Seth Gecko is a complex man, witty, obviously capable of making the right moral choice and he doesn't want to do what he perceives as 'unnecessary' harm to others. But none of this means he isn't selfish, brutal and incapable of seeing other people's viewpoints. He wouldn't have cared had someone else's brother died through no fault of his; why would someone else care if his brother died through no fault of theirs? He fundamentally lacks empathy. He may have good qualities, they may come more to the fore as the picture goes on but these facts don't stop Seth Gecko from being a bad human being who does terrible things out of utter selfishness.

It is also worth noting that Seth's semi-redemption in the face of evil alters his use of language; he doesn't decrease the amount of swearing he does but by the end of the film a man who said that God could 'kiss my ass' and mocked Jacob Fuller's profession is using the word 'Godless' as an insult.

Richie is a less complex and less appealing personality than Seth, but then he's meant to be. It's tempting to see the addition of his more obnoxious character traits in re-drafting (see below) as an attempt to distinguish him more from his brother and to cast his brother in a subtly more appealing light. Richie's sociopathy is obvious and he has difficulty telling the difference between fact and fantasy. He seems to genuinely believe that Kate sexually propositioned him in the hotel room, whereas he actually imagined it. The aftermath of Richie's rape and murder of the innocent hostage Gloria (Brenda Hillhouse) is the film's most unpleasant and disturbing scene. On the page this is the point where Richie stops being, even partially, a comedy character. After this moment the audience is terribly aware of how dangerous and dislocated from reality he is. Interestingly, in Tarantino's pre-fame draft of the screenplay, Richie was a less monstrous character, neither a convicted sex offender nor an obvious sociopath, simply a wise-cracking career criminal more like his brother. In that draft he was allowed to survive the final massacre in the Titty Twister, along with the entire Fuller family. Tarantino's later pre-production rewrite also revised this aspect so that only Kate, Scott and Seth escaped and Seth and Kate went off together at the end. (In simple terms, the two innocents and the redeemed Seth survive and Seth's reward for his redemption is that he gets the girl.)

This was later revised *again* to make Seth and Kate the only survivors but they do not go off together. This is a reversal of standard film plotting logic in that it doesn't unite the final two characters left standing – both played by actors known as sex symbols – into a romantic, or at least sexual, union. This absence of 'reward' also make Seth's redemption more muted (as it perhaps needs to be, given his tolerance for Richie's more appalling actions) but at the same time allows him to comment on it himself; he recognises that to take the exhausted, traumatised and largely innocent Kate with him – especially given the obvious sexual implications of what she says at the end of the picture – would be wrong to the point of being abusive. Hence his comment, 'Honey,

I'm a bastard. But I'm not a *fucking* bastard.' By turning down the girl his brother fantasised about he's even more clearly delineating himself from Richie in the minds of the audience. It's a small thing, but it works.

There were other, smaller, less thematically interesting changes made to the script during production. They include the characters of Sex Machine and Frost being rewritten to fit the perceived personas of the actors playing them (originally Sex Machine was the biker character) and the fact that one of the film's most memorable lines of dialogue is Clooney's Seth responding to Santanico Pandemonium's 'Welcome to slavery' with 'No thanks, I already had a wife' was improvised by George Clooney on set.

CASTING: Most of the casting in *From Dusk Till Dawn* works by a process of casting against type in order to work against the audience's expectations of what the characters will – even *should* – be like. In addition, the actors director Rodriguez and producer Tarantino selected are largely people associated with their earlier productions, fostering the idea of a 'talent pool' which was so integral to the contemporary perception of Tarantino's work as a new, but familiar, kind of cinema. George Clooney had found fame, and indeed fortune, as roguish 'nice guy' paediatrician Doug Ross in NBC's TV series *ER*. His casting as a ruthless, gun-happy gangland figure, albeit the 'nicer' and more stable of the two brothers in the Gecko-sibling partnership, is both a repudiation of this image (Seth is not anything like Doug Ross) and yet also plays along with the idea, fostered by his TV role, that however badly Clooney seems to behave his character can ultimately be trusted to do the right thing. (Tarantino had, interestingly, written the role of Seth with actor Robert Blake (*Lost Highway*, David Lynch, 1997) in mind but became drawn to Clooney and his possibilities as the character after observing the obviously intelligent and intense actor talking on the panel on the cultural and political discussion/entertainment show *Politically Incorrect*.)

Harvey Keitel's casting (he had been in *Reservoir Dogs*) is another piece of almost-revisionist actor positioning. Keitel's profile was – indeed is – largely dominated in the public mind with 'hard' roles and playing tough, if complex, characters and violent men in pictures such as *Bad Lieutenant* (Abel Ferrara, 1992). To cast him as a compassionate, if flawed, man of God and committed father is another, more major, piece of casting against type. Indeed one of the unsung subtleties of the script is that, on first viewing, most movie-literate audiences will side with the monstrous Richie during his first encounter with the Fullers. What is Keitel's character hiding? What is the deal with him being a preacher according to his papers? Why is this odd-looking man travelling with two teenagers of widely different ethnicities, both of whom he insists are his children? In most road movies he'd turn out to be a cult leader or a criminal on the run, and the casting of Keitel plays along with the audience's assumptions. (He had, after all, been incendiary as the ultimate betrayer, Judas Iscariot, in Martin Scorsese's *The Last Temptation of Christ* (1988) only a few years before.) Ultimately, though, Jacob Fuller is exactly who he claims to be and Keitel's small and homely performance overcomes the audience's assumptions. Also feeding into the ideas of 'perception subversion' and working from a 'palette' of actors was the casting of Juliette Lewis. Lewis had been in Oliver Stone's production of Tarantino's script *Natural Born Killers* (1994) and it's that performance (perhaps even that film) as well as her appearance in *Kalifornia* (Dominic Sena, 1993) that her casting here seems designed to comment on, even repudiate. For although Lewis had been acting since childhood and had appeared in a number of films as 'daughter' figures (Martin Scorsese's *Cape Fear* 1991 remake, Woody Allen's 1992 *Husbands and Wives*, Jeremiah S Chechik's 1989 *National Lampoon's Christmas Vacation*, etc.) those two pictures had come to dominate perceptions of her and she was associated with playing a certain kind of 'nasty' young woman – poor white-trash girls with a secret. While Kate is not a *total* repudiation of that archetype she is a far more 'normal' girl; it's almost an ingénue role. Her innocence of the very idea that she *can* drink alcohol even though she isn't actually 21 (it's physically possible, it's just against the law) is a big character indicative moment. She's also both a character placed in a very difficult situation who does not become a victim and a teenage female character whom the picture itself does not sexualise even while some of the characters do (and that's even harder than it sounds).

In keeping with this theme of subversion of actor perception there was some thought given to either Steve Buscemi or Tim Roth playing the character of Pete Bottoms (the store worker killed in the opening scene). The filmmakers felt that the audience would not expect a character played by a Tarantino regular to be killed off so quickly and arbitrarily, adding another surprise to the picture. Interestingly there seems to be an element of deliberate Steve Buscemi pastiche to John Hawkes's performance as Bottoms.

The casting of Cheech Marin in no less than three (widely disparate) roles (although the decision for him to play the third role Carlos was arrived at when another actor proved unavailable) seems to have other motives entirely: it's designed to demonstrate the performer's undoubted but undervalued versatility. Best known for his writing and acting in the 'Cheech and Chong' series of 'marijuana comedy' films beginning with *Cheech and Chong's Up In Smoke* (Lou Adler, 1978), Marin had enjoyed some cross-over success in providing voices for animated films like Disney's *The Lion King* (Roger Allers, Rob Minkoff, 1994). Following *From Dusk Till Dawn* he gained second billing on the TV series *Nash Bridges* (1996–2001) for which he was nominated for half-a-dozen awards.

Also multitalented is Michael Parks (Earl McGraw). He had been the star of *Then Came Bronson* (1969–70) on television as well as a successful country music artist. He combined the two careers when the James Hendricks-penned theme tune for *Bronson* became a top-twenty hit. He'd also been a frequent guest star on *Twin Peaks* (1990) as Jean Renault, spent a year (1987) on the *Dynasty* spin-off *The Colbys* and came near to qualifying to represent the United States at the 1972 Munich Olympics as a runner.

Salma Hayek had been a soap star in her native Mexico and appeared in director Rodriguez's *Desperado* (1995) and (in a small role) in his section of *Four Rooms*. *Desperado* and *From Dusk Till Dawn* made her a pin-up, but from these inauspicious beginnings she has gone on to a wide and varied career incorporating blockbusters, romantic comedy, serious drama and an Oscar-nomination (for *Frida* (Julie Taymoor, 2002)). What is less well known is that her character, Satanico Pandemonium, is named after the film of the same title, which is also known as *La Sexorcisto* (Gilberto Martinez Solares, 1975).

A writer/director as well as an actor, Fred 'The Hammer' Williamson (Frost) is the kind of actor who is instantly recognisable to the average moviegoer while his name continues to elude them. He was Captain Jones in *M*A*S*H* (Robert Altman, 1970) and has been a constant presence on American television. His turn in the 1969 *Star Trek* episode 'The Cloud Minders' must, like most episodes of that series, be on somewhere in the world every day of the year. He was a huge star of African-American targeted cinema of the 1970s, including *Black Caesar* (Larry Cohen, 1973) and *Hell Up In Harlem* (Larry Cohen, 1974); while his talents have never truly been recognised by the mainstream it is to be hoped that his hilarious turn in *Starsky and Hutch* (Todd Philips, 2004) will lead to a higher profile for him.

Of course, one of the most famous pieces of casting in *From Dusk Till Dawn* is Tarantino's own appearance as Richie Gecko. This has been much criticised. However, anyone who seriously believes that Tarantino has no real acting ability should consider how very different Richie Gecko is from *Four Rooms*'s Chester Rush. Tarantino's body language is as different as his voice is distinctive. Richie is a small performance, couched in looking down at the floor and speaking slowly (compared to Tarantino's own rapid-fire speech anyway). His body language is unconfident, repressed, angry, obscure. Nothing like the expansive, inviting, silly, flamboyant Chester Rush and even less like the engaging, enthusiastic, impressive Quentin Tarantino. There is a disturbing air about Richie even before the audience has reason to be horrified by his actions, a dislocation from reality which is conveyed by Tarantino's very earnest performance in the role. Tarantino's own contention that people who see him act have criticised him because they can't get past their perceptions of his own, very public persona, has some validity. In *From Dusk Till Dawn* his work as an actor suggests that, while he will never be as great a performer as he is screenwriter or director, he is a very much better actor than any of his critics have been prepared to suggest.

QUOTES:

Seth: 'Let me tell you what "low profile" is not. It is not taking girls hostage. It is not shooting police. It is not setting fire to a building.'

Kate: 'Don't you believe in God any more?'

Jacob: 'Not enough to be a pastor . . . yes, I do believe in Jesus. Yes, I do believe in God. But do I love them? No.'

Seth: 'Those acts of God really stick it in and break it off, don't they?'

Seth: 'I know that I put you all through hell . . . but from here on in you are all in my cool book.'

Seth: 'These guys are not spic firecracker salesmen from Tijuana.'

Seth: 'You can change the name of this place to Benny's world of blood'

RECURRING ELEMENTS: Several of Tarantino's fictional brands turn up in *From Dusk Till Dawn*. The Gecko brothers eat Kahuna burgers (the same takeaway brand evangelised by Jules in *Pulp Fiction*) in the hotel room. Red Apple cigarettes are visible on the dashboard of Seth's car. Seth says, 'OK ramblers, let's get rambling' to Jacob; Joe Cabot says much the same thing in the first scene of *Reservoir Dogs* although Seth develops it into a whole set of recurring phrases culminating in 'OK vampire killers, let's kill vampires.' Again, as in most Tarantino scripts, the topic of cunnilingus is mentioned – this time inside Richie's fantasies about Kate. Seth steps out in front of the Fullers' wagon causing it to stop – someone doing this to a slowly moving vehicle is also common in Tarantino films (think Marsellus Wallace in *Pulp Fiction*) and seems to have been drawn from *Psycho* (Alfred Hitchcock, 1960). The very odd way that newscaster Kelly Houge tries to be sexy while reporting an appalling number of crimes echoes the concerns of *Natural Born Killers*. Seth's line 'Are you absolutely positively clear about rule number one?' very nearly recurs in *Kill Bill – Vol. 1*.

SPURIOUS INTERTEXTUALITY: Kate and Seth's conversation about bullets just before the vampires' final attack is a paraphrase of dialogue from *Assault on Precinct 13* (John Carpenter, 1976; (remade) Jean-François Richet, 2005). Scott actually wears a T-shirt with 'Precinct 13' on it all the way through the film. Sex Machine's gun is very like one of the weapons in El Mariachi's guitar case in Rodriguez's *Desperado* (1995). While it's never been confirmed by anyone involved surely the Fuller family are named after director Sam Fuller? Equally the Gecko family must be named after Gordon Gecko, as played by an Oscar-wining Michael Douglas in *Wall Street* (Oliver Stone, 1987). (The word 'gecko' does have a literal meaning, a kind of lizard, but that doesn't seem to have any application here and Tarantino has said that *From Dusk Till Dawn*, like *Kill*

Bill exists in a world where the only meaningful references are to other movies.) Peter Cushing who, as various incarnations of Van Helsing, fought vampires in *Horror of Dracula* (Terence Fisher, 1958), *The Brides of Dracula* (Terence Fisher, 1960), *Dracula AD 1972* (Alan Gibson, 1972) and *The Satanic Rites of Dracula* (Alan Gibson, 1973) is invoked by Seth as an example of a vampire killer. The Fullers drive down a road called Deguayo. This is also the name of a song played by the villains to John Wayne in *Rio Bravo* (Howard Hawks, 1959). If that seems like a bit of a stretch, then it's worth pointing out that Quentin Tarantino has said that *Rio Bravo* is one of his three favourite films ever made. (The others are *Blow Out* (Brian de Palma, 1981) and *Mean Streets* (Martin Scorsese, 1973).) Chongo beer (from Rodriguez's *Desperado* (1995)) is on sale in the Titty Twister bar. 'I've got six little friends and they can all run faster than you can' is a line from *That Darn Cat!* (Robert Stevenson, 1965), equally Kate saying 'What's in Mexico?' and Richie's replying 'Mexicans' is a line from the spectacularly violent western *The Wild Bunch* (Sam Peckinpah, 1969) which Seth also refers to when he threatens to turn the store into 'the fucking Wild Bunch'. The semi-crippled Jacob Fuller turning into the enemy even as he helps his friends defeat them seems drawn from *Dawn of the Dead* (George Romero, 1979). One of the film's taglines 'Vampires. No Interviews' is, of course, a reference to *Interview with the Vampire: The Vampire Chronicles* (Neil Jordan, 1994), the Tom Cruise-starring adaptation of Anne Rice's tedious novel. *From Dusk Till Dawn* takes a completely different angle on the use of vampires within a plot. Rice's book and Jordan's film concentrate on the loneliness of long-lived beings and the supposed allure of the mythic, sexually potent vampire; Tarantino's script presents them as relentless evil which must be destroyed.

CRITICAL REACTION: In the *New Yorker*, Terence Rafferty felt that the writer's and director's approaches didn't 'so much mesh as simply take turns' with the first half feeling like a Tarantino picture and the second half like a Rodriguez movie. Finding the film 'rather self-conscious' as well as 'cheesy, derivative, and ultimately, a little wearying' he at least conceded it was 'unpretentious' and 'insanely cheerful'. Janet Maslin of the *New York Times* saw the film as 'high-stakes poker' in which Tarantino gambled his reputation (already damaged in many eyes by *Four Rooms*) and Clooney and Rodriguez tried to establish themselves as a movie star and a first-rank director respectively. She liked the 'promising if down-and-dirty first hour' which she considered to be clearly good enough for the writer, director and star to win their metaphorical card game. However, the film's detour into horror in the last quarter posed a problem for her; she felt that the script's origins (commissioned by an effects company to demonstrate its workers' skills) caused problems – 'visual tricks are a lot of the finished film's raison d'être. But they're tricks that narrow its audience to viewers who enjoy watching flesh melt.'

THE NUMBERS: Released in the United States on 19 January 1996 on 2,004 screens the picture took around ten million dollars over the course of its opening weekend. While this may not seem a great deal when compared to genuine blockbusters, it's a sizeable portion of the movie's estimated $20m above-the-line budget. Total US rentals exceeded $24 million leaving the movie to make a handsome long-term profit in video and DVD rentals and sales, as well as international admissions.

FINAL COMMENT: Quite why anyone would want to find the exact middle ground between *Badlands* (Terrence Malick, 1974) and *Buffy The Vampire Slayer* is anyone's guess, but that's where *From Dusk Till Dawn* takes place. It's tremendous fun and more subtle than it has been given credit for (to be fair, more subtle than it chooses to appear to be) but it couldn't be said to achieve anything beyond laughs and visceral thrills. It isn't particularly big and it isn't particularly clever, but it's very entertaining.

However, *From Dusk Till Dawn* suffers terribly from having its best feature, the shocking dogleg of its plot, being the most famous thing about it. If the film's sudden switch from a sort of buddy boy cross between *Badlands* (Terrence Malick, 1973) and *48 HRS.* (Walter Hill, 1982) into a vamped-up, bar-set version of *Dawn of the Dead* (George Romero, 1979) hadn't been expected by the audience, it would be a glorious piece of sleight of hand. But it isn't, because every viewer is waiting for it to happen right from the very beginning of the first scene.

Texas Blood Money (1999)

'If your dog died, we'd have ourselves a country song.'

Following the success of *From Dusk Till Dawn* Miramax set upon the idea of producing straight-to-video sequels that could be made under the 'supervision' of (and sold using the names of) director Robert Rodriguez and writer Quentin Tarantino. The writer/director of the film that became *From Dusk Till Dawn: Texas Blood Money* was Scott Spiegel. Spiegel was another old-time friend of Tarantino's who had known Quentin pre-fame. The two met in 1989 through Sheldon Lettich, a writer on *Rambo III* (Peter Macdonald, 1988) and the director of *Double Impact* (1991) who Tarantino had encountered while working at Imperial Entertainment making sales calls. Tarantino asked Spiegel for advice relating to limited partnerships and independent financing – at the time he was trying to get one of his self-penned screenplays, either *True Romance* or *Natural Born Killers*, made as a small-scale production. Spiegel was impressed by the Tarantino screenplays he read and the two became friends.

Years later, Spiegel accompanied Tarantino on an impromptu visit to the Cinerama Dome, Hollywood, to see *From Dusk Till Dawn* one Friday night shortly after the film's release. The actor/writer wanted to see the movie with a paying audience who were unfamiliar with the picture. (Spiegel had visited the set during production.)

The two of them bumped into Bob Weinstein who had had much the same impulse. The next week Weinstein called Spiegel and asked him if he would be interested in writing and directing a companion-piece/sequel to the film.

Tarantino had shown the Weinsteins Spiegel's *Intruder* (1988) in order to persuade them that Spiegel was the man for the job. Spiegel and Boaz Yakin wrote a storyline which Spiegel then worked into a screenplay co-written with Duane Whitaker whose *Stripteaser* (Dan Golden, 1995) both Tarantino and Spiegel admired. Spiegel's original story featured both Seth and Richie Gecko. Seth was to die in a hail of bullets while trying to meet up with a criminal gang (composed of the same characters who are actually in the film as shot) and they would then head to the Titty Twister because they knew that Richie and Seth had gone there shortly after crossing into Mexico. There they'd meet Richie, who was now a vampire, and become involved in the same event that transpires in the released version. This version of the storyline got far enough to be mentioned in Miramax brochures in late 1997 but ultimately George Clooney chose not to participate and the script was rewritten to exclude Seth Gecko.

The films new lead, playing the character of Buck, whose role had been expanded in the redraft, was Robert Patrick. Then best known for his chilling, near silent performance as the T-1000 in *Terminator 2: Judgement Day* (James Cameron, 1991) Patrick went on to star in the later seasons of *The X-Files* as FBI Agent John Doggett. Also in the cast were Danny Trejo (playing a similar, but not the same, character as he had in *From Dusk Till Dawn* – Razor Eddie as opposed to Razor Charlie), co-writer Duane Whitaker and James Parks. Parks's father Michael played Texas Ranger Earl McGraw in *From Dusk Till Dawn*. In *Texas Blood Money* James plays Deputy McGraw, the son of the character his father played in the earlier film. Both men would reprise these roles in *Kill Bill – Vol. 1* in 2003.

Spiegel shot his film in South Africa in the early months of 1998. It was a generally smooth shoot, occasionally beset by local problems, such as the difficulty in finding left-hand drive cars. Bruce Campbell, the star of the *Evil Dead* trilogy and an old friend of Spiegel's agreed to do a cameo and flew over from New Zealand where he was directing and guest-starring in episodes of ABC's popular Sam Raimi produced *Hercules: The Legendary Journeys* and *Xena: Warrior Princess* TV series.

It's entertainingly daft; a low-rent action-horror film firmly in the tradition of the higher-end exploitation movies with a high body count, lots of blood and a solid, witty script. Spiegel's direction is smart and unobtrusive, with lots of point-of-view shots and enjoyable set pieces. Patrick is hugely entertaining in something which is a slick production that knows not to outstay its welcome. Despite taking its characters and concepts from a Tarantino script it's not really Tarantino-pastiche but is instead a separate person's take on the same kind of films that often inspire Tarantino's fervent devotion. The work of a kindred spirit.

The film was released straight to video in March 1999 in the United States, rated 'R' and with a running time of 88 minutes, and only ever released on DVD in the UK.

The Hangman's Daughter (2000)

The second 'sequel' to *From Dusk Till Dawn* was actually a prequel which set out to explain the history of the character Satanico Pandemonium as played by Salma Hayek in the original *From Dusk Till Dawn*. The screenplay was written by Alvaro Rodriguez (a cousin of Robert's) from a story by both Robert and Alvaro. (An earlier treatment by Aint-it-Cool webmaster Harry Knowles was rejected; its contents are largely unknown).

Unlike Scott Spiegel who was an old friend of Tarantino's the director for *The Hangman's Daughter*, PJ Pesce, first met Tarantino during the shooting of *Jackie Brown* in order to discuss his taking on the third *From Dusk* film as a project. PJ was selected by Robert Rodriguez on the basis of his western *The Desperate Trail* (1995) which both Rodriguez and Tarantino admired.

In addition to the not-yet-vampiric Satanico Pandemonium (her human name was Esmeralda and she's the eponymous hangman's daughter) the Rodriguezs' script uses Ambrose Bierce as a character. Bierce is a historical figure, a real-life horror writer who disappeared in Mexico in 1913 while searching for Pancho Villa's revolutionary forces.

Pesce set out, with Rodriguez's blessing, to make a film that had some sympathy with the concerns of Bierce's work; a more supernatural-inclined film than either *From Dusk Till Dawn* or *Texas Blood Money* both of which were largely crime pictures. The period setting demanded a different aesthetic anyway and the script's use of a central female character and the trope and furniture of the standard western placed it in a very different genre to the other two films in its series.

The Hangman's Daughter is very much in Rodriguez's image in the same way that *Texas Blood Money* is obviously the work of someone who shares tastes and methods with Tarantino. After preview screenings the ending was reshot but you couldn't call the finished film a success. Rated 'R' it was released on 18 January 2000.

The Man From U.N.C.L.E.

In the mid 1990s Quentin Tarantino stated in a few interviews that he was looking into the possibility of acquiring the rights to the 1960s TV series *The Man From U.N.C.L.E.* The series was a super-cool globe-trotting spy thriller show which starred Robert Vaughn (one of *The Magnificent Seven*) as Napoleon Solo and British actor David McCallum as Ilya Kuriyakin, an American and a Russian respectively working together against international terrorists and criminal organisations. The series was huge, running for four seasons (1964–68) and 105 episodes and spawning a spin-off series *The Girl from U.N.C.L.E*, which ran concurrently for a single season. Tarantino suggested that he would script the film himself, and possibly direct it. He would play Kuriyakin while George Clooney would play Napoleon Solo.

Sadly, whatever negotiations were undertaken came to nothing. This is something of a shame as Tarantino's take on the world of U.N.C.L.E would surely have been at least an interesting diversion among the many films-based-on-old-TV-shows, and the idea of Clooney as the suave Solo is something to relish.

Rolling Thunder

In the period that saw the explosion of his fame, and the value of his name rise to new heights post-*Pulp Fiction*, Quentin Tarantino set up a film- and VHS-distributing label under the Miramax imprint. It was called Rolling Thunder. Tarantino explained the logic behind the move to *LA Weekly* in June 1997: he had, he said, become bored with one particular aspect of going to the cinema. It was going to movie festivals, seeing what he thought 'were interesting movies, telling Harvey or Bob [Weinstein] about them and having one of their acquisition people say, "Nah, it's not for Miramax".' The final straw for Tarantino was Miramax's rejection of the idea of distributing Wong Kar-Wai's (masterful) *Chungking Express*. He quoted himself as telling the Weinsteins that 'I'm the best acquisition guy you've got.' What he proposed for Rolling Thunder was that they should allow him to release around four films in every calendar year; they would all be films that Miramax would only have to pay a low amount for the right to distribute, meaning no real risk to the company. Rolling Thunder would be a kind of Tarantino-branded speciality label inside Miramax; 'It won't cost you a thing,' he reportedly told the brothers Weinstein. So keen was Tarantino on the project that he agreed not to be paid for it.

Releasing a combination of new films that excited Tarantino (such as the aforementioned *Chungking Express* and 'Beat' Takeshi Kitano's explosively wonderful *Sonatine*) and older films that no longer had deals, Rolling Thunder had, in Tarantino's view, it's own distinctive personality. 'We're here to bring back the glory of 70s chopsocky movies, Italian crime films, blaxploitation! Have the fun of watching them in a movie theatre!' Philosophically accepting of the fact that some of the movies would do well and some wouldn't, Tarantino simply decided to trust his own instincts, reasoning that if these were movies he wanted people to see, the least he could do was give them the opportunity to see them, even if it was an opportunity he couldn't be sure they'd take up.

Rolling Thunder releases also included *Mighty Peking Man* (a Shaw Brothers movie from 1977 starring Evelyne Craft as a kind of Sheena, Queen of the Jungle girl) and the Jet Li-starring remake of Bruce Lee's *Fists of Fury*. The company was the first American distributor to release a film by Italian filmmaker Mario Brava with subtitles, instead of dubbed into American English, putting out his *Blood and Black Lace* (1964). Rolling Thunder also put out Tarantino's friend Richard Linklater's then unreleased, earliest pre-fame feature, a super-8mm semi-professional piece both written by and starring the director and entitled *It's Impossible to Learn to Plow by Reading Books* and Lucio Fulci's *The Pyschic*. The widely disparate nature of these pictures indicates that, while Tarantino felt 'Rolling Thunder' should have a personality, that personality was always going to reflect the joyous, expressive eclecticism of his own tastes. (Rolling Thunder also sponsored a number of releases of 70s 'blaxploitation' films in the UK.)

Not all Tarantino-backed, discovered or revived pictures have carried the Rolling Thunder imprint and it seems unlikely that the use of the, now increasingly infrequent, imprint would survive beyond the brothers Weinstein's departure from Miramax. It's existence, though, is a demonstration of Tarantino's higher calling: the need to share with others his passionate love of film – 'You can't lament that you wish that more people would see this, that and the other kind of film. You can't make the people see it – it's just your job to turn on the lights.'

The X-Files, Episode 86: 'Never Again'

Tarantino was forbidden by the Director's Guild of America (of which he is not a member) from directing an episode of *The X-Files* TV series ('Never Again' written for Tarantino to direct by regular *X-Files* writers Glen Morgan and James Wong). Their reasoning was that he had directed his episode of *ER* without compensating the union for, they argued, putting one of their members out of work.

Morgan and Wong's script was an oddity within the series of which it is a part because it concentrated on Gillian Anderson's Scully to the almost total exclusion of her co-star, David Duchovny's Special Agent Fox 'Spooky' Mulder. The character of Mulder is on holiday, having been informed that he legally has to take a week's vacation because he hasn't had a day off work in four years.

Scully heads to Philadelphia on what she regards as a pointless case. Once there she meets a man, Edward Jerse (Rodney Rowland), whose tattoo (of a

Betty Boop-type girl) is talking to him. Scully meets Jerse and becomes attracted to him. There is much flirtation and, with Mulder absent, the more-hidden 'bad girl' aspects of Scully's persona surface; despite saying that she's 'not a one night stand' girl she probably does go to bed with Jerse and she also takes time out to get a tattoo herself (it's of an Ouroborous, the mythical snake eating its own tail. The tattoo is actually real; Anderson herself already had it before production began in the episode).

That the script was written for Quentin Tarantino is occasionally betrayed by dialogue, which seems to be trying to emulate his style. For example, Scully says, 'Your contact, while interesting in the context of Science Fiction, was, at least in my memory, recounting a poorly veiled synopsis of an episode of *Rocky and Bullwinkle.*' Equally Mulder's holiday takes him on a 'spiritual journey', which turns out to be a visit to Elvis Presley's home and grave at Graceland. Meanwhile, director Rob Bowman borrows a shot from Alfred Hitchcock's late classic *Frenzy* (1972) and the talking tattoo is voiced, in a Tarantino-style piece of self-referentiality, by Jodie Foster. Foster, of course, won an Oscar for playing Special agent Clarice Starling in Jonathan Demme's adaptation of Thomas Harris's *The Silence of the Lambs* (1991). That character, and in particular Foster's portrayal of her, was the model for *X-Files* creator Chris Carter when he was creating Scully.

This was one of the cleverest, and certainly the sexiest, episodes of *The X-Files'* fourth season and, going by Tarantino's work on *ER*, it seems likely that he could have brought something extra to the episode. The episode was transmitted on 2 February 1997.

Jackie Brown (1997)

Miramax Films Presents
A Band Apart
A Film by Quentin Tarantino
Jackie Brown
Costume Designer: Mary Clare Hannan
Editor: Sally Menke
Production Designer: David Wasco
Director of Photography: Guillermo Navarro
Co-producer: Paul Hellerman
Executive Producers: Bob Weinstein, Harvey Weinstein
Executive Producers: Richard N Gladstein, Elmore Leonard
Based on the novel *Rum Punch* by Elmore Leonard
Produced by Lawrence Bender
Written and Directed for the screen by Quentin Tarantino

TAGLINES: 'Be Prepared.'

'This Christmas, Santa's Got A Brand New Bag.'

'Six players on the trail of a half a million in cash. There's only one question . . . Who's playing who?'

CAST: Pam Grier (Jackie Brown), Samuel L Jackson (Ordell Robbie), Robert Forster (Max Cherry), Bridget Fonda (Melanie Ralston), Michael Keaton (Ray Nicolette), Robert De Niro (Louis Gara), Michael Bowen (Mark Dargus), Chris Tucker (Beaumont Livingston), Lisa Gay Hamilton (Sheronda), Tommy 'Tiny' Lister Jr (Winston), Hattie Winston (Simone), Sid Haig (Judge), Aimee Graham (Amy, Billingsley Sales Girl #1), Ellis E Williams (Cockatoo Bartender), Tangie Ambrose (Billingsley Sales Girl #2), T'Keyah Crystal Keymah (Raynelle, Ordell's Junkie Friend), Venessia Valentino (Cabo Flight Attendant), Diana Uribe (Anita Lopez), Renee Kelly (Cocktail Waitress), Elizabeth McInerney (Bartender at Sam's), Colleen Mayne (Girl at Security Gate), Laura Lovelace (Steakhouse Waitress)

SUMMARY: Forty-something air stewardess Jackie Brown is busted by the airport police and the ATF for trying to smuggle money into the United States. This is something she does for gun-runner Ordell Robbie in order to add to her meagre paycheck. Offered a deal to avoid jail by the authorities, but afraid that Ordell will kill her while she's out on bail, she decides to pretend to accept the deal while actually playing the ATF and Ordell against each other. Convincing both that she is working *them* against the other she gets Ordell to agree to let her smuggle his entire life savings, around half a million dollars, into LA. However she tells the ATF that she's bringing in much less money, and keeps the balance for herself, while provoking a situation in which Ordell is killed by Ray Nicolette, the ATF agent who first arrested her, leaving Jackie free to get on with her life.

DEVELOPMENT: Following up *Pulp Fiction* can surely not have been easy. In making his third directorial film Tarantino was faced with two problems that should, in any sensible world, have found it impossible to coexist. Thanks to the vagaries of public expectation and the way celebrity functions, they managed to exist together without cancelling each other out. The first was that he had made, in *Pulp Fiction*, a film that was obviously great; a film that would find itself, in short order, being hailed as the film of the decade and among the best American movies ever made; a film that was joining the list of films that people shook their heads at come Oscar time and wondered how they'd not won Best Picture at the Academy Awards. How does any filmmaker, no matter how talented, cope with that level of expectation? The second problem was the Tarantino backlash that was a response to, but managed to exist alongside, the adulation he received for *Reservoir Dogs* and *Pulp Fiction*.

Tarantino had actually hit on the idea of how to follow *Pulp Fiction* relatively early; speaking on the *Charlie Rose Show* on 14 October 1994 he said he was thinking 'What I might end up doing now is, maybe what would be cool . . . would be taking, like a novel, and adapting it. That still requires me to write, still requires . . . my voice but it's also coming from somewhere else.' Deciding to write and direct an adaptation of a novel was not the only solution to Tarantino's problem. He could have chosen to work as a more discrete director-for-hire (he turned down LM Kit Carson's offer to direct his screenplay *The Moviegoer*, for example). This would not have been as out of character as it sounds. After all, many contemporary directors regarded as distinctive and individualistic, from Terry Gilliam to Tim Burton and David Lynch, have come aboard projects generated by other hands later in the day and turned them into something they could 'own'. (Say, 1995's *Twelve Monkeys*, 1994's *Ed Wood* and 1999's *The Straight Story* respectively.)

However, adaptation was the course Tarantino chose. Which novel to adapt was a more complex matter; but when the answer to this question presented itself it was entirely elegant.

ELMORE LEONARD: Leonard was born in New Orleans in 1925. A graduate of the University of Detroit he worked as a copywriter before starting a fiction-writing career that has endured to this day (he's been writing professionally since 1951). Starting out as a writer of westerns and crime stories for magazines he soon 'graduated' to novels, principally cheap 'pulp' paperbacks although he firmly and irrevocably broke into the mainstream with *Glitz*, a 1985 top ten *New York Times*'s bestseller. By 1960 he'd written thirty western stories and five western novels. *The Big Bounce* (1966) was his first crime novel. He writes roughly a novel a year. Praised for his wit, characterisation, arch social observation and plotting, *Time* magazine called him 'The Dickens of Detroit' in 1985.

SCREENPLAY: Tarantino was a long-time fan of Elmore Leonard and claimed that as an adolescent he'd been picked up by a book store's security for trying, and obviously failing, to take a copy of Leonard's *The Switch* without paying for it. Throughout the early 90s Tarantino quoted Leonard as an influence on his style of filmmaking (for example, on the *Charlie Rose Show*, in magazines like *Projections* and *Film Threat* and when talking to the *Chicago Sun-Times*'s Roger Ebert; his comment 'his style *dictated* my style to some degree'). Perhaps as a consequence of this public endorsement Tarantino was sent, during pre-production on *Pulp Fiction*, a galley proof copy of the then as yet unpublished Elmore Leonard novel *Rum Punch* and, while reading it, as he recalls, 'it just kind of presented itself to me as a low-budget anti-Hollywood action picture'. The idea of turning it into that film appealed to him and he considered contacting Leonard in order to acquire the rights. However, as he was in the middle of sorting out *Pulp Fiction*, this never happened; partially because Tarantino was aware that whatever films he wanted to make after *Pulp Fiction* may be very different to the kind of films he wanted to make before having gone through the process of making it.

Later, after the completion of the *Pulp Fiction* project and his decision to make an adaptation of a novel, Tarantino acquired the rights to three, rather than one, Elmore Leonard novels. One was *Rum Punch* (1992), and the other two were *Freaky Deaky* (1988) and *Killshot* (1989). His intention was, at this point, to get another director to shoot *Rum Punch* and to make one of the other two into a film himself; but then he reread *Rum Punch* and 'That same movie I saw years before came back in my head.' Faced with such a compulsion, he felt he had no option but to make the film.

Before beginning work on the screenplay Tarantino talked to Leonard about it but rather than bother the novelist with endless questions, queries and requests during the writing process he decided to simply ask a few technical questions, retire to write the screenplay and then present Leonard with the finished article for his approval. While writing he was buoyed up by Leonard's reassuring words, 'You're the filmmaker – use what you want and make your movie.'

As an approach Tarantino's deliberate estrangement from Leonard worked. After Tarantino finally sent the novelist the completed screenplay Leonard later stated publically that it was not only the best screenplay adaptation of one of his own works that he'd read, it was possibly the single best screenplay he'd ever read full stop.

Tarantino's adapted screenplay is a generally faithful rendering of the novel. All the main set pieces are there, the plot is there more or less in full and much of the dialogue is there. (Leonard lovers may, however, mourn the loss of (the black) Ordell's speech about how he can manage to be friends with a Klansman due to the fact that they both believe in racial segregation. It is hilarious that two men of different skin tones can work together because their common ground is that they despise other ethnicities.) Writing the dialogue presented an especial challenge for the screenwriter. A screenplay of a novel will, almost by default, contain more dialogue than the novel itself because it has to convey information that is contained within the prose of the novel through dialogue or action. Tarantino later expressed pride that the dialogue in the film was about 50 per cent his and 50 per cent Leonard's – and challenged people to tell the difference without checking.

The major changes Tarantino did make to *Rum Punch* in order to turn it into *Jackie Brown* were that he moved the location of the story from Florida to California and – most famously – changed the main character from being Caucasian to being African-American. He also changed her name from Jackie Burke to Jackie Brown and made that name the title of his screenplay, later saying that this was a deliberate tribute to the movie *Foxy Brown* (Jack Hill, 1974), as by then he'd already decided to cast Pam Grier.

Tarantino said that he did not initially consciously decide to change Jackie's race; he just assumed that she was black when first reading the novel – having never noticed that she was described as being Caucasian. He may have subconsciously made this mistake for a simple reason. On other occasions, he has described an older black woman, Jackie, a friend of his mother's during his childhood, as being a major influence in his life, indeed a 'second mother'. (Her brother 'Big D', incidentally, was the basis for the character played by Samuel Jackson in *True Romance* and the man who, in real life, informed Tarantino that 'Sicilians were spawned by niggers'.)

A terrific example of Tarantino's screenwriting on this picture is the scene where Max heads over to Jackie's to get his gun back. The two of them sit and talk and she makes him coffee. The dialogue, which is Tarantino's not Leonard's in this instance, is ever so gently suggestive and yet it's played by the actors as if it isn't. Max has clearly already fallen for Jackie in a big way, and she knows it. When she asks him about how he feels about getting old he assumes she's flirtatiously digging for a compliment. She isn't, but she wants him to think he is so she can push him away gently. She's already asked him 'You want some sugar?' – the implications of which are obvious if you've a passing grasp of 70s slang; and he's tried to be flirtatious while not being concerned about the lack of milk for his coffee – 'Black is fine,' he says, trying to acknowledge he's emotionally grasping towards romance with this woman. When he compliments her, saying that he's sure she doesn't look any different to how she did when she was 29, he's emboldened enough, when she semi-bitterly complains that her 'ass . . . is bigger', to smile and say 'nothing wrong with that'. It's simply beautiful screenwriting from Tarantino even if it is based on another man's work; it's not crass, yet it's still suggestive, and it avoids being grotesque or silly or seeming as if it's meant to be so. It's lovely, one of the nicest scenes in the film.

Of course, before and after this, the really attentive viewer will realise that Jackie is telling Max a slightly different story about the previous night than she told Ordell. While *Jackie Brown*'s plot isn't hugely complex, and its structure is straightforward, it does require absolute concentration in some key scenes; more than one person of my acquaintance only worked out on a second or third viewing just how early Jackie comes up with her plan to scam everyone else. Jackie does lie – lightly and infrequently to everyone except Ordell (who deserves it). She's clever, good at the game she's playing, because she knows it's her last chance to escape prison and to get any kind of fortune out of life. 'It's not like it's somebody's life savings,' says Jackie when talking to Max about the money she intends to steal. Actually it *is*. It's Ordell's life savings, and that's the kind of lie that she tells throughout the movie; lies which make life easier for her, and easier for people to side with her – lies that are entirely acceptable because of the desperation of her situation.

Jackie Brown is a warm and charming script even when dealing with obnoxious characters like Ordell and even he is, arguably, just trying to survive. In fact, his plan is to make $1 million and then retire (in the script, he's going to retire to the Philippines) which could be the plot of a movie in which Ordell is the hero; there are plenty of crime films about gangsters who simply want out, after all.

CASTING: Tarantino wrote his screenplay envisaging Pam Grier in the title role. Before *Pulp Fiction* Tarantino had actually called Grier to tell her that he wanted to work with her and that he would write a film for her to star in. Grier was understandably initially sceptical, later saying she thought 'He's gonna write for me. Surrrrrre. It won't be that he won't want to do it, it'll just be that Kevin Costner will call him first. Quentin'll have to do some big megabuck movie, and he won't be able to write for me before my teeth fall out and my breasts sag.' He auditioned Grier for the roles of both Mia and Jody in *Pulp Fiction* but didn't feel she fitted either; more, she deserved better. His adaptation of *Rum Punch* was the ideal opportunity to fulfil his original intention with a role which was perfect for her. 'Jackie had to be forty-four but look thirty-four, and seem . . . as if she could handle anything.' The very concept of *Rum Punch* struck him as a the ideal 'mature' Pam Grier movie; a way of allowing her to demonstrate her skills as an actress while playing a role which would utilise the screen persona and status she'd acquired in the 70s in a surprising way; 'It's like putting Clint Eastwood in *Unforgiven* (Clint Eastwood, 1992): an icon used in an un-iconic role. She's a real human being stuck in this situation.' Grier had acquired that 'iconic' status through the genre which is often called 'Blaxploitation', films made cheaply and primarily for urban black American audiences. Grier appeared in some terrific examples of the genre including *Coffy* (Jack Hill, 1973), *Scream Blacula Scream!* (Bob Keljan, 1973), *Sheba, Baby* (William Girdler, 1975) and *Hit Man* (George Armitage, 1972). The latter is a remake of *Get Carter* (Mike Hodges, 1971) which stars Bernie Casey. A thousand times better than the Sylvester Stallone remake of 1999 it's one of the 70s most underrated films. Grier also made many appearances in films of the 'women in prison' subgenre including *The Big Doll House* (Jack Hill, 1971), *Women in Cages* (Gerardo de Leon, 1971 – as the warder this time) and the attempt at a Roman epic 'women in prison' film *The Arena* (Steve Carver, 1974). Grier saw her work in cinema as an attempt to establish a filmic presence that was 'assertive yet feminine' and said her archetypal screen character could, and would, 'work on a construction site . . . wear a dress after coming home' and 'love our man all night long'. Jackie Brown was 'none of that' but instead a normal person whom she could use the 'wisdom and emotionality' of middle age to play. Grier had started out as a receptionist at Roger Corman's production company and her first film was Russ Meyer's camp trash classic *Beyond The Valley of the Dolls* (1970).

In the film's second leading role, Ordell Robbie, Tarantino cast his friend Samuel L Jackson. This was an easy choice for the director, but not an easy task. While writing the screenplay he had come to identify strongly with Ordell whom he felt was the kind of person he might have become had he had no artistic ambitions. If he did briefly consider playing it himself he has never said so, and he passed the role to Jackson. Jackson is brilliant as Ordell, giving a completely different performance to that in *Pulp Fiction* while still working within the same genre. Jackson's performance creates an audience sympathy for Ordell even though he's plainly a bad man, while his decision to show the character in increasing states of *dishabille* as he descends into greater cruelty adds a great physical element to what could be a generally talk-heavy role.

Robert Forster was Tarantino's first choice for the role of bail bondsman Max Cherry. Tarantino had written the part of Vincent in *True Romance* with Forster in mind, and the actor had also auditioned for Joe Cabot in *Reservoir Dogs*. Tarantino had long admired Forster, who had impressed as enlisted serviceman Williams, object of Elizabeth Taylor's lust in *Reflections in a Golden Eye* (John Huston, 1967) and proven his brilliance in the difficult *Medium Cool* (Haskell Wexler, 1969) in which he played a cameraman desensitised to the horrors of modern life through observing and recording them. Like *Pulp Fiction*'s John Travolta he had fallen out of public view despite his obvious talent and his last notable movie was probably Disney's expensive and hollow *The Black Hole* (Gary Nelson, 1979). He has said that in the five years prior to *Jackie Brown* he'd only worked for scale on small projects and had mostly made money giving motivational speeches. Tarantino bumped into Forster in a restaurant and noted that with the 'dark calm power' he had shown in his film roles there was an 'underlying sweetness' that middle age had brought to the actor's persona. Tarantino told him he intended to use him and asked him to read *Rum Punch* as preparation before receiving the script. His brilliant performance in *Jackie Brown* would earn him an Oscar nomination and reignite his career (he publicly hoped for '. . . just get *ten per cent* of what Travolta got out of *Pulp Fiction* . . .' during production). Later work includes a splendid cameo in *Mulholland Drive* (David Lynch, 2001), a role in Gus Van Sant's 1998 *Psycho* remake, major roles on television in *Karen Sisco* (2003) and the mini-series *The Grid* (2004) and a part in the ludicrous blockbuster *Charlie's Angels: Full Throttle* (McG, 2003). 'This is the best part of success,' Tarantino told the *New York Times*, 'it lets you cast Robert Forster.' More so even than John Travolta – who has arguably thrown away his comeback through bad film choices – Robert Forster's return to prominence is one thing that anyone who really loves films should be enduringly grateful to Tarantino for.

As Ordell's beach bum girlfriend Melanie, Tarantino cast another personal friend – Bridget Fonda, daughter of Peter, granddaughter of Henry. She had previously been noticeable in *Single White Female* (Barbet Schroeder, 1992), barely present in *The Godfather – Part III* (Francis Ford Coppola, 1990) and highly entertaining in *Army of Darkness* (Sam Raimi, 1993). Fonda saw her character as 'a real conniving bitch' with few redeeming features and saw the key to playing her as being an understanding of how both Melanie and Ordell enjoyed the adversarial nature of their relationship – 'In that kind of relationship, nothing is small,' she commented on MTV, quoting the two characters quarrel about who should answer the phone as emblematic of the whole piece.

Tarantino cast Fonda after a chance meeting on a plane, but acquiring the services of Micheal Keaton was much more difficult, with the actor convinced he wasn't right for the role of Ray Nicolette. Tarantino knew he was and persuaded him to take it, although it took time. Keaton will probably always be known as Beetlejuice in Tim Burton's 1988 comedy or as Batman in that director's two comic book adaptations of 1989 and 1992 respectively although if you want to see what he can really do try out *Clean and Sober* (Glenn Gordon Caron, 1988) or – at the very other end of the scale – *Much Ado About Nothing* (Kenneth Branagh, 1993).

The picture also contains an outstanding character appearance from Robert De Niro. Star of around a dozen great movies (Scorsese's 1980 *Raging Bull* or 1995 *Casino*, Coppola's *The Godfather – Part II* (1974), etc.) De Niro is stunning in *Jackie Brown*. His near wordless, stumbling performance as the seemingly mellow but clearly crazed ex-con Louis is a delight. De Niro met Tarantino at Munich Film Festival but they didn't initially talk about De Niro acting for Tarantino; instead they discussed a project that De Niro might bring to Miramax. It was actually producer Lawrence Bender who passed a copy of the script to the actor who, on reading it, became very interested in playing the small, but interesting, role of Louis.

He is, for much of the picture, oddly reminiscent of the Mole from *The Wind in the Willows*, blinking and stretching as he discovers the world around him, playing a piece of human wreckage with remarkable perspicacity.

The judge at Jackie's arraignment is played by Sid Haig; Haig was one of the white stars of 70s exploitation films, and appeared with Pam Grier in *The Big Doll House* (Jack Hill, 1971), *The Big Bird Cage* (Jack Hill, 1972), *Black Mama, White Mama* (Eddie Romero, 1972) and *Foxy Brown* (Jack Hill, 1974). Known for playing 'hard' roles the Judge isn't the kind of part you'd expect to see Haig in. A long-time admirer, Samuel L Jackson was thrilled to appear in a scene with Haig, even though they didn't share dialogue.

KEY SHOTS: *Jackie Brown* was shot across the summer of 1997 in and around the South Bay area of Los Angeles. This is a change from the book, which is set in Florida. Tarantino made the decision to alter the setting from Florida to California for a simple reason. Part of the joy of Leonard's novels is their elaborate, detailed understanding of their settings, be it Florida or Michigan. They always take place in areas that Leonard knows well and for where he can create an air of reality through incidental details. Tarantino felt that to recreate this element of Leonard's world was more important in spirit than in terms of the actual location, and moved the story's action to Los Angeles in order to set it in an area he himself knows well. The South Bay is where Tarantino grew up. The South Bay area is, despite its reasonable proximity to Hollywood, not used in motion pictures all that often; Tarantino reinforces the specifics of his setting through use of captions cards throughout. These repeatedly tell the audience that they are in, say, 'The City of Carson', rather than a generic, homogenised 'movie world' part of America. (The City of Carson was so thrilled with Tarantino, incidentally, they presented him with the key to the city on completion of the movie.) The movie begins at LAX airport and all the film's locations are within twenty minutes drive of there; most of the last hour and a half of the film is shot in and around, and takes place in and around, the Del Amo mall – where Tarantino used to work as a clerk.

The LA shoot lasted ten weeks. Samuel L Jackson found that the great success of *Pulp Fiction* hadn't affected his friend's approach to his cast and crew: 'He was more confident in what he was doing than he was during *Pulp*,' says Jackson. 'But it was basically the same old Quentin.' The director himself, though, felt there were significant changes to his working methods between *Pulp* and *Jackie Brown*. 'It's not an epic, it's not an opera. It's a character study,' said Tarantino of his screenplay. He also said that he felt he'd 'gone about as far as I could with my signature shooting style' and that *Jackie Brown* was deliberately shot in a different way as a result. 'I knew I didn't want to go bigger than *Pulp*, so I went underneath it.' He also commented that he made a conscious decision to listen to his actors more on *Jackie Brown*, allowing scenes to unfold at the pace set by the performers rather than choreographing the performers around specified camera moves. He later said he'd heard his actors referring to the process as 'moment by moment' meaning that 'instead of having everything predestined, you let each moment happen. We weren't rushing to get to a result; we were enjoying the journey.'

Jackie Brown is certainly different to look at than Tarantino's two previous directorial pictures. In it the camera generally lurks in low mid-shot, as a hidden presence seemingly observing the characters' lives unfold, almost documentary style. There are diversions from this (see below) and Tarantino both utilises extreme close-ups and pulls off ambitious luxury shots when he has to, but generally *Jackie Brown* is much more low key in terms of its camera movement. The camera doesn't zip around as much, it focuses and refocuses far less than is the case in, say, *Pulp Fiction*, and Tarantino rarely uses the technique, frequently demonstrated in his two earlier films, of having two objects each in sharp focus even while one is in the near foreground and one the far background (think Marvin Nash talking to Mr Orange after the latter has killed Mr Blonde in *Reservoir Dogs*).

Jackie Brown is the first Tarantino film to begin with characters in camera but no dialogue. It has an opening scene where the movie's key themes are established almost entirely through the actors' physical action, cutting and camera movement. Against a colourful background of tiles in different shades of blue, Jackie moves into shot from the right. She's smartly but theatrically dressed and strikingly beautiful. Her clothes are also blue. The credits come up in a font which is strikingly retro 70s in its associations. The music playing is 'Across 110th Street' by Bobby Womack. Cutaways to X-rays and close-ups of personal metal detectors let the audience know that she is in an airport, and still the music just keeps zinging. Jackie struts in long shot, then from the front, then in tight close-up. She's cool and she's lovely – the music is one of the best records of the 70s and it's so exciting and soulful the viewer doesn't know whether to cheer, cry or dance. She, it and, by that peculiar osmosis that allows audiences to absorb film, the *audience* is so cool. So, so cool; and then the scene changes, turns round. Jackie is no longer strutting, instead she's rushing. She's panicking and dashes, glancing out of the window at a moving plane. The bravado and power seem to have gone out of her. It's something the audience realises with a shock, as the mundane nature of the job she's about to do hits. 'She ain't none of *that*' said Tarantino on MTV, she's, after all, 'just trying to get to work'.

The audience hasn't so much been tricked as fed a slightly false set of associations in order to create, in this wordless sequence, something which is a segue from the characters Grier played in the 1970s to the character she's playing now; not the icon that is Foxy Brown, but Jackie Brown, a woman described by Grier as a 'real woman getting through a real day'. The actual physical rushing, the speeding up that Jackie does as she begins to literally run out of time – the time she needs to get to work – establishes a key theme of the movie: the realisation of some of its characters that they are getting older, that they are running out of time. The last shot of the scene is of Jackie brightly issuing platitudes ('Welcome aboard' etc.) to the customers of the airline; in this shot the audience is also suddenly aware that Grier has aged since her 70s heyday. That isn't to say she isn't still beautiful, she is. But she has aged, something that was not apparent as she stalked the airport corridors with power a mere ninety seconds before. After Jackie's glorious, iconic entrance we realise that she has a very dull life and, thanks to the obvious connection Pam Grier's presence gives to her earlier films and what they represent in the evolution of American culture and politics, we also remember that the 70s didn't achieve as much as they should have and that society still has a long way to go. Why else would this woman be in this position? In a few minutes, she's going to be serving peanuts, after all. This sequence is not quite four minutes, but it's some of Tarantino's very best work.

Tarantino's use of close-ups has been mentioned before. Here when they come they often arrive in the middle of otherwise long uninterrupted takes. There are lots of short close-ups on characters' fingers or toes. There's a lengthy close-up on Melanie's feet as she wordlessly flirts with Louis right under Jules's nose at the beginning of the picture. In fact, the first scene with Fonda, De Niro and Jackson is a great indication of the film's general style. Jackson dominates the film in terms of dialogue and the sound mixing, but visually he's rarely there, the camera focusing on other things in the room, creating a three-dimensional space which the drama can operate in but which is somehow separate from it. It also, early on, features a fantastic example of Tarantino's unorthodox manner of not shooting coverage. When we first see Ordell and Louis sitting on the sofa discussing guns, the way the scene is set up encourages the audience to think that they are the only people in this scene. Because there's been no establishing shot of the whole room the audience doesn't know that Melanie is there also, and won't know until Ordell starts to talk to her. This should be, indeed is, a violation of basic film grammar, but in this instance Tarantino's disruption of the rules works because it's so clearly deliberate and so clearly there to create a specific effect, in this case an indication of the emotional space between Melanie and Ordell and her isolation from, and lack of interest in, his 'business' affairs.

Tarantino has called *Jackie Brown* a 'hang out movie', one where the audience 'hangs out' with the characters as though they are their friends. The almost laconic camera of *Jackie Brown* often seems to be simply hanging out with the characters itself. The fact that it's a window onto this world for an audience doesn't seem to concern it, so casually right is its movement.

The 'Beaumont' sequence is a short film in its own right, as Elvis Mitchell of the *New York Times* once pointed out. It's also Jackie Brown's own story in microcosm: what would happen to Jackie if she, not Ordell, won out in the end. Beaumont is, like Jackie, someone out on bail on Ordell's money, someone whose existence threatens him.

Ordell dispatches Beaumont with a brutal dispassion which allows Tarantino to demonstrate what Anthony Lane in the *New Yorker* called some 'ice-cold Hitchcock distance'. Initially the audience is unsure what Ordell's plan is. It seems he's getting Beaumont out of prison because he needs him and his scene with Beaumont appears to be setting up a plot thread which will run and run. But it isn't. In something which feels like another Tarantino nod to *Psycho* (Alfred Hitchcock, 1960) the whole plot that Ordell lays out to tempt Beaumont into his car is, despite its many incidental details, there only to be abandoned. Beaumont gets into the boot of Ordell's car and the car drives away into the back of the shot, almost dropping out of focus it's so far away. At the same time the music Ordell's car stereo is playing becomes fainter as the car gets further away from the screen. The car then turns left and something extraordinary happens: the camera cranes up and to the left to show the audience that Ordell has simply driven into a lot. The audience knows that Ordell has a gun on him because he was seen to take it out of the glove compartment before he drove off. However, the audience has been encouraged to see that gun as something Ordell is carrying to the meeting with 'Asians' that he has just said he and Beaumont are going to. In short order the viewer realises it's a set-up. Ordell gets out of the car and goes to the back of it. He opens the boot and shoots Beaumont dead, coldly and without comment. The camera still lurks in its stationary position hundreds of feet away from him as he does it, lurking at an angle in the sky and anterior presence which makes the audience feel voyeuristic, as if trespassing on Ordell's area of crime. It's chilling and thrilling and the audience is no longer in any doubt as to what kind of man they're observing in Ordell.

One scene which has been much discussed is when Max first sees Jackie walking towards him out of the prison, shimmering in distant light like Omar Sharif coming out of the desert in *Lawrence of Arabia* (David Lean, 1962). This is a beautifully shot scene of which the effect, all diffused light and shifting light sources, is – despite Tarantino's protestations – chiefly romantic in nature. The use of 'Natural High' by Bloodstone seems to be indicative of Max's state of mind as he sees Jackie and falls for her; the camera reflects this, nudging forwards to reflect Max's reaction to seeing Jackie for the first time. Tarantino has said that this scene divides audiences. That 'black audiences' see this scene and understand it, that it's about Jackie and her power. While I wouldn't presume to doubt the director's intentions, it's a valid question as to why so much of the scene focuses on Max if that's the case.

Tarantino also finds a non-gimmicky and entirely story appropriate use of split screen – which might be a first. It occurs 48 minutes in when Ordell goes to Jackie's apartment in order to kill her. Ordell's visit to Jackie carries on on the right-hand side of the screen while on the left the audience sees Max driving home and realising that he no longer has his gun in his glove compartment. The audience realises that it's gone just as he does, and exactly at the moment that Jackie threatens Ordell with the weapon, saving herself from being picked off by him. What's remarkable about this is that it's difficult to envisage any other way of shooting this scene that would be so effective. To see her take the gun earlier would remove the suspense; to explain it later would be crude; to intercut from Max to Jackie would ruin the scene's deliberately slow pace and disrupt the general tenor of the film.

Fifty-one minutes into the film the light fades down, fades back up again in Jackie's apartment. Tarantino has used a lot of fades in the films so far, but always to emphasise shifts of locations, not time. Jackie walks back into shot from the direction she walked out of it, and the lighting tells us that it's a different time as does her dressing gown. What's neat is that the shot doesn't let the audience see who is at the door. The more attentive audience member may conclude that dramatically it has to be Max but Tarantino may want to subvert that. In the end it is, as we realise when she wearily, casually, yet flirtatiously, asks him, 'Do you want your gun back? Come on in, I'll get it for you.'

The audience seeing the handover of the money from three different angles is the sequence that elongates the movie to its sizeable length. While showing the same scenes from multiple perspectives will usually be referenced to *Rashomon* (Akira Kurosawa, 1950) by a film-literate audience, what *Jackie Brown* does is different. While we see the scene from different perspectives, these perspectives aren't filtered through the prejudices or personalities of their protagonists. They're objective fact. The triple-fold heist is just another example of Tarantino teasing his audience with the release of information on his terms and at his pace. The triple-back also tricks the audience into thinking, initially, that Jackie's scam has gone wrong and Tarantino the director gets to have his cake and eat it, unsettling his audience with the unhappy ending before comforting them with the happy one, and the reassuring presence of Robert Forster. This is the only real diversion from linear narrative in the film although there are a few small flashbacks here and there (to Jackie meeting Max for the first time when they discuss that night or to Jackie's dinner with Ray Nicolette) but there's nothing as convoluted as the basic shape of *Pulp Fiction* or *Kill Bill* in evidence.

The scene in which Ordell and Louis quarrel and which ends with Ordell murdering Louis is shot from behind. This increases the tension because, although the audience knows that Ordell has a gun, we can't see his hands, or most of his face, and have no idea when, if or how he will choose to use it.

One of the smartest, and smallest, directorial tricks is in the first mall scene. There Max Cherry is seen exiting a movie theatre while the music for the ending credits is playing. This is, in fact, the closing music for the movie *Jackie Brown*.

The ambiguity over whether Jackie will find a way to get Max to join her – he's already refused once but he seems to regret it as soon as she's gone, promising to write to him – is reflected by his disappearing out of focus at the end; his future is uncertain and the way he's shot reflects that. Her fate is set and the way she's shot reflects *that*. His future is ambiguous, but hers is, like the lighting cast across Grier's beautiful face in the movie's very final shot, quite simply golden.

QUOTES:
Ordell: 'That shit is going to rob you of your ambition.'
Melanie: 'Not if your ambition is to get high and watch TV.'

Ordell: 'Add them mother fucking figures up and tell me this ain't the business to be in.'

Louis: 'I didn't look like a bum.'
Ordell: 'Come on, man, you know you had that Salvation Army thing going on.'

Ordell: 'What the fuck happened to you, man? Your ass used to beautiful.'

RACE: Although it would spawn controversies of its own over its depiction of racial politics and its use of the N-word, Tarantino's screenplay for *Jackie Brown* contains some small indication that he had taken on board what people had said about the racial epithets that littered *Pulp Fiction*. Here, unlike there, the word 'nigger' is used exclusively by black characters (Jackie, Ordell, Beaumont) and can be considered, generally, to fall under the category of 'reclaimed' language (see **Pulp Fiction**).

Of course the single fact most worthy of initial comment relating to race in *Jackie Brown* is the casting of Pam Grier in the role of a character, Jackie Burke, who is, in Leonard's novel Caucasian. While this could partially be said to be simply casting the best actress for the part, the screenplay contains numerous references to Jackie's race. This is not simply colour-blind casting, it's the redrawing of a character's background. Making Jackie a black woman rather than a white woman does, as has been noted by Tarantino, increase the character's desperation when she's placed in the situation of having to play the ATF off against Ordell or face jail or being killed. The initial scenes of Jackie being bullied by the police have slightly more force than they might otherwise have had because the audience cannot help but know that for a 45-year-old black woman to start again with a criminal record is harder than for a 45-year-old white woman.

Ordell's use of race in his conversations is also interesting. He uses 'nigger' liberally, often several times in the same sentence, but he uses it in a variety of contexts: to denigrate his customers; to convince Beaumont he's on his side; and to mock others. Ordell also 'plays' with the concept of race in his dialogue. He explicitly asks Max Cherry who the black man in the picture on the wall is and then tries to uncover what he can about the relationship between Max and Winston. He implies that Max hasn't told him that he's Winston's boss in order to not have to tell him, Ordell, a black man, that he, Max, a white man, is Winston's superior in the firm.

After trying to unsettle Max like this, Ordell also then implies that Max had the photograph taken for the same reason. Max is unimpressed by this and the next time Ordell tries to manipulate him shoots back 'Is white guilt supposed to make me forget I'm running a business?', after which Ordell stops trying to play games with Max. There's no real sensible suggestion in the film that Max has a picture of himself and Winston on the wall for any reason other than as an *aide memoir* of their very enjoyable fishing trip.

It's not just Max that Ordell treats like this. When Jackie accuses him of attempting to kill her, he begins to declaim on how the police have 'messed' with her and how they've clearly been successful in 'pitting black against black', but she tells him to shut up, aware that he's abusing their shared history as African-Americans in order to try and gain an advantage over her.

SPURIOUS INTERTEXTUALITY: The indebtedness that Tarantino's own 'shared universe' approach to fiction has to Leonard's has earlier been noted and Tarantino has gone on record to say that he regards *Jackie Brown* as taking place in some celluloid Leonard World rather than the Quentin World of his own. At the time of *Jackie Brown*'s production Leonard adaptations were virtually a popular subgenre of Hollywood picture so common were they. An exciting opportunity therefore presented itself to have an actor play the same character in two largely unconnected pictures.

In 1998, *sex, lies, and videotape* (1989) director Steven Soderbergh made an adaptation of another Elmore Leonard novel, *Out of Sight*. Ray Nicolette, who features in *Rum Punch*, also features in *Out of Sight* as the boyfriend of the lead character Karen Cisco. Tarantino and Soderbergh agreed that if Ray were to appear in both movies, and Michael Keaton was amenable, he should be played by the same actor.

This kind of thing has been attempted before. *Supergirl* (Jeannot Szwarc, 1984) features a lot of the same supporting cast and characters as the earlier *Superman* (Richard Donner, 1978; Richard Lester, 1980) films. It also features, when a picture of Superman is needed, a photograph of Christopher Reeve in character which is treated as 'real'. This was partially possible because both the *Superman* and *Supergirl* films were produced by the Salkinds. Quite often opportunities which could arise for this sort of action are prevented by legal contracts. For example: reporter Ben Urich is a supporting character in both Daredevil and Spider-Man comic books on a semi-regular basis. He could therefore appear in both films and if he did it would obviously be to the benefit of the Marvel Comics films' brand that he be played by the same actor. However, the licensing of the film rights to those two heroes to separate studios means that the character can only appear in one film (*Daredevil*, in which he's played, rather brilliantly, by Joe Pantoliano) despite employees of the parent company (Marvel Comics) being interested in seeing the character appear twice over and the actor himself being amused by the idea. For *Spider-Man* fans the *Daily Bugle* without Ben Urich is a very strange place, but we abide.

Keaton's buzzy little cameo in *Out of Sight* is something of a joy; audiences always respond well to it but it was actually difficult to arrange legally, both studios (Universal and Miramax) objected, until Tarantino condemned their objections as 'bullshit fucking nonsense' and insisted that there was surely no good reason to *not* do it.

The copyright information for the film is placed directly under the title as was often the case with 70s films, but is rarely the case today. The design of the logo too is obviously planned to evoke the logo for *Foxy Brown* (Jack Hill, 1974) probably Pam Grier's most famous role.

In the closing credits, Tarantino gives special thanks to 'Bert D'Angelo's Daughter'. This is coded reference to his then girlfriend, the actress Mira Sorvino. Her father Paul appeared in the 70s TV series *Superstar* as a character called Bert D'Angelo; therefore 'Bert D'Angelo's Daughter' is Mira Sorvino. The copyright holder of the film is Mighty Mighty Afro-dite productions (yes, spelled exactly like that) – a reference to Sorvino who played the female lead in *Mighty Aphrodite* (Woody Allen, 1995) for which the actress won an Oscar for her portrayal of the squeaky-voiced prostitute and mother to Woody Allen's adopted son as well as a pun on 'Afro'. Ordell refers to 'Roscoe's House of Chicken and Waffles', a real resturant that is also featured in *Swingers* (Richard Linklater, 1992) and mentions stoner comedians Cheech and Chong, the former of whom appeared in *From Dusk Till Dawn*.

The Killer (John Woo, 1989) is credited by Ordell as having an impact on what kind of guns his criminal customers want to buy.

No aficionado of 70s American cinema could watch the scene of Jackie going into an LA country prison without thinking of Pam Grier's many roles in 'women in prison' movies, especially *The Big Doll House* (Jack Hill, 1971). Max reads *Berlin Game* by Len Deighton while Melanie watches *Dirty Mary, Crazy Larry* (John Hough, 1974). This movie starred Peter Fonda, father of the actress who plays Melanie. Which is weirdly, pleasingly intertextual.

Susanville prison, previously given a namecheck in *Reservoir Dogs*, is mentioned here too. Tarantino includes a shot of the camera staring out of the trunk of a car in the films eighteenth minute. Teriyaki Donut is the same fictional chain of Chinese donut restaurants visited by Marsellus in *Pulp Fiction*. Jackie drives the same white Honda Civic driven by Butch in *Pulp Fiction*. It's not even just the same make it's actually the same car, a leftover prop from that film which was bought in the first place as a nod to Tarantino's own first automobile.

MUSICAL NOTES: The use of 'Across 110th Street' as the opening music is a nod to the eponymous 70s movie starring the great Yaphet Kotto as a gangster who disguises himself as a cop in order to pull off robberies. It was directed by Barry Shear in 1972. This is indicative of a use of music that is slightly different from that which Tarantino put in his earlier directorial films. While tracks such as 'Stuck in the Middle with You' were used to provide counterpoint to the actions on screen, *Jackie Brown* uses music from other films in order to simultaneously add thematic musical accompaniment and provide an external reference. An example of this is the use of Pam Grier's own 'Long Time Woman' which she recorded for *The Big Doll House* (Jack Hill, 1971). This song not only accurately reflects Jackie's predicament when in prison but also links Jackie and Grier to Grier's other earlier roles while reminding the audience of the amount of time that has passed since the early 70s. (Another example is the use of Randy Crawford's 'Street

Life' which was featured in *Sharkey's Machine* (Burt Reynolds, 1981).)

Tarantino took take this approach a step further in *Kill Bill*, where he uses instrumental music written for other movies (as opposed to songs written for or featured in other movies) to score most of the picture. *Jackie Brown* actually uses the odd snatch of the Roy Ayers score for *Coffy* (Jack Hill, 1973) towards the end of the picture. This was a last-minute decision, but the sheer effectiveness of the approach obviously had an effect on Tarantino, hence most of *Kill Bill* being scored like this.

In the film's last hour, as the three separate groups of people involved in the con converge at the mall, Tarantino uses three separate songs to score the shots featuring each of the three groups. These are the aforementioned 'Street Life' (for Jackie), 'Didn't I (Blow Your Mind This Time)' by the Delfonics for Max and 'Midnight Confessions' by the Grass Roots for Louis and Melanie. Each record is very carefully chosen. 'Midnight Confessions' is Melanie's choice of music; it winds Louis up, adds to his increasing drug-addled agitation and it pre-figures him losing his temper with her later. The use of the Delfonics track, which Jackie introduced Max to earlier in the movie, is an indication that Max is really doing all this for Jackie rather than for himself, and that she is never far from his mind, while the pulsing power of 'Street Life' is pure empowerment music for the sequence where Jackie puts one over on everyone and finally and absolutely empowers and frees herself.

Perhaps the most effective use of a record in the film is the playing of 'Strawberry Letter 23' by the Brothers Johnston as Ordell puts on his gloves and prepares to murder Beaumont. It's a great record and the high-pitched opening notes seem, in this context, faintly reminiscent of the opening to *The Twilight Zone* theme and have the same shudder-inducing effect.

The soundtrack also includes Johnny Cash's awesome performance of 'Tennessee Stud'; this isn't particularly relevant, but it's an amazing recording and deserves noting.

CRITICAL REACTION: On their TV show *Siskel and Ebert at the Movies*, the two venerable reviewers were broadly in agreement. The film, said Ebert, 'shows Quentin Tarantino at his best' demonstrating that he could make a film that was 'sweet and understated'. Ebert also praised the 'chemistry' between Forster and Grier and felt this was that rare thing: a film that was all about the 'process not the payoff' of telling its story. Ebert's partner Siskel praised Grier's performance extensively seeing that she was playing someone who 'is a characterisation' rather than the archetype(s) she played in the 70s. In the *New Yorker*, Anthony Lane didn't really agree, considering Jackie Brown to be exactly that archetype and noting that he felt Grier didn't 'do quite enough to drag her down to Earth'. 'Jackie Brown has touched down in Tarantinoland,' he said, indicating a certain feeling of the film being 'business as usual' for the director. He also felt the whole picture had a tendency to 'drag a bit' and that at times the director seemed to be 'going through the motions'; things he liked about the film included its nature as an ensemble piece and how when the camera is pointed at a particular character they are the most important person in the film. Writing in the *Village Voice*, J Hoberman was generally more positive about the film but not really its lead actress's performance, calling the picture 'a brilliantly cast homage' but suggesting that Grier was 'more a presence than an actress'. The film's good qualities, though, were 'mitigated by indulgence' of both his actors and himself by Tarantino. His conclusion was that Tarantino should 'make movies more often' – a backhanded compliment which, while implying that he'd enjoy seeing more Tarantino movies, also suggests he thought they'd be better if the writer/director was made to work harder and more often. In *Rolling Stone*, Peter Travers was unabashedly enthused, calling it 'knockout, loaded with action, laughs, smart dialogue and potent performances'. He was particularly impressed with how Tarantino adapted *Rum Punch* 'without losing the author's compassion'. Travers's general feeling about the film was that, packed as it was with homages to blaxploitation movies while being an Elmore Leonard novel adaptation, it was Tarantino 'acknowledging his debts' in order to begin the process of 'moving on . . .'

THE NUMBERS: *Jackie Brown* opened in the USA on Christmas Day 1997 having been shot across that summer for a budget of roughly $12 million. It took nearly $9.3 million across its official opening weekend (over $12 million if you include the days before the weekend) having been released to 1,370 screens (by far the largest number for a Tarantino film up to that point). The UK opening weekend took £85,244 (22 March 1998) which sounds less impressive until you realise that's a London exclusive opening on a single screen.

FINAL COMMENT: 'Yeah, that really hit the spot.' *Jackie Brown* is the kind of film that you'd expect a fifty-year-old Quentin Tarantino to make. It's languidly paced (if beautifully shot), and generally deals with calmer, less brutal people than his earlier work does. These are all people who just want to get along or away or out. 'It's a love story,' said Tarantino of his script. 'A love story with older people and an older sensibility.' It's certainly *about* older people and it really does have a much older sensibility. Its characters are mostly middle-aged and have difficulties with money, with growing older and with their place in a world that they don't quite fit into. Perhaps the film's only dissatisfaction is that the love story between Max and Jackie goes unconsummated and they don't disappear together; or maybe not. Just because the audience wants Max and Jackie to be together doesn't mean it's artistically right, even if we would prefer it as human beings.

Jackie Brown also genuinely grows more enjoyable with the rewatching and, unlike *Pulp Fiction* or *Reservoir Dogs*, it is a film that is easy to love as well as appreciate and admire. Tarantino has stated that he doesn't think anybody could honestly think that *Jackie Brown* is his best movie. He's probably right, but it could honestly be someone's favourite Tarantino film, and that's not really the same thing at all.

Blaxploitation?

Thanks to Tarantino the public seems to be fully aware of the term 'blaxploitation' to describe a certain subgenre of film.

Though the term is not without its controversies, these do not concern which particular films constitute that 'canon': 'blaxploitation' is used to describe low-budget films of the early 1970s made predominantly to appeal to poor, urban black audiences, and which used predominantly black talent both in front of and behind the camera.

It is generally agreed that *Sweet Sweetback's Baad Asssss Song*, written, directed by and starring Melvin Van Peebles was the first film that could accurately by described as 'blaxploitation'. It grossed $15 million despite being made for $150,000 and did so because it was a massive hit with underprivileged, low-income, urban-based African-American audiences who had, up until that point, been horrendously under-represented not only in cinema but in pretty much all mainstream American cultural media. The success of *Sweet Sweetback's Baad Asssss Song* led to not only a whole slew of imitators but also numerous films which were, while different from both it and each other, designed to appeal to – and therefore profit from – exactly the same audience that made *Sweetback* such a colossal money spinner.

While, in the minds of many, 'blaxploitation' films are associated with gangster, crime and revenge pictures, these were obviously not the only films that this now-being-served audience wanted to watch. There are also comedies, romances and horror films amongst the vast catalogue of such pictures. Although it is unquestionably the likes of *Coffy* and *Foxy Brown* (both of which starred *Jackie Brown*'s Pam Grier) that are best remembered, the best films of this period include the less-well-known likes of George Armitage's 1972 *Hit Man* (a remake/reworking of *Get Carter* which, as a result, becomes about empowerment) and *Blacula* (William Crain, 1972), a much more subtle and intelligent vampire film than the cheerfully ludicrous title might suggest.

Writer/director and actor Fred 'The Hammer' Williamson, the star of *Black Caesar* (Larry Cohen, 1973) and who later featured in Tarantino's *From Dusk Till Dawn* has expressed a strong personal dislike of the term 'blaxploitation'.

Hammer has argued that the term, by the late 90s almost universally applied, was misleading and unfortunate. He argued that nobody involved in such films was exploited, the actors and crews were being paid fairly for employment in their chosen profession and audiences were paying a reasonable price for a film which presented, on screen, things that they wanted to see. Speaking on MTV in December 1997 Pam Grier indicated that she had some sympathy with his views.

The term 'blaxploitation' evolved out of the terminology of 'exploitation' filmmaking, and, while the exact origins of *that* term are difficult to define, it is probable that it refers to the exploitation of available resources, i.e. the nature of such films as fundamentally inexpensive with their producers often having to 'make do' with few sets and small casts and shoot principally on location, rather than the exploitation of human beings, or a group of human beings. Hammer, however, clearly has a point that, in the context of the historical treatment of black Americans, the term has a certain other resonance. He has also pointed out that no similar terms exist to describe other kinds of filmmaking explicitly targeted at other ethnic or social groups (after all, nobody would refer to *Black Caesar* director Larry Cohen's 1976 'second coming'/serial killer movie as 'Catholicsploitation'). For these reasons as well as Hammer's own creative contribution to film his complaint must be both respected and given some credence. For that reason an attempt has been made not to use the term in these pages, although its use is sometimes unavoidable.

James Ferman

James Ferman, for more than a decade Britain's chief film censor as director of the British Board of Film Classification (BBFC) spoke out against *Pulp Fiction* in 1998, intimating that he regretted not cutting certain elements from the film's UK release when it first came out: 'We didn't cut the film, and I don't know, looking back, whether that was a good idea.' He claimed that he saw the film as glamorising drugtaking and suggested it could have contributed to increases in heroin abuse as a result: 'I still wonder whether injection has increased since this film was out, because it was going to increase the glamour of injection considerably.' He labelled the picture 'socially irresponsible' for, in his perception, doing this and criticised the director for referring to the sequence as 'the best shooting-up scene in the world'. In doing this he seemingly missed the point that Tarantino had said that every time he shot something (say about 'X') he wanted it to be 'the best "X" sequence in the world' as a matter of professional pride.

Ferman, who had made drug education films for schools before moving to the BBFC, was speaking to the Institute for the Study of Drug Dependence when he made his remarks. Despite his obvious professional expertise in the arenas of both film and drug-related matters, it's difficult to see how anyone could see Mia's drool-encrusted face and see Vincent jabbing a syringe full of adrenalin into her heart in order to save her life, and come away with the idea that drugs were 'glamorous' or that trying heroin would be a good idea.

Wait Until Dark

'You're belittling my acting aspirations' Tarantino told Roger Ebert when, during an interview, the critic expressed surprise that the director would choose to spend six months playing a smallish role in an off-broadway theatrical production. 'I'm serious about it. It's not me screwing around, all right? It's not some ego thing. It's a need – all right? It's one of my colours; it's one of my palettes.'

While his semi-comic chiding looks harsher in excerpt than it does at the conclusion of a good-humoured interview, Tarantino's reaction was arguably in response to the disbelief some people felt when the project was announced. Many felt, indeed still feel, that while Tarantino is inarguably a superb filmmaker – perhaps one of his generation's best and most important – he is an indifferent to mediocre actor. The follow-up criticism is, obviously, that Hollywood has plenty of indifferent to mediocre actors to spare, but distinctive and brilliant writer/directors are in worrying short supply.

In short, Tarantino's acting aspirations *had* been mocked, albeit not by the ever-genial Ebert, and he had every right to feel wounded by the mocking, just as his critics had every right to suggest that they would personally prefer it if he stuck to doing what they thought he was best at. Given the huge gaps between *Pulp Fiction* and *Jackie Brown* and then *Jackie Brown* and *Kill Bill*, audiences and critics could be forgiven this impatience both then and now, and there's certainly a valid argument that every Tarantino project outside his (still very small) core directorial canon (*Dogs, Pulp, Brown, Bill*) stripped a little lustre from his reputation. It's an argument that Tarantino seems to have developed some belated sympathy with if the large credit 'The 4th Film by Quentin Tarantino' as included on *Kill Bill – Vol. 1* is anything to go by, but in the late 90s, well, he saw things differently.

So it was then that early 1998 saw him living the life of the jobbing stage actor, playing eight shows a week at the Brooks Atkinson Theatre on West 47th Street, New York (a lovely old theatre, built in 1926, just off Broadway), in a revival of the thriller *Wait Until Dark*. The play would seem, on the face of it, to be an odd choice for someone who had spoken of a 'need' to act and the choice of role even stranger. *Wait Until Dark* is a convoluted, badly plotted and fundamentally not terribly memorable play. Few can recall the 1967 movie adaptation (directed by Terence Young) even though it starred Audrey Hepburn. It's also somewhat challenged in the sense department, something that the presence of masterful screenwriter Tarantino in the cast surely can't have failed to draw attention to.

Wait Until Dark is about a blind woman, Susy, who is bullied, charmed, stalked, lied to and threatened by a gang of three petty criminals who are trying to get her to part with a doll which is stuffed with heroin and which has somehow found its way into her possession. (An example of its lack of logic would be that at one point one of the thugs disguises himself to fool said blind lady.) Playing the lead in the production that featured Tarantino was the beautiful and exceptionally talented Marisa Tomei, who had won an Oscar for *My Cousin Vinny* (Jonathan Lynn, 1992). New York stage actors, such as Broadway veteran Stephen Lang filled out the small cast of the piece, which is set entirely within the confines of a New York apartment building. Tarantino took the role of Harry who was played, with considerable success it must be said, by former Inspector Clouseau and future *Sesame Street* regular Alan Arkin in the film.

Critics weren't kind to the play's revival or Tarantino's place in it, with reviews being virtually unanimous in condemning the script's lack of logic, the production's accelerated, almost farce-like pace, the cast generally (few took to Tomei's Susy) and Tarantino's performance in particular. A lot of critics even took time to suggest that he'd put on rather a lot of weight – a particularly cheap shot that is (along with its polar opposite, the accusation of an eating disorder) a journalistic stock-in-trade for any celebrity a publication deems out of favour.

The *Village Voice* felt that Tarantino had 'all the menace of a dentist's receptionist' despite being in what was, after all, 'a role meant to be scary'. The *New York Post*'s regular Broadway critic Clive Barnes damned with the faintest of praise saying Tarantino was '. . . far better than I had been led to expect – in fact he was merely terrible. *Entertainment Weekly*'s criticism may have been the harshest considering Tarantino's comment (again to Ebert) that 'I don't think [critics] see the work because you're just seeing me.' It claimed Tarantino came across as an uncomfortable understudy who'd unexpectedly had to go on with the 'proper' actors and not been able to cut it.

Despite all this negativity the play was a modest success and tickets, which at their most expensive hovered at the $60 mark, tended to sell in sufficient quantities to make the whole exercise financially worthwhile.

God said 'Ha!' (1998)

Comedienne Julia Sweeney talks to camera about difficult times in her life,
dwelling on the time when her brother was diagnosed with cancer and moved
into her spare bedroom shortly after her parents had also moved into her home.
The result was, for her, an extended tragedy-laden rerun of the homelife of her
childhood, living in a version of her original nuclear family. The difficulties of
such a life are obvious; the changed power ratios between parents and children
make life difficult and adds extra complications to pursuing potential romantic
relationships, coping with her brother's cancer or just living her professional
life. Tarantino is a credited Executive Producer, who helped get the project off
the ground and arrange for the performance to be recorded.

'Quentin Tarantino presents *Hero*'

Directed in China by Zhang Yimou in 2002, *Hero* is a sweeping tale of sacrifice,
assassination and empire building told in elaborately structured, astoundingly
colourful flashbacks. What makes it especially interesting, apart from the
presence of the Western-audience friendly Jet Li in the central role, is that it
takes the approach to narrative taken by *Rashamon*, Akira Kurosawa's 1954
film that examines an event from multiple, and contradictory, perspectives.
While Kurosawa's film has proved massively influential in a number of ways –
and was remade as *The Outrage* (Martin Ritt, 1964) – *Hero* can fairly be called
the most direct subsequent use of its central conceit (even taking into account
the use of 'false' flashbacks in Brian Synger's 1995 *The Usual Suspects*).

Having seen *Hero* and been disappointed by its failure to find release in the
United States ('I think they lost faith in it,' he noted), Tarantino offered to lend
his name to the picture in order for it to attract box-office attention. He also
advised that the film be released uncut, rather than have its length trimmed for
the sake of English-speaking audiences.

The credit 'Quentin Tarantino presents' was appended to the trailer and
posters for the English-subtitled version of the picture and Tarantino's celebrity
certainly assisted in getting people into theatres to see it. Tarantino announced
himself 'very proud' of helping the movie to secure US (and more mainstream
UK) release and stated that he'd 'had to fight' in order to convince the
distributors to put it out at all.

Hero is a superb film, at times seeming almost impossibly beautiful, and it
contains some of the most elaborate and impressive sword fights ever seen in
film. Tarantino's championing of it is to be entirely applauded. After the film's

cinematic release Tarantino went on to record an interview with its director that was included on the American DVD edition; a further way of using his celebrity to boost the film's profile and – hopefully – profits further.

In the face of this philanthropy, the fact that the film, the most expensive ever made in China, is also entirely unashamed, profoundly aggressive Chinese nationalist propaganda in a manner both sanctioned by the country's government and clearly designed to question the morality and humanity of anyone who doubts the wisdom of their leaders doesn't really matter. Well, hardly.

Alias

One of Tarantino's more high-profile, pre-*Kill Bill – Vol. 1* projects was his decision to appear in a number of episodes of the JJ Abrams-created TV series *Alias*. *Alias* concerns a seemingly ordinary college-age girl, Sydney Bristow (played by Jennifer Garner), who is recruited for the CIA. Or so she thinks. Upon graduation she goes to work for a bank, Credit Dauphine (ostensibly a cover organisation for the CIA), and is seconded to a secret section of the CIA called SD-6. In the series' very first episode she discovers that SD-6 is not a part of the American secret service at all but is, in fact, a criminal organisation with a vast agenda of its own, which is merely pretending to be a part of the CIA. Only the very highest-placed SD-6 employees know the truth, with the majority of its agents and support staff believing they are working for their country rather than a vast, ancient conspiracy. At the end of the series' premiere Sydney turns herself in to the CIA and becomes a double agent. So she's now a CIA agent working undercover in a criminal organisation that is pretending to be a part of the CIA, most of the employees of which believe themselves to be CIA agents as well. As a basis for a series it's not exactly uncomplicated, is it?

In the two-part first season story 'The Box' (transmitted 20 January 2002 and 10 February 2002) Quentin Tarantino made his first appearance as McKenas Cole. Cole is a former SD-6 agent left for dead by the series' regular antagonist Arvin Sloane (Ron Rifkin) when the helicopter that was sent to collect him from a mission in Grozny didn't wait long enough for him and his team to get aboard. (It later transpires that the reason Cole and his team were late was because they were attempting to carry an injured man back to the contact site in defiance of SD-6 procedure.) Cole was captured by the Russians and tortured, but when he told them he was an American citizen they contacted the CIA who promptly denied all knowledge of SD-6. This is how Cole discovered that SD-6 was not part of the US Government.

In 'The Box' Cole returns, backed up by a crack team of mercenaries, to the SD-6 headquarters in the Credit Dauphine building both for a reckoning with Sloane, who he feels betrayed him, and in order to acquire the titular box, which is in the building's vault. At the end of the spectacular and bloody double episode (which includes scenes of fingers being severed, the consumption of champagne and some kick-boxing) Cole is captured by the CIA. That's the real CIA, by the way.

Tarantino is fantastic as Cole, playing on his public persona in a different way to his characters of Jimmie in *Pulp Fiction* or Richie in *From Dusk Till Dawn*. Cole is super-cool and also super-repellent, dressed like a Reservoir Dog, handy with weapons and creepily fascinated by Garner's Sydney. He also has a just cause in his need for revenge against the monstrous and odious Sloane, but the details of his new employment (he is literally working for someone called 'The Man') and his brutal methods ameliorate audience sympathy.

Cole (and Tarantino) returned to the series in its third season. Appearing as an uncredited voiceover only in 'Full Disclosure' (11 January 2004), Tarantino made a fuller appearance in 'After Six' (15 February 2004): Cole was still seeking revenge on Sloane, while working for The Covenant, yet another secret organisation. 'After Six' also featured an appearance by *Kill Bill – Vol. 1*'s Vivica A Fox.

Kill Bill – Vol. 1 (2003)

Shaw Scope
Our Feature Presentation
Miramax Films presents
A Band Apart
The 4th Film by Quentin Tarantino
Editor: Sally Menke
Martial Arts Advisor: Yuen Wo-Ping
Casting: Johanna Ray, CSA, and Koko Maeda
Special Make-up Effects: KNB EFX Group, Inc.
Associate Producers: Dede Nickerson, Koko Maeda
Costume Designers: Catherine Thomas, Kumiko Ogawa
Original Music: The RZA
Production Designers: Tohei Taneda, David Wasco
Director of Photography: Robert Richardson, ASC
Executive Producers: Harvey Weinstein, Bob Weinstein,
Erica Steinberg, E Bennett Walsh
Produced by Lawrence Bender
Japanese Anime: Production IG, Tokyo, Japan
Written and Directed by Quentin Tarantino

TAGLINES: 'In the year 2003, Uma Thurman will kill Bill.'

'The Fourth Film by Quentin Tarantino.'

'Here comes the bride.'

'On October 10th, speak softly and carry a big sword.'

'On October 10th . . . a Quest for Revenge begins.'

CAST: Uma Thurman (The Bride), Lucy Liu (O-Ren Ishii), Vivica A Fox (Vernita Green), Daryl Hannah (Elle Driver), David Carradine (Bill), Michael Madsen (Budd), Julie Dreyfus (Sofie Fatale), Chiaki Kuriyama (Gogo Yubari), Sonny Chiba (Hattori Hanzo), Gordon Liu (Johnny Mo), Michael Parks (Earl McGraw), Michael Bowen (Buck), Jun Kunimura (Boss Tanaka), Kenji Oba (Bald Guy (Sushi Shop)), Yuki Kazamatsuri (Proprietor), James Parks (Edgar McGraw), Sakichi Satô (Charlie Brown), Jonathan

Loughran (Trucker), Yoshiyuki Morishita (Tokyo Business
Man), Tetsuro Shimaguchi (Crazy 88 #1 (Miki)), Kazuki
Kitamura (Crazy 88 #2), Yoji Boba Tanaka (Crazy 88 #3),
Issei Takahashi (Crazy 88 #4), So Yamanaka (Crazy 88 #5),
Juri Manase (Crazy 88 #6 (Girl)), Akaji Maro (Boss
Ozawah), Goro Daimon (Boss Honda), Shun Sugata (Boss
Benta), Zhang Jin Zhan (Boss Orgami), Xiaohui Hu (Young
88 (Spanked Boy)), Ambrosia Kelley (Nikki Bell), Sachiko
Fukii (The 5, 6, 7, 8's), Yoshiko Yamaguci (The 5, 6, 7,
8's), Ronnie Yoshiko Fujiyama (The 5, 6, 7, 8's), Shu Lan
Tuan (Okinawa Airline Ticket Agent), Ai Maeda (O-Ren
(animé sequence – voice)), Naomi Kusumi (Boss Matsumoto
(animé sequence – voice)), Hikaru Midorikawa (Pretty
Riki (animé sequence – voice))

4th FILM?: The sizeable presence of the title card **The 4th
Film by Quentin Tarantino** at the beginning of *Kill Bill –
Vol. 1* seems designed to eject *Four Rooms* from any serious
consideration of being part of Tarantino's directorial career.

SUMMARY (IN CHRONOLOGICAL ORDER): Brutalised
and beaten into a coma by the Black Viper assassination
gang on her wedding day four years ago, a nameless bride
wakes up in hospital and sets about orchestrating her
revenge on those who she believes nearly killed her,
slaughtered her wedding party and caused her to miscarry
her child. She's going to kill the gang in order ending with
Bill, their leader, and the father of her lost child. Travelling
to Okinawa, she meets a revered sensei, Hattori Hanzo,
who, once she has told him who she plans to kill, breaks his
vow of three decades, trains her and makes a sword for her.
Bill was one of his pupils, and he feels he bears some
responsibility for his actions against The Bride and others.
She attacks the Japanese mob, fighting and killing hundreds
of followers, before besting O-Ren in hand-to-hand combat.
She sends O-Ren's right-hand woman, now crippled, back to
Bill as a message that she is coming for him, before returning

to America to kill Vernita Green the second of Bill's henchwomen. As the end credits roll, Bill wonders aloud if The Bride is aware that her child, *their* daughter, is still alive.

QUOTES:

The Bride: 'Just because I have no wish to murder you in front of your daughter doesn't mean that parading her around in front of me is going to inspire sympathy . . . you and I have unfinished business.'

The Bride: 'It's mercy, compassion and forgiveness I lack, not rationality.'

Hattori Hanzo: 'I can tell you with no ego, this is my finest sword. If on your journey, you should encounter God, *God* will be cut.'

The Bride: 'I have vermin to kill.'

The Bride: 'Wiggle your big toe.'

O-Ren: 'Silly Caucasian girl likes to play with samurai swords'

Hattori Hanzo: 'You like samurai swords? *I* like baseball!'

SCREENPLAY: The 222-page final combined script for both parts of *Kill Bill* reportedly took Tarantino a year, writing virtually every day, but its origins go back much further in the director's life.

While shooting *Pulp Fiction* and indulging in an (entirely platonic) 'major artistic love affair' with Uma Thurman, Tarantino came up with the notion of a pastiche revenge gangster flick which he wanted the actress to star in. This, he decided, would begin, as the film as released does, with a black-and-white shot of a woman being taunted by a man's off-screen voice insisting that there is no sadism in his actions. He would then shoot her through the head.

The title came a little later as the director found himself explaining to his intended leading lady that he'd like her to

'Kill Bill!' (the rhyme of the title was an early decision). Thurman, though, went one better than Hollywood's wunderkind. As he described his opening scene to her she threw back the question 'What if [in that shot] I'm in a wedding dress?' Thurman's suggestion was seized by Tarantino and incorporated into his ideas for the picture. So integral did he think Thurman's additions became to the character's and the film's construction that he later arranged for the credit 'Based on the character "The Bride" created by Q and U' to be included on both volumes of the film as released.

Later in 1994, and while exhibiting *Pulp Fiction* at the Stockholm Film Festival, Tarantino had a burst of *Kill Bill*-related inspiration and wrote thirty pages of the screenplay in one sudden writing session; so enthused was he, he found himself calling up Miramax head Harvey Weinstein excitedly in the middle of the night, reading sections of the screenplay to him. Weinstein compared the scenes to the work of Polish filmmaker Kieslowski (although based on the finished film it's not easy to see why after a gap of a decade). Time was not on the writer/director's side, however, as he needed to return to America shortly to begin work on *Four Rooms*, and was booked in to act in Robert Rodriguez's production of his own pre-fame vampire/road movie script, *From Dusk Till Dawn*. Returning to America, Tarantino put *Kill Bill* aside, not wanting to work on another 'full-on, lurid exploitation movie experience' immediately after the Rodriguez film, which was intended to be entirely that. When the question of what to make as his third directorial project eventually presented itself, *Kill Bill* was not an option he chose to explore (see **Jackie Brown**).

The long years between *Pulp Fiction* and *Jackie Brown* were followed by an even longer creative silence from Tarantino. When asked about his long lay off, Uma Thurman pondered aloud, 'I didn't really assume he was stuck, but . . . creative work is kind of mysterious . . . people do get lost . . . people do lose the fire . . . people's energy does go elsewhere.' Even during production of *Jackie Brown*, Tarantino had repeatedly assured the press that he was never going to be the kind of filmmaker who made a picture a year (or more, as some particularly workaholic directors do) as he didn't see how he could do that and still live 'a life'. As the kind of director who generates his own work rather than jumping on board projects already in development he was placed in the position of having to start from scratch after each break after completion of a project. It may also be true that the criticism that he had received for the non-directorial projects he'd pursued between *Pulp Fiction* and *Jackie Brown* had ameliorated his enthusiasm for doing anything other than writing and direction and that he could only write/direct when he had exactly the right project which he felt was ready.

It was a chance meeting with Uma Thurman that led Tarantino to dig out, finish and rework his unfinished screenplay as his fourth directorial project after such a long delay. Further delays were created when, on the verge of shooting the script, Uma Thurman became pregnant. Tarantino pretended to consider recasting the part for a week, just so that the studio wouldn't think he was completely insane, and then announced he would wait. As he later told the BBC, 'If Josef Von Sternberg is getting ready to make *Morocco* and Marlene Dietrich gets pregnant, he waits for Dietrich!'

The screenplay to *Kill Bill – Vol. 1* is, fascinatingly, very reminiscent of, while almost being almost entirely unlike, Tarantino's earlier screenwriting efforts. Two of Tarantino's major trademarks (the intrusion of reality on genre clichés and his smart, witty dialogue) feature hardly at all in *Kill Bill – Vol. 1*. Indeed the dialogue is functional, to the point and occasionally, languidly, randomly prosaic, often in clear imitation of the kinds of films that *Kill Bill – Vol. 1* is seeking to pastiche.

Having abandoned these core principles of his writing, Tarantino does retain some others. The progression of the plot is defiantly anti-linear, but, in another departure, there are no attempts to confuse or befuddle the audience as to chronology (compare with Vincent's death in **Pulp Fiction**) and everything is clearly and slowly explained through a combination of on-screen captions and the list that The Bride constantly refers to.

Nevertheless here's the order the film is in (yes, Chapter One really is called (2)):

Prologue
Chapter One – (2)
Chapter Two – The blood-splattered BRIDE
    1 – 'Four years and six months earlier in the city of El
       Paso, Texas'
    2 – (No Title)
    3 – Four Years Later
Chapter Three – The Origin of O-REN ISHII
Interlude
Chapter Four – The MAN from OKINAWA
Chapter Five – Showdown at the House of Blue Leaves
Epilogue

This is the order the events occur in dramatically speaking:

Chapter Three
Prologue
Chapter Two
Interlude
Chapter Four
Chapter Five
Epilogue
Chapter One

Chapter Two begins 'Four Years and Six Months' before Chapter One. The Bride wakes up Four Years after Bill orders Elle to abort her attempted murder of The Bride when the latter is comatose. As Chapters Four and Five take place before Chapter One we can assume that that rogue six months is partially used up between sections 1 and 2 of

Chapter Two and also in Chapters Four and Five. There are a few other complications, however. (For example, the first chunk of 'The MAN from OKINAWA' is a flashback to O-Ren assuming control of the yakuza, which takes place a year after the first attempt on The Bride's life – so, if you wish, between Chapter Two – 1 'Four years and six months earlier in the city of El Paso, Texas' and Chapter Two – 2 (No Title).

What this structure does for Tarantino this time out is not, in fact, what it has done for him in the past. It isn't used to create shocking narrative twists (the narrative is simple) or changes of dramatic tone (which changes, but not shockingly, and not really around these points). Instead it's used to give something that seems like a straightforward Hollywood movie action structure to (half of) a story which doesn't naturally have that structure at all. Robert McKee and Don Simpson would both heartily approve of the structure of *Vol. 1* as you watch it. It has a small prologue that sets up the main character, has a huge action sequence, then drops off in pace as it builds up the characters again, before ending in an enormous climactic and cathartic fight sequence.

Tarantino's abandonment of his smart dialogue (there are no characters who are deliberately funny in *Kill Bill*, a departure for the screenwriter) doesn't mean that the dialogue that is there isn't specifically chosen to achieve certain effects. Take, for example, Bill's explanation that there is nothing sadistic in his actions towards The Bride in the prologue. What he means, and this is actually true, is that he takes no pleasure in killing The Bride. It's just something that he thinks he *has* to do. The audience may disagree with this, but it's true from the character's point of view. Indeed what he's trying to tell The Bride is that in fact these actions are masochistic. It actually pains *him* to cause pain to someone who has worked for him, who he's cared for who – as we will shortly discover – has been his lover. He's not clichéd enough to say that it hurts him more than it hurts her, but he wants her to know that there is no pleasure in this for him, only pain.

'There's nothing sadistic in my actions' also sounds like a plea from the director/writer. Nobody ever said that making movies was easy and to make a film is clearly more difficult than to watch one. If anyone suffers as a result of Tarantino making a film, it's only ever going to be him or the cast or the crew, not the audience – who merely offer a small some of money and a tiny expanse of their time.

There are also recurring threads that run through the dialogue; little handovers of words and moments that reflect back on earlier ones. For example, we discover in *Vol. 2* that the Bride's name is Beatrix. Now, when towards the end of *Kill Bill – Vol. 1* O-Ren asks The Bride, 'You didn't think it was going to be that easy, did you?' and The Bride replies in the affirmative, O-Ren says, 'Silly Rabbit, Trix is for kids.' This isn't just a slogan for some cereal and an allusion to The Bride's as yet unknown name, it's also a marrying of Beatrix and Rabbit – which should remind most people of an author who wrote animal stories. Names also provide another of Tarantino's little dialogue tricks. The Bride's surname is Kiddo. Bill calls her this more than once in *Vol. 1* but it seems to the audience to be merely an incongruously affectionate term like calling someone 'honey' or 'mate'. No one suspects that the question of The Bride's identity, which Tarantino goes so far as to use bleeps on the soundtrack to drown out when Uma Thurman and Vivica A Fox say it, has been half answered already. When Earl McGraw says 'hold their piece' in relation to the massacre at the wedding it's a weak pun ('peace' from the wedding service, 'piece' as the slang for gun). Not a pun the audience would find amusement in, but an insight into his character nonetheless.

The word 'bitch' occurs and re-occurs many, many times in *Kill Bill – Vol. 1*. In some ways it serves a similar function to 'nigger' in Tarantino's earlier scripts, being a multi-purpose epithet thrown around by characters who could claim it as 'reclaimed' (women) and those who couldn't (men). It's interesting that its use hasn't proved controversial.

Bill doesn't appear much in *Vol. 1*, but his use of language is also interesting and uniquely his own. It's littered with sentimentalities and clichés ('beautiful blue eyes', 'I love you very much', 'I'm the man') and also the coldly functional language of the organiser of murders ('You will abort the mission').

A number of Tarantino's influences can be detected at script level in *Kill Bill*. There are two principal senses in which this is true. One is the now normal Hollywood sense of quoted lines or pastiched dialogue. Examples of this in *Kill Bill* include Buck the nurse's line, 'My name is Buck, and I came here to fuck' – which is a quote from Robert Englund's character (Buck, naturally) in *Eaten Alive* (Tobe Hooper, 1976). Another example is Bill's comment, 'I'm kind of particular who my girl marries' which is taken from *His Girl Friday* (Howard Hawks, 1940), and a third is Edgar McCraw's 'Son Number One' which is a reference to Charlie Chan. (Incidentally, starring in a recontextualised Charlie Chan revival – as his granddaughter and successor sleuth – is Lucy Liu's dream project.)

Kill Bill also, and this is far less common, features a character from another person's project who is imported in wholesale, albeit with permission: Sonny Chiba's character is Hattori Hanzo the swordmaker. This character is intended by the filmmaker to be another member of the dynasty of characters named Hattori Hanzo which Chiba played on television in the long-running series *Hattori Hanzô: Kage no Gundan*. In this Chiba played many generations of the same heroic family in a manner that is probably most easily comprehensible to British audiences through being compared to Rowan Atkinson's portrayal of the Blackadder family across 515 years of English history between 1983 and 2000. In an extra twist on top of that, when Hattori Hanzo gives The Bride her sword the words he says to her (see **QUOTES**) are taken from *Makai tenshô* (Kinji Fukasaku,

1981) in a scene where a character played by Sonny Chiba *receives* rather than gives away a sword.

Tarantino wrote and rewrote the script during production, adding and subtracting elements as he saw fit. One aspect that was lost was Yogo's sister (see **Vol. 2**), another was Bill's character as an alchemist who used potions to induce certain behaviours in other people (interrogating Sophie with one called 'The Undisputed Truth', for example). Another smaller change is the Yakuza character Mr Barrel, who had his role reduced substantially and became Johnny Moe.

CASTING: The years since *Pulp Fiction* hadn't really seen Uma Thurman add significantly to her list of accomplished performances. She had appeared in the financially, critically and artistically disastrous *The Avengers* (Jeremiah Chechick, 1998) and the only slightly less so *Batman & Robin* (Joel Schumacher, 1997) with only her splendid turn in *Sweet and Lowdown* (Woody Allen, 1999) to remind viewers of what she was capable of. Thurman herself would dismiss all these projects as 'whatever I did in those seven years'. *Kill Bill* gives the actress her best onscreen role to date, and it's hard not to feel that her prompting Tarantino to revive the project (see **SOURCES TO SCREEN**) was caused by a self-awareness at how little her career had advanced since she last worked with Quentin. That said, if Thurman affirms anything in *Kill Bill*, it's that in no way can her lack of onscreen form be put down to her talents or her commitment. It's impossible to imagine any other A-list Hollywood actress subjecting herself to the training and fitness regime required by the part of The Bride, or accepting quite so readily camera angles that, say, dwell on the hairs on her toes or a tired, bruised, bloodied countenance.

New Yorker Lucy Liu exploded into the consciousness of the American public via her role as Ling Woo in TV's *Ally McBeal*, a supporting character who became a recurring presence, then a regular character and then one of the series' biggest assets. So much so that the series didn't long survive her departure to take on other roles. These roles included Alex in the *Charlie's Angels* films (McG, 2000, 2003), a hugely amusing performance in *Shanghai Noon* (Tom Dey, 2000) – the performance that won her the *Kill Bill* role in fact – and a stellar turn that was one of the few redeeming features of dull Best Picture Oscar-winner *Chicago* (Rob Marshall, 2002). There was also an unheralded, but stunning, cameo in *Sex and The City*.

David Carradine, star of the television series *Kung Fu* (a childhood favourite of Tarantino's) was cast after both Warren Beatty and Kevin Costner were considered for the role of Bill. It wasn't that Carradine wasn't Tarantino's first choice, it was that the role of Bill grew in the writing to a more physically demanding part with more screen time than the one Beatty had been expecting, and expected, to play. 'I thought Bill really wouldn't come into the movie until the end, almost like Brando in *Apocalypse Now* [Francis Ford Coppola, 1979]' Tarantino told the BBC. The part was, with the martial arts training that would also be necessary '. . . just a bigger deal than I had led Warren to believe'. Tarantino had read Carradine's autobiography while working on the draft screenplay and judged the actor's memoirs to be 'beautifully written'.

Chiaka Kuriyama had appeared in the explosively wonderful *Lord of the Flies*-a-like *Battle Royale* (2000) with Takeshi Kitano. It was a film Tarantino greatly admired – the last in the career of the octogenarian-during-its-production Japanese director Kinji Fukasaku. 'It's a sad cliché that most every director ends their career with a whimper . . .' noted Tarantino, quoting Fukasaku's final picture as one of the very few exceptions he could think of. Kuriyama was cast by Tarantino on the strength of her performance in that film.

Darryl Hannah's performance as the punningly named Elle Driver is one of Tarantino's least heralded pieces of 'redemption casting'. A star in the 1980s through movies like *Splash* (Ron Howard, 1984) Hannah had, by 2000, essentially disappeared from view entirely. *Kill Bill* doesn't just show that's she still gorgeous (sexier than ever, in fact), it shows that she can do so much more than the light comedy she was previously known for so that all casting directors should be embarrassed for not using her before.

KEY SHOTS: During publicity duties for *Pulp Fiction*, Tarantino told TV interviewer Charlie Rose that 'one of the things I love most about filmmaking is that you can make a left turn in the narrative and suddenly you're in a whole new film'. *Kill Bill – Vol. 1* is, consciously or otherwise, the logic of that approach taken to its ultimate conclusion. *Kill Bill* seems to, as cinema, have three essential aims: 1) To make the audience feel the ferocity of The Bride's need for revenge to the extent that the audience will sympathise with her method; 2) To work through a number of genres and cinematic landscapes; 3) To combine the above two elements to create a world; to do what Sergio Leone arguably did for the American western and turn a world which essentially only existed on film anyway into a self-consciously mythic, heightened reality that the audience can absolutely believe in while knowing it simply isn't real; a place that only exists by reference to other fictions – other movies.

Each section of *Kill Bill* could be called pastiche. Each takes the photography, lighting and editing conventions of the kind of film that its imitating and copies them. Except it doesn't, not quite, because all the various sections of *Kill Bill* are obviously, even as they are wildly different from each other on almost every stylistic point, the work of Quentin Tarantino. This is because he retains his propensity for long, long takes that allow the actors to play a scene out at their own pace; because he continues to use sampled music over dialogue-free scenes to create atmosphere; because he continues to use close-ups to establish information about where a scene is set; and because he continues to open scenes without the traditional establishing shot almost demanded by conventional post-Griffith film grammar. He also chooses to shoot a lot of the film from directly above. This isn't a part of his own previous directorial style or an aspect of any of the things he's copying. It's something new he's brought to the table himself to demonstrate his individuality even in a pastiche film like this. *Kill Bill* shows that Tarantino can make anything his own while allowing it to remain itself. 'I wanted to see how good I am,' Tarantino told an interviewer. Looking at the astoundingly visual *Kill Bill* it's safe to say he found out he's exactly as good as he always thought he was – he can do pretty much anything and make pretty much anything he chooses cinematically beautiful.

Vol. 1 begins with a bleached out black-and-white shot of The Bride's bloodied face; Uma Thurman's face. This has the crushing immediacy of newsreel even though the blood on her face is horribly black. It's a sudden intrusion of real emotion and real horror after a few moments of jokey, parodic, colour-filled messing around. It's the first shock 'reversal' of *Kill Bill – Vol. 1* and the shock is profound; audiences inevitably collapse into utter silence in less than a moment. After the credits, Tarantino borrows from the beginning of Orson Welles's *Citizen Kane* (1941) for the (still black-and-white) shot of the light seeping into The Bride's hospital room before detouring into a glossy fight scene in a kitchen that mingles Hong Kong action with the Technicolor vibrancy of TV shows like *Alias*. Scenes in the kitchen in this section are often shot from above, with the screen bisected by the wall that separates the 'cooking' and 'eating' areas of the kitchen, creating something which is not unlike 'split screen' but which has an ostensible in-camera cause. At the end of the scene there's a brilliant shot where, having killed Vernita Green, The Bride kneels to touch the body, revealing to the audience that Vernita's four-year-old daughter is standing in the doorway behind (she has previously been obscured by The Bride herself) and has seen her murder her mother. Every time I've seen this film someone in the audience gasps at this moment. (Also note that the box of cereal Vernita has a gun hidden inside is called 'Kabooom!')

The scenes at the hospital begin in full-on Brian de Palma mode, pastiching Hitchcock without obviously actually copying any of his shots before descending into split-screen and Tobe Hopper parody (as The Bride attacks Buck).

The O-Ren Ishii flashback is presented in animated form. Tarantino commissioned Production IG, based in Tokyo, to realise the sequence. Founded in 1987 by Mitsuhisa Ishikawa and Takayuki Goto, the house has been responsible for several of the most prominent animé films of recent years including *Kôkaku kidôtai (Ghost in the Shell)* (1995), *Patlabor* (1990) and *Blood: The Last Vampire* (2000). Full of visible screen action effects, loud noises and a visual tribute to Hitchcock's *Psycho* (1960) (the close-up of the eye), it's absolutely astounding and would be even if it wasn't backed by entirely inappropriate spaghetti western music.

Tarantino has said that he opted to give the audience '. . . shit they can't even believe they're seeing'. Even if he wasn't talking about this scene when he said it, it is this sequence which comes closest, on first viewing, to simply defying the audience's ability to comprehend what's going on. The last time most people saw a film which turned into a cartoon halfway through it was *Mary Poppins* (Robert Stevenson, 1964).

The Yakuza scenes are shot like a high-budget Yakuza movie but after The Bride arrives at the House of Blue Leaves we're in full-on exploitation massacre territory. Before we get there though, there's one of the most outrageously long shots in Tarantino's career. After The Bride moves away from O-Ren's floor, the camera follows her down the stairs, through the bar, past the kitchen and into the lavatory. The camera then ducks out of the lavatory and back up the stairs to follow Sophie. What's really remarkable is the way the camera (it's on a crane) moves in huge arcs as it makes this movement, rising and then falling again, with huge amounts of visual information visible on what should be the periphery of the camera's vision – we can see there are rooms that we can only see the edge of. This long, long shot isn't just showing off, it gives the audience a real feel for the House as a three-dimensional space.

What is also worth noting is how Tarantino's camera usually finds Uma Thurman. It puts her face in *extreme* close-up more often than not, so the long slowly curving lines of her undeniably beautiful face seem to stretch so far up and down we can hardly see where she begins and ends. For some reason this gives her image enormous immediacy and power. Equally when his camera goes wide and shows the whole of her body, usually already decked in clothes which emphasise her not inconsiderable height, she simply seems to stretch away towards an infinite sky, becoming more and less than human.

Kill Bill – Vol. 1 is also the first Tarantino film made after the CGI revolution kicked in in earnest (which is arguably after *Star Wars: Episode I – The Phantom Menace* (George Lucas, 1999) when Lucasfilm and ILM made the technology developed for that film available to those using them as an effects house). Tarantino uses CGI fairly extensively in *Vol. 1*. Not just for the overhead shots of the planes carrying The Bride from place to place, but also for the cityscapes and shots of the plane sweeping low over Tokyo. These beautifully rendered shots combine with the vibrancy of the Tokyo scenes to create something which is bracing to watch.

VIOLENCE: The *Village Voice* called *Kill Bill – Vol. 1* 'probably the most violent movie ever made by an American studio'. While that's perhaps an overstatement (is it even as violent as *Natural Born Killers* or is a single death as nakedly sadistic as the opening killings of *Jaws* (Steven Spielberg, 1975) or *Scream* (Wes Craven, 1996) to pick two almost random examples? I personally think not) the movie is certainly very violent indeed. Whereas *Jackie Brown* saw all four of its killings (Beaumont, Melanie, Louis, Ordell) occur off-screen (with the camera focusing on something else in the scene as the bullets struck their victims) and gave such emotional weight to each murder that the audience is left feeling distressed at the death of the monstrous Ordell simply because he was ultimately human, *Kill Bill – Vol. 1* features a literally uncountable number of on-screen deaths and few, if any of them, contain any emotion at all, even the killing of a mother in front of her child. Whereas *Reservoir Dogs* and *Pulp Fiction* punished their already ambiguous, murderous characters, or redeemed them through showing their renouncing of violent means (i.e. Jules), *Kill Bill – Vol. 1* has a heroine who slaughters her way through a multi-ethnic cornucopia of multiple men and women with only the occasional shudder while the audience is only rarely given an emotional context to these acts of violence. This is usually when they relate to The Bride herself, in fact. Viewers are far more likely to recall the grim opening of the movie with horror than they are to react in such a way to the playful, Technicolor balletic brutality of what transpires in the House of Blue Leaves. Much of the violence in *Kill Bill – Vol. 1* is rendered in terms of, and is best understood in terms of, its function as aesthetics. The cutting off of one of the arms of one of the Crazy 88 killers has no more connection with what it would be really like to cut someone's arm off in the 'real world' than Oliver Hardy treading on a rusty nail in *Saps at Sea* (Gordon Douglas, 1940) has with the perforated skin and blood infection that would result if someone did this in 'real life'. 'This is definitely not taking place on planet Earth,' commented Tarantino when asked. Where did it take place then? 'Fantasy Land'.

In order to achieve the kind of fights he wanted in his movie, Tarantino hired Master Yuen Wo-Ping and Sonny Chiba to train Uma Thurman. 'Yuen Wo-Ping will choreograph the Chinese kung fu action and Sonny Chiba will choreograph the samurai action,' Tarantino announced. 'They are going to put Uma through training, where she will have to learn the kung fu animal styles.' At that time the

plan was for both Chiba and Yuen Wo-Ping to also take
acting roles in the film, but scheduling made it impossible for
Wo-Ping to play the part that had been written for him (see
Vol. 2). Yuen Wo-Ping had become well known in the West
for his acclaimed work as fight choreographer on *Crouching
Tiger, Hidden Dragon* (Ang Lee, 2000) and *The Matrix*
(Andy Wachowski, Larry Wachowski, 1999) but he had had
a long career in Eastern cinema as a director of action scenes
for movies like *Wong Fei-hung ji yi: Naam yi dong ji keung*
(Hark Tsui, 1992). Sonny Chiba had been described in
Tarantino's script for *True Romance* as, 'The finest actor
working in martial arts cinema today.' A very fine actor as
well as a man capable of making physical action appear
tremendously exciting on-screen he's made an amazing
number of films including the legendary *Street Fighter*
(Sakae Ozawa, 1974) – the first movie to be rated X for
violence in America. His acting performance in *Kill Bill* has
a gravitas, dignity and power that you'd normally associate
with someone like the great Toshiru Mifune or Alec
Guinness. (Could there be a higher compliment?) Yet his
role also incorporates some highly camp messing around in a
sake shop that seems more like the sort of thing Jackie Chan
would do on an off-day. That Chiba manages to incorporate
both into a recognisable, indeed admirable, human being is
remarkable. If anyone deserved an Oscar for their acting
work in *Kill Bill*, it's he.

Chiba and Yuen Wo-Ping trained Thurman so well that
Tarantino was able to improvise numerous action scenes
while shooting and experiment with new ideas on a daily
basis. 'I was only safe from stuff I thought an insurance
company wouldn't let him do,' Thurman noted, 'only when
it was definitely, positively illegal.'

'I have done violence before but never in such an
outrageous way,' commented Tarantino, not without relish.

SPURIOUS INTERTEXTUALITY: The film then proceeds
to a caption which reads 'Revenge is a dish best served cold'

and then labels it as an 'old Klingon proverb'. It's actually, of course, a line from the French novel *Les Liaisons Dangereuses* by Pierre Choderlos de Laclos, filmed many times in both English and French. What Tarantino is referring to is the moment in *Star Trek II: The Wrath of Khan* (Nicholas Meyer, 1982) where the titular vengeance-obsessed maniac (Ricardo Montalban) quotes this and labels it an 'old Klingon proverb'. It's a clever thing for Tarantino to do. He's placing his film in metaphorical inverted commas from the very start. It's not just a quotation, it's a deliberately funny use, which is also actually a paraphrase (Khan says 'That revenge is a dish that is best served cold'), of a *translated* misquote that is in itself a joke (to the audience, though not the characters) in the (not terribly highbrow, but also brilliant and thus terribly under-appreciated) film in which it is used. The whole logic of *Kill Bill – Vol. 1* is present in this caption.

When making *Reservoir Dogs*, Tarantino had expressed admiration for the French gangster films of Jean-Pierre Melville and Jean-Luc Godard (indeed, his production company A Band Apart is named after one of Godard's) and the way they translated an American artform (the gangster film) into something uniquely French. *Reservoir Dogs* was supposed to be an American gangster film that took what the French gangster films added to the genre and then filtered them through other cinemas (including Hong Kong cinema) to produce something new. The 'Klingon' caption represents that process in its totality; the process whereby an American crime novel by Dashiell Hammett became the Kurosawa film *Yojimbo* that was subsequently remade as *Per un pugno di dollari* (*A Fistful of Dollars*) (1964) by Sergio Leone. This is a film which is a western set in America, starring an American, but shot by an Italian, partially *in* Italian, but made in Spain, a film which then went on to influence virtually every western made in America after it. The spirals of multiple cultures and multiple influences and remakes reflect into the distance like the many Charles Foster Kanes in the mirror in Welles's *Citizen Kane* (1941) (which is referenced by Tarantino in the very next shot).

Here are some of Tarantino's many borrowings, riffs and influences as represented by that opening caption.

The domino masks worn by O-Ren's bodyguards (massacred by The Bride) are clearly indebted to those worn by Bruce Lee as Kato in the TV series *The Green Hornet*. Given that Uma Thurman's yellow tracksuit is, obviously and self-confessedly, a deliberate look-a-like for that worn by Bruce Lee in the unfinished *Game of Death* (Robert Clouse, 1978) one is faced with the image of Bruce Lee massacring an army of Bruce Lees.

The sudden 'blink' into black and white for the massacre in the House of Blue Leaves is a reference to the habit of US television stations of showing black-and-white copies (or merely black-and-white copies of some scenes) of violent Eastern films in order to disguise the gore content.

Tarantino also references himself in *Kill Bill – Vol. 1*. The Bride draws a rectangle (not a square, oddly) with her fingers when saying the word 'square' – Mia (also Uma Thurman) did much the same thing in *Pulp Fiction* although there the action was accompanied by an on-screen line, here it isn't.

Conceptually, the Deadly Viper Assassination Squad is clearly a riff on the notion of 'Fox Force Five', the TV show that Mia has shot a pilot for in *Pulp Fiction*. (The members of the Deadly Viper Assassination Squad are, of course, all named for snakes: Sidewinder, Black Mamba, Cottonmouth, Copperhead and California Mountain King.)

The characters of Edgar and Earl McGraw appear in *From Dusk Till Dawn 2: Texas Blood Money* (Scott Spiegel, 1999) and *From Dusk Till Dawn* (Robert Rodriguez, 1996) respectively, played by the same actors, James Parks and Michael Parks as here. The actors are, like their characters, son and father.

Often a close-up of The Bride's eyes is shown and then immediately followed by flashback footage of a massacre in black and white. This is a conceit taken from the majestic, yet violent Lee Van Cleef western *Da uomo a uomo* (*Death Rides A Horse*) (Giulio Petroni, 1968).

One character is mockingly referred to as Charlie Brown because he ostensibly looks like the Charles Schultz cartoon character from *Peanuts*.

Budd is apparently named after Budd Boetticher, the director of *The Rifleman* (1958), *Arruza* (1972) and *Bullfighter and the Lady* (1951) amongst others. Though it's also worth noting that if you put Budd and Bill together you nearly get Billy Budd – the title of the Herman Melville short story filmed in 1962 starring Terence Stamp and directed by Peter Ustinov.

The glass floor in the House of Blue Leaves is borrowed from Seijun Suzuki's *Tokyo Drifter* the head-curdling 1975 psychedelic gangster epic.

The basic concept seems to have been borrowed from Truffaut's *La Mariée était en noir* (1967) which itself borrowed extensively from three Hitchock classics, *Foreign Correspondent* (1940), *Notorious* (1946) and *Rear Window* (1954); making *Kill Bill*'s concept an American riff on a French film influenced by American films featuring all of the many, many influences above.

Oh, and finally, what is The Bride being awoken by the vampiric sucking of a mosquito but a particularly nasty twist on Sleeping Beauty being awoken by a kiss? A point which is reinforced when, a few minutes later, she is likewise kissed by the redneck who has paid $75 to sexually assault her comatosed form.

CRITICAL REACTION: Reviewers (and indeed viewers) were and are split about the film. The essential dividing line seems to be between those who felt the picture was beautifully made and very exciting, but essentially lacked humanity, emotion and real merit, and those who felt its aesthetic qualities marked it out as a great film due to the inspired combination of them and the film's seemingly almost awe-inspiring total lack of human content. 'It's a slasher flick, a revenge comedy and a work of frivolous art that establishes Tarantino as the most indiscriminate film cannibal of them all,' wrote James Christoper in *The Times* of 9 October 2003. He went on to comment that 'One puff of cold reality and this house of cards will fold. But Tarantino never allows us a decent interval to draw that fatal breath. At least not when we are watching', arguing in essence that the film was a conjuring trick, only a distraction while being performed. Fellow Miramax filmmaker Kevin Smith (director of *Clerks* (1994) and *Chasing Amy* (1997)) posted excitedly to his own message board on 30 September 2003 saying it '. . . made me so insanely happy [it] delivers in ways few movies ever do . . . proof positive that Quentin's a mad genius . . . the kinda flick that makes me remember why I got into filmmaking in the first place.' AO Scott in the *New York Times* of 10 October called the film 'above all an exercise in style' and a glimpse into a 'looking-glass universe that reflects nothing beyond . . . cinematic obsessions'. It was, overall, oddly 'endearing' with The Bride's massacre of 88 foot soldiers 'as insouciant and elegant as a show-stopping musical number'. Roger Ebert of the *Chicago Sun-Times* called Tarantino a 'virtuoso violinist racing through the Flight of the Bumble Bee'. The movie he pointed out '. . . is all storytelling and no story' with that non-story taking place in a 'parallel universe in which all of this makes sense in the same way that a superhero's origin story makes sense'. In the *Village Voice* of 15 October 2003, Matthew Wilder stated the obvious but in clearer terms than any other reviewer: 'I had no idea that Tarantino possessed the skills to sustain . . . near-unbearable emotional intensity . . . in its meticulous craftsmanship and jacked-up cinephilic energy [*Kill Bill*] might be the most viscerally and emotionally overwhelming B-movie ever made'. Two weeks earlier his colleague J Hoberman had called the film 'more exhausting than invigorating' and noted that if there was no limit to the actions possible in the movie's extreme world of gangland violence 'neither is there any real consequence' of those actions.

In *LA Weekly* John Powers called the film 'a grindhouse Ulysses' in tribute to its dazzling variety of influences and allusions and the way they led an attentive audience to other works of art. It was also, to him, 'an astonishing piece of movie-making and, quite possibly, an Olympian folly' with a plot which was basically 'Charlie's Angels in Hell' told 'with the glee of a flea who's discovered a new kennel'.

MUSICAL NOTES: The first original music composed for a Tarantino feature was created for *Kill Bill – Vol. 1* by The RZA of the Wu-Tang Clan. Tarantino and RZA had met socially and instantly connected through their shared love of grindhouse cinema. Tarantino has since stated that he didn't even have to ask The RZA to work on *Kill Bill*, it just naturally happened as a result of their growing friendship. RZA's music is generally used in the Tokyo sequences of the film and includes the creepy refrain used to underscore O-Ren's argument with the council of bosses (the soundtrack contains a version of this that he raps over, which is brilliant).

For the most part Tarantino continues his use of 'found music'. He does this both in the manner he's been using since *Reservoir Dogs* (of using songs) and also in the form he tentatively began on *Jackie Brown* of using pieces of scores for other films rather than songs to assist in the creation of the appropriate mood for his scenes. For example, the tune whistled by Darryl Hannah's character as she sets off to murder The Bride is part of the score used to signify Hywell Bennett's murderous character in *Twisted Nerve* (Roy Boulting, 1968); this then builds into an actual use of the score itself, which is by Hitchcock maestro Bernard Hermann. Also used is the theme from the *Ironside* TV series (1967–75) which starred Raymond Burr as a wheelchair-bound police detective. This is used cheekily for underscoring the scene in which The Bride rolls herself around in a wheelchair. Tarantino also borrows the theme from *The Green Hornet* (yet another Bruce Lee reference) and Luis Bacalov's spaghetti western theme 'The Grand Duel – (Parte Prima)' to underscore some anime. 'Super 16' the theme from *Du bi quan wang da po xue di zi* (Yu Wang, 1975) is also used.

Elsewhere the genre and cultural cut and paste continues as Tarantino uses a pan-pipe version of James Last's 'Zamfir' and a Mexican guitar version of 'Please Lord Don't Let Me Be Misunderstood' (B Benjamin, S Marcus, G Caldwell) most famously recorded by rock group The Animals. This last one is a particularly extreme cultural mish-mash. A song in a medium (rock 'n' roll) which is essentially American (albeit formed from the elements of African culture redolent in America as a result of slavery) made famous by a British band, re-recorded by a Latin American sound group and then used to score a fight between a Chinese-Japanese-American and a Caucasian American that takes place in a pastiche Japanese stone garden with samurai swords.

What is most perfect though is the entirely un-arch use of Nancy Sinatra's cover version of Sonny Bono's 'Bang Bang (My Baby Shot Me Down)', the lyrics of which get right to the conceptual heart of The Bride's story with such calm power that the song feels like it was written for the film. Which is probably the idea.

THE NUMBERS: *Kill Bill – Vol. 1* took $22.7 million at the US box office in its opening weekend, a hugely impressive hit for half of a movie that cost – according to most estimates – between $55 and $65 million.

VOL. 2?: It's difficult to pin down the exact moment when the decision was made to cut *Kill Bill* in half. Tarantino has implied in interviews that it was discussed early on in production between him and Harvey Weinstein but certainly when the decision was made public there had been no real media speculation about it happening beforehand (and the first trailer for the film contains moments that were eventually used in *Vol. 2*).

The news that the film would be released in two volumes was made public on 17 July 2003 and Tarantino later said that it was simply a matter of him not wanting to release either a four-hour version of *Kill Bill* or a three-hour version that would be compromised. 'I wouldn't have had the balls, the first time out, to come out with a four-hour movie.' He also feared a four-hour grindhouse revenge epic would be seen as 'pretentious' and that 'the average moviegoer would overdose' when faced with three hours of trash aesthetic.

The Weinsteins concurred with Tarantino's decision, perhaps aware that they had hobbled Martin Scorsese's *Gangs of New York* (2002) by asking it to be cut down to a more audience (and Academy) friendly length. Of course they can't also have been discouraged by the possibility that releasing it as two films would virtually double the potential revenue from the picture without coming close to doubling the costs of something already shot.

Having seen the film, some critics didn't approve of the decision. 'Cutting the film in half is a real mistake,' commented John Powers in *LA Weekly*, saying that after seeing *Vol. 1* he felt 'cheated . . . not by what I'd seen but by what I hadn't'.

There was much speculation that the version of *Vol. 1* that was released was more than simply the first half of the film that Tarantino had originally been going to release; speculation that expanded when *Vol. 2* proved to be so very different to *Kill Bill – Vol. 1*. The speculation generally centred around the idea that the 'chapters' would have been arranged in an entirely different (albeit equally anti-chronological) order so as to create a film that was paced differently. All this speculation briskly disappeared when Tarantino's complete version turned out to be pretty much the two films joined together with minimal – indeed barely noticeable – alterations.

This isn't to say that the editing of *Kill Bill* as a project wasn't influenced by the decision to release it in separate volumes though. If released as one film it would have had to run around three hours. The 'complete' version runs at very nearly four. Releasing the film in two 'halves' enabled Tarantino to keep in shots, jokes and moments that would have been sacrificed had he simply cut the film to 180 minutes and put it out. He got to keep his 'grace notes' he commented; scenes he would have dropped or shortened (in *Vol. 2*) include Budd's hapless encounters with the other staff at the bar where he works and the Pai Mei flashback, which he estimated would have been cut by two-thirds of its length.

FINAL COMMENT: 'You didn't think it was going to be that easy, did you?' An epochal, masterful piece of filmmaking, a sort of Noah's Ark of pop culture clichés, archetypes and scenarios, all rendered with an astonishing beauty, *Kill Bill – Vol. 1* is a bit like being stylishly beaten around the head with an eclectic aesthete's video library. 'I'm giving you a revenge movie . . . no apologies,' said Tarantino on release, but the artistry of the man actually gets in the way of this ambition. Stanley Kubrick long speculated what it would be like to make a pornographic film with a fantastic film crew, the best actors of the day and the best script the best screenwriter could muster. Even if it kept the 'storytelling' conventions of pornography and descended into hardcore every fifteen minutes, surely the skills of those involved would make it distinct from standard 'top-shelf' exploitation material? *Kill Bill – Vol. 1* is, in a sense, like that. It's a film which is too lavish and beautiful to actually be that which it's aping, but which ends up as so much more as a result. In a similar way to how *Raiders of the Lost Ark* (Steven Spielberg, 1981) is actually vastly better than any of the serials it's based on, *Kill Bill* is too beautiful, too considered (and took far too long to make) to be an actual exploitation movie; it's like Andy Warhol's portrait of Superman turned into a film – and isn't that cliffhanger just astoundingly great?

Quentin Tarantino presents: My Name is Modesty: A Modesty Blaise Adventure

Tarantino's friend and collaborator Scott Spiegel (whom Tarantino credits with giving him 'the greatest gift of all, a career') shot a film based on Peter O'Donnell's Modesty Blaise character which went straight to DVD in 2003. The plot revolves around a hostage situation in a casino in Tangiers which prompts Modesty to reveal some of her past to her fellow hostages. Lee and Janet Scott Batchler's screenplay deliberately acts as a 'prequel' to all of O'Donnell's self-penned Modesty Blaise adventures, taking references to what the character's life was like *before* the Network and before meeting Willie Garvin. Alexandra Staden is a good match for Romero's original Modesty illustrations and gives an appealingly strong yet vulnerable performance. It's the most successful screen presentation of the beloved character to date, though this is perhaps somewhat less of an achievement given the tedious, joyless camp of Joseph Lodey's 1966 *Modesty Blaise*.

'In Shaw Scope'

Kill Bill – Vol. 1 begins with the 'Shaw Scope' logo. The familiar, Warner Bros-inspired 'badge' of the Shaw Brothers company opened many of the classic films made by and at the brothers' 'Movie Town' complex in Hong Kong. 'Movie Town' was 46 acres of purpose built movie studio in Clearwater, comprising no less than 12 sound stages, 16 standing backlot sets and countless cutting rooms, creative departments and film processing labs. The complex even had dormitories for employees who found themselves working too late to return home.

The Shaw Brothers were Tan Sri Dr Shaw (born 1901) and his younger brother Run Run (born 1907), entrepreneurs who eventually settled permanently in Hong Kong following the Communist takeover of mainland China.

Before World War Two they had owned more cinemas than anyone else in Asia (139 by 1939) having moved into movie theatre ownership via a sideways step from their original business as stagers of theatrical spectaculars, which they had begun while Run Run was still a teenager.

The Japanese invasion of Singapore (the surrender was 15 February 1942) should have posed a problem for the brothers' fortune – and indeed many of their portable assets, such as lighting equipment, were seized by the Imperial forces – but the brothers had simply converted their assets into gold and buried it. At the end of the war they dug it up and started again.

The free-market atmosphere of Hong Kong, as opposed to Nationalist post-war, pre-Long March China, was an attraction to the brothers, who set up 'Movie Town' on the British-administered island in 1957. As film fans and the 'hands on' operators of an increasingly vast chain of cinemas, the Shaws felt they knew what audiences would respond to. They were right.

The average Shaw Brothers picture cost five or six times what their nearest rivals were willing to pay out for a film; lavish production, impressive sets and proper feature-length motion pictures, running in excess of ninety minutes – most Chinese language films were then still, at most, around an hour in duration – saw them quickly establish their studio's logo as a brand of quality in the region. They also made their films in widescreen when most Chinese films were made in the television ratio of 4:3. The term 'Shaw Scope' was quickly coined.

The studio's output was colossal in terms of quantity – over forty films a year at their peak – and varied in terms of genre. Highly rated Shaw Brothers movies include the musicals *Qian Jiao bai mei (Les Belles)* (Qin Tao, 1961) and *Xiang Jiang hua Yue Ye (Hong Kong Nocture)* (Umj Inoue, 1966) and dramas like *Liang Shan bay u Zhu (Love Eterne)* (Han Hsiang Li, 1963) and *Yang Kwei Fei (The Magnificent Concubine)* (Han Hsiang Li, 1964).

Odd as it may seem from the perspective of the early twenty-first century, when the Shaw Brothers are best known for their contribution to martial arts cinema, until the mid-60s 'Shaw Brothers' was primarily thought of as the brand leader in what were called 'women's pictures'; a Chinese language studio-sized equivalent of the great Douglas Sirk, if you will.

The Shaw Brothers' cinemas still screened films produced by other companies and in other countries and it was the popularity of Japanese swordplay epics that led, in 1966, to Run Run Shaw commissioning *Da zui xia (Come Drink With Me)* (King Hu, 1966). While this still had a female lead (the beautiful Pei-pei Cheng) it was an action epic, a two-fisted fight-filled spectacular, which proved a massive success at the box office.

A sequel was commissioned but King had left Shaw and so the film was directed by Chang Cheh (1923–2002) instead. Cheh is the most important figure in the history of Hong Kong action movies – he discovered Bruce Lee. John Woo, who considers Cheh his 'mentor', says that Cheh encouraged him to become a personal artist. Woo fills his films with tribute's to his former teacher's style.

Paired with his screenwriter friend Ni Kuang, Cheh developed a muscular, aggressive, masculine style of action movie for the studio, making films about vengeance, honour and Chinese history with dynamic male leads and epic fight sequences. Stylistically he dabbled with the use of hand-held cameras, dolly shots and slow-motion effects and was openly influenced by American movies – he cited *Bonnie and Clyde* (Arthur Penn, 1967) and *The Wild Bunch* (Sam Peckinpah, 1969) as favourite American films – and Japanese production methods.

It was Cheh who pushed for the development of an entirely unarmed combat style fighting movie – creating what even a casual audience would recognise as a Kung Fu film in the process.

Kung Fu classics made for the Shaws by Cheh include *Fang Shiyu xing Hong Xiguan (Heroes Two)* in 1974 and *Sap saam taai bo (The Heroic Ones)* in 1970). Those made without him include *Mao Shan Jiang Shi quan (The Shadow Boxing)* (Chia-Liang Liu, 1979), a film which is credited as being the first comedy Kung Fu picture and thus the foundation of not only an entire subgenre but also the career of international superstar Jackie Chan.

Run Run Shaw was also involved in international co-productions including the Hammer Horror/Kung Fu crossover (and camp classic) *The Legend of the Seven Golden Vampires* (Roy Ward Baker, Cheh Chang, 1974) and Ridley Scott's SF masterpiece *Bladerunner* (1980).

The Shaw Brothers studio closed in 1983 after nearly four decades of continuous operation. Tan Sri Dr Shaw was by then 82 and Run Run was 76. Age and the desire to enjoy a retirement rather than artistic or business problems seems to have been the major factor in their decision to call it a day after so long in the business; certainly their fans would like to think so. (The last Kung Fu great from the studio was also perhaps the greatest – *Wu lang ba gua gun* (Eight Diagram Pole Fighter) (Chia-Liang Liu, 1983). Other late classics include *Wu Guan (Martial Club)* (Chia-Liang Liu, 1981).

Tan Sri Dr Shaw died in 1985. Run Run continues to administer the Shaw Brothers charity foundation to this day.

As a Hong Kong citizen Run Run was, indeed is, a British subject. He was knighted in recognition of his charity work; it is to be hoped that a sneaking admiration for the many artistic achievements of his studio, and the enjoyment they brought to millions, also played a part in his being awarded this honour.

Untitled Mandarin Kung Fu Project

While most of Tarantino's fans were certain that his next project after *Kill Bill* would be the much-delayed *Inglorious Bastards*, in November 2004 Tarantino spoke to the BBC and, in the process, disabused the public of this notion: 'Everyone still thinks I'm doing *Inglorious Bastards* next, but, before I do that, I want to do something much smaller,' he said. He went on to comment that shooting the Japanese language section of *Kill Bill* had inspired him so much that he intended to make another film in a foreign language, but this time entirely in a foreign language – '. . . this whole film will be entirely in Mandarin'. The idea for the picture was to make a Kung Fu action movie, one which could, in part, use up ideas for set-pieces that there had been no room for in either volume of *Kill Bill*, while paying renewed tribute to the influences of his childhood, especially the Shaw Brothers. Acknowledging the difficulty for American audiences with watching subtitled films he also announced that 'If you're not up to watching it with subtitles, I really want to do a full-on dubbed version.'

By early 2005 it seemed as if Tarantino's plan might have changed again. He was publicly discussing *Inglorious Bastards* more frequently than his untitled Mandarin Kung Fu project. However, by late March 2005, trade papers were reporting the casting of the Chinese-born actress/model Li Xin (who appeared in *Double Zéro* (Gerrard Pires, 2004) and martial arts hero Donnie Yen (who appeared in *Shanghai Knights* (David Dobkin, 2003) and *Blade II* (Guillermo Del Toro, 2002) in major roles and suggesting that shooting was due to begin in the summer of that year.

Officer of Arts and Letters

While serving in his capacity as President of the Jury at the Cannes Film Festival, Quentin Tarantino was presented with a civilian honour from the French government. He was handed the award, which made him an Officer of Arts and Letters, by French culture minister Renaud Donnedu at the same time as the minister also handed the award to director Milos Forman, who won an Oscar for *One Flew Over the Cuckoo's Nest* (1975). Standing next to Forman and the minister, Tarantino told a reporter that he was, unusually for him, 'speechless' at the honour. He told the, mostly French, audience about his love for France and French cinema, citing Jean-Pierre Melville as a particular influence. Melville (1917–73) had directed films such as *Bob Le Flambeur* [*Bob the Gambler*] (1955) and *Le Doulos* [*The Finger Man*] (1962) and left an indelible mark on world cinema. Melville's work, Tarantino felt, 'gave the impression that if you love movies you can't help but make a good one'. (Tarantino had already talked of his love of Melville since the early 1990s so there could be no question that he was simply playing to the crowd.) Talking of growing up poor in America, with no option to visit other countries, he explained how cinema had given him a love of other countries and cultures. Film was 'how I became a Francophile . . . going by going here . . . [because] I couldn't.'

Anti-Britain?

In May 2005 the British tabloid press had a minor field day by claiming that Quentin Tarantino was anti-British. This was due to some remarks he'd made at the beginning of the month at the press conference to publicise his role as President of the Jury at the Cannes Film Festival. In these largely non-inflammatory remarks Tarantino talked of how British films, and the British film industry as a whole, faced a very specific problem: 'As soon as people become stars in Britain they get out of there and go to Hollywood' he said. While he was specifically talking about actors, it's also worth considering that the same is arguably true of British film directors who 'come up' through UK television series (such as *Trainspotting*'s Danny Boyle) often taking (the usually higher-paying) jobs in America rather than choosing to work within the ever struggling industry producing homegrown British films. Tarantino did take the time to put his remarks in context, something those reporting his comments rarely did, by comparing British cinema to Indian and Hong Kong filmmaking. In each of those countries, as in America, a strong domestic film industry dominated by domestic talent provides the films that make the most money and are seen by the most people. In Britain, as a general rule, the films that make the most money are American, with the British Film Industry (and a lesser extent British television) feeding Hollywood ideas, actors, writers and directors in the way that American independent cinema does. One only has to look at the career paths of the stars of British hit *Bend it like Beckham* to see the truth in Tarantino's statement. Parminder Nagra went on to a regular starring role in top US TV drama *ER* while Keira Knightley achieved pin-up status and roles in Hollywood fare like *Pirates of the Caribbean: The Curse of the Black Pearl* (Gore Verbinksi, 2004). What Tarantino was arguing for was for the British film industry to try and act more like the cinemas of Asia in creating popular home-grown product. This is something it had once done, with the successful Hammer series of horror movies and popular, successful comedy series such as the *Carry On* range.

Any controversy over his remarks should have been ameliorated when a spokesman for the film-funding board, the UK Film Council, publicly agreed with much of what Tarantino had said. 'He said something which was absolutely true. Anyone in their right mind is going to go to Hollywood, because that's where the money is.' Tarantino's portrayal in the press must have been particularly infuriating for him, a director who has worked with British stars like Tim Roth, declared his love for British films like *Get Carter* (Mike Hodges, 1973) and even tried to persuade people that the *Carry On* films had merit: 'No-one ever said the *Carry On* movies were art but they were very funny.' While one cannot doubt his enthusiasm and sincerity, one might question his taste in comic pictures.

Vol. 2 (2004)

Miramax Films Presents
Vol. 2
A Film by Quentin Tarantino
Based on the character 'The Bride' created by Q & U
Edited by Sally Menke
Casting by Johanna Ray
Original Music by Robert Rodriguez and the RZA
Produced by Lawrence Bender
Executive Producers: Erica Steinberg, E Bennett Walsh,
Bob Weinstein, Harvey Weinstein
Director of Photography: Robert Richardson, CSA
Written and Directed by Quentin Tarantino

TAGLINES: Revenge is a dish best served cold.

The Bride is back for the final cut

This Spring, It's Not Over Till It's Over

Back With A Vengeance

Here comes The Bride

She will kill Bill

CAST: Uma Thurman (*Beatrix Kiddo*), David Carradine (*Bill*), Gordon Liu (*Pai Mei*), Michael Madsen (*Budd*), Daryl Hannah (*Elle Driver*), Michael Parks (*Esteban Vihaio*), Bo Svenson (*Reverend Harmony*), Jeannie Epper (*Mrs Harmony*), Stephanie L Moore (*Joleen*), Shana Stein (*Erica*), Caitlin Keats (*Janeen*), Chris Nelson (*Tommy Plympton*), Samuel L Jackson (*Rufus*), Reda Beebe (*Lucky*), Sid Haig (*Jay*), Larry Bishop (*Larry Gomez*), Laura Cayouette (*Rocket*), Clark Middleton (*Ernie*), Claire Smithies (*Clarita*), Perla Haney-Jardine (*BB*), Helen Kim (*Karen Kim*), Venessia Valentino (*1st Grade Teacher*), Thea Rose (*Melanie Harrhouse*), William P Clark (*Soda Jerk*), Vicki Lucai (*Trixie*), Stevo Polyi (*Tim*), Al Manuel Douglas (*Marty

Kitrosser), Jorge Silva (*Bartender/Pimp*), Patricia Silva (*Hooker #1*), Maria Del Rosario Gutiérrez (*Hooker #2*), Sonia Angelica Padilla Curiel (*Hooker #3*),Veronica Janet Martinez (*Hooker #4*), Lucia Cruz Marroquin (*Hooker #5*), Citlati Guadalupe Bojorquez (*Hooker #6*), Graciela Salazar Mendoza (*Hooker #7*), Maria de Lourdes Lombera (*Hooker #8*)

SUMMARY: The Bride tracks down Bill, fighting her way through the squabbling and scared remnants of the Deadly Viper Assassination Squad in the process. Elle Driver kills Budd, meaning that The Bride doesn't have to and The Bride spares Elle's life, though she blinds her after she discovers that Elle killed her old master Pai Mei. On discovering that her daughter is still alive, The Bride initially talks to, rather than fights, Bill – they discuss their relative perspectives on his betrayal of her and her betrayal of him. The Bride kills Bill and leaves for a new life with their daughter.

QUOTES:

Beatrix: 'I roared and I rampaged and I got bloody satisfaction. I've killed a hell of a lot of people to get to this point . . . and when I arrive at my destination I am gonna kill Bill.'

Bill: 'I've never been nice my whole life, but I'll do my best to be sweet.'

Bill: 'You hocked a Hattori Hanzo sword? It was priceless.'
Budd: 'Not in El Paso, it ain't. In El Paso I got me $250 for it.'

Bill: 'There are consequences to breaking the heart of a murdering bastard . . . was my reaction really that surprising?'

Bill: 'I am truly and utterly incapable of believing anything you say.'

SCREENPLAY: As with *Kill Bill – Vol. 1*, *Vol. 2* has a non-chronological structure. This is the order the events are shown in the film:

Introduction by The Bride
Chapter Six – Massacre at Two Pines
Interlude (Budd and Bill)
Chapter Seven – The Lonely Grave of Paula Schultz
Chapter Eight – The Cruel Tutelage of Pai Mei
Interlude (The Bride rises from the Grave)
Chapter Nine – Elle and I
Last Chapter – Face to Face

In chronological order they would run:

Chapter Eight – The Cruel Tutelage of Pai Mei
Chapter Six – Massacre at Two Pines
Interlude (Budd and Bill)
Chapter Seven – The Lonely Grave of Paula Schultz
Interlude (The Bride rises from the Grave)
Chapter Nine – Elle and I
Introduction by The Bride
Last Chapter – Face to Face

This is essentially correct, although 'Last Chapter – Face to Face' contains a flashback that occurs between Chapter Eight and Chapter Six chronologically speaking. If interspersed with *Vol. 1*, so that the whole film happens in chronological order, it would go:

Chapter Three – The Origin of O-Ren Ishi
Chapter Eight – The Cruel Tutelage of Pai Mei
Chapter Six – Massacre at Two Pines
Prologue ('My Baby Shot Me Down')
Chapter Two – The blood-splattered BRIDE
Interlude (The Bride wakes up)
Chapter Four – The MAN from OKINAWA
Chapter Five – Showdown at the House of Blue Leaves
Epilogue ('Soon be as dead as O-Ren')

Chapter One (2)
Interlude (Budd and Bill)
Chapter Seven – The Lonely Grave of Paula Schultz
Interlude (The Bride rises from the Grave)
Chapter Nine – Elle and I
Introduction by The Bride
Last Chapter – Face to Face

Got that? Good.

During production, what would have been an additional chapter, 'Yukie's Revenge', was cut from the script and subsequently went unfilmed. This would have featured the character of Yukie Yubari, the sister of *Kill Bill – Vol. 1*'s Gogo Yubari coming after The Bride in order to revenge her sister's death. Some reports have indicated that Yukie was originally to appear in *Vol. 1* as well, sharing her sister's dialogue and plot function in the scene set as the House of the Blue Leaves. When 'Yukie's Revenge' was removed, all of her relevant dialogue was handed over to the character of Gogo and incorporated into hers. It has been suggested that the 'Pussy Wagon', which The Bride steals from Buck in *Vol. 1*, would have been destroyed in this sequence, hence The Bride no longer having it with her in *Vol. 2*. (The only explanation offered in the finished film is 'My Pussy Wagon died on me'.)

Another change made to the script during production was to shift the location of where Bill relates stories about Pai Mei to The Bride. As scripted, this was to take place in their Jeep as they journey to Pai Mei; rewrites set the scene around a campfire with Bill telling the story in a less instructive (or even cautionary) way, relaying the tale in a more indulgent manner. It's a key scene because it softens Bill in the audience's mind. The scene is warm and the two characters seem happy and contented with one another's company in a way that isn't easily achievable if they're both seated in a moving vehicle (in which case, with one of them driving, it's not as if they could look at each other).

There has been much discussion of a version of the final scene which, rather than a brief, seated sword duel between Bill and The Bride, was the dawn fight on a vast wide beach that Bill proposes. No one involved has verified this, however, and it would seem odd if the bathetic ending of the film as shot wasn't what was always planned, as it's so very apt. Earlier drafts of the screenplay had The Bride kill Elle Driver rather than merely blinding her.

Additionally, Bill's truth serum – 'The undisputed truth' – was originally scripted as appearing in *Vol. 1*, with Bill using it on Sophie Fatale.

What is most interesting about the script to *Vol. 2* is that, whereas *Kill Bill – Vol. 1* is powerfully vacuous, a rollercoaster of sensations and adrenaline rushes with little or no emotional context (or a context that isn't noticeable because there's not enough of it to outweigh the spectacular action going on), *Vol. 2* is a film which consists almost entirely of that kind of context.

More than that, though, *Vol. 2* recontextualises and deconstructs *Kill Bill – Vol. 1*, forcing an audience to reassess and re-evaluate much of the earlier film by providing new information about things the audience already think they know or understand.

What makes it certain that this is a deliberate conceit is that this approach carries over to even some of the smallest aspects of the production, indicating a confluence of approach on a macro and micro level. Examples of the latter include, say, Bill's revelation to Budd that there weren't actually 88 people in the 'Crazy 88', that they just called themselves that because 'it sounded cool'. Though a small example, it is a recontextualisation and subversion of what the audience were told in the previous film. Another example is the Hattori Hanzo sword: in *Vol. 1* this is an object of utter reverence; in *Vol. 2* Budd jokes about pawning one for a measly $250, a mockery unthinkable in *Vol. 1*. The audience also sees one of Budd's lines from *Vol. 1* in a different context: in *Vol. 1* his line 'That woman deserves her revenge, and the audience deserve to die' is given enormous weight. It's one of the last lines in the film and leads the audience to believe that Budd is a wistful, weighty figure. In *Vol. 2* the audience sees this scene again and sees that he grins immediately afterwards, then quips 'Mind you, so does she' – at that point, the audience realises that he's a cunning, corpulent yob. (In *Vol. 1* the audience are never told that Budd is Bill's brother either, this revelation waits until *Vol. 2*.)

The way the film does this in a larger sense is that *Vol. 2* demonstrates things that *Vol. 1* often chose to ignore – that every act of violence has repercussions. Bill even says those exact words. The biggest, most important way this is expressed is through Bill's real regret at what he did to Beatrix when he tried to kill her on her wedding day. As he says to their daughter, 'I was very sad . . . and that's when I learned: some things, once you do, they could never be undone.' This makes his refusal to let Elle Driver kill The Bride in *Vol. 1* a part of that regret, and his statement that The Bride 'deserves better' emerges as an excuse his minion will accept.

Vol. 2 is where the audience discovers Bill as a character. They are told that 'like most men who never knew their fathers . . . Bill collected father figures', and are then introduced to Esteban, the first of Bill's father figures. This not only assists in their understanding of him (he grew up in a brothel, the fatherless son of a prostitute raised by her pimp), it also contextualises him in a way he wasn't before, and changes the way the audience regard his relationships with his two teachers they have already seen, Hattori Hanzo and Pai Mei. (There's a smart exchange between Bill and Beatrix on this topic towards the end. 'How is Hanzo-san?' he asks. 'He's good,' she replies, meaning both that he's well but also that he is morally good . . . and Bill's not.)

The tale Bill tells of Pai Mei is interesting in and of itself and also as a reflection on him. It's a vile story: the story of how Pai Mei demanded the slaughter of hundreds of Shaolin monks because it was possible, although not certain, that one of their number had disrespected him by not returning the cursory nod he had given him when walking past him in the street. The story is filled to the brim with the ludicrous concept of absolute respect and firmly establishes Pai Mei as a fundamentally unreasonable person. His punishing of an accident which may or may not have happened, and the grotesquely disproportionate nature of the punishment he demands is basically the insane action of an evil, bloodthirsty man, disguised as a story about 'respect'. What is interesting is that Bill approves of these unconscionable actions.

This reflects on Bill's own actions towards Beatrix after she runs away while pregnant. These are events that the audience have already seen, but which, when Bill relates the story, haven't happened to him yet. The following massacre at the wedding chapel rehearsal is also a vile, disproportionate reaction to a perceived insult/injustice. It's clear which of his teachers, out of the dignified and noble Hattori Hanzo and wilful, cackling and cruel Pai Mei ('I kill at will!'), Bill got his moral sense from.

There is another parallel with Bill and Pai Mei. When Bill says of Pai Mei that, 'like all rotten bastards', he became lonely when he got old, the audience will obviously think of the older Bill, lonely after the disintegration of his Deadly Viper Assassination Squad. This is especially relevant as it is Bill's out-of-proportion act of revenge (the massacre in El Paso) that leads to that disintegration of the Deadly Viper Assassination Squad and Bill ending up old and lonely. The lesson Bill took from Pai Mei is the wrong one, and it leads to him ending up in the same situation. They are also both murdered by a woman they abused beyond endurance.

The idea that the massacre in El Paso is what caused the collapse of the DiVAS is worth more examination because it isn't stated outright in *Vol. 2* that this is the case. It is instead left for the audience to work out, although there's plenty of evidence to make it a clear 'fictional fact'. Budd, the only one of the DiVAS who expresses any regret at what happened in El Paso, has never left there, living as trailer trash and working as a bouncer. He is 'still mad' at his brother Bill for an unspecified reason, one which the audience can assume is related to the slaughter in the wedding chapel. At the time of the massacre, Vernita Green is either pregnant or already a mother (see **VERNITA GREEN'S BABY**) and she clearly leaves Bill's employ shortly afterwards. From *Vol. 1* the audience learn that, less than a year after the massacre, O-Ren Ishii had become the head of the Japanese Yakuza. By the actual 'present' timeframe of the film, Bill is relying on Elle Driver alone to carry out his wishes and is living in seclusion with BB.

Perhaps the most important context that *Vol. 2* provides to *Vol. 1* is very simple: it gives the audience a context for Bill's actions in El Paso. He tells The Bride that he thought she was dead and that he was hunting the people who he thought killed her, not her. This changes the audience's angle on Bill and their general impression of him. He still did the terrible things he did, but the different perception of his reasons shifts the audience's feelings about him, as does the clear demonstration that he's a loving and affectionate father to BB.

Bill's own use of language continues to be very precisely monitored by Tarantino. Bill spells out the word 'job' as 'Jay Oh Bee' like he's a child spelling out swearwords. It's a reflection of his contempt for 'normal' people. He's very picky about The Bride's playful use of the word 'promise' in connection with him, when he himself never said it. Bill's also selfish enough to lack self-awareness at times; he condemns The Bride for letting him think she was dead when she was alive as 'quite cruel'; he's seemingly unaware or unconcerned as he says this that, by letting The Bride think that her daughter was dead, he is equally as guilty of this as she is.

Whereas *Vol. 1* has an action movie structure to go with its action movie sequences, the opening of *Vol. 2* is very,

very slow and, except for the peak of the fight between Elle Driver and The Bride, it never really picks up pace. It's a slow, talky contemplative film, punctuated by occasional acts of brief violence.

This leaves less space for Tarantino's characteristic reversals, but there are a few. The snake leaping out of the suitcase at Budd is one; Bill pulling a gun on Beatrix and shooting her with a dart is another.

Tarantino does, however, use the non-chronological structure to build tension. The sheer dread of the conversation in the chapel that led up to a massacre – that the audience knows is inevitable but the characters don't expect – is horrifying (the moment when it's suggested it's bad luck to see a Bride in her dress before the wedding is *horrifying*). The position of the Pai Mei flashback provides a 'sensible' (OK, plausible) way for The Bride to escape from being buried alive. This is not dissimilar to how Republic serials would insert whole scenes to explain how someone escaped a cliffhanger ending. This also happens between *Frankenstein* (James Whale, 1931) and *The Bride of Frankenstein* (James Whale, 1933). This positioning is, of course, an example of the recontextualisation that is absolutely at the centre of the way that this script unfolds.

CASTING: Several characters who did not appear in *Vol. 1* are featured in *Vol. 2*, while others who have minor roles in *Vol. 1* feature in *Vol. 2* more strongly. Pai Mei, the Master who teaches The Bride, was originally to be played by Yuen Wo-Ping (Master Woo Ping) and Tarantino reported his casting as fact to the BBC in an interview. It was his intention that Master Woo-Ping, who choreographed the 'chinese' action film, should also play this sizeable speaking part, much as Sonny Chiba has both been responsible for the look of the samurai action and taken/reprised (it really depends on how you want to see it) the part of Hattori Hanzo.

Gordon Liu, who had already played Johnny Mo in *Vol. 1* was cast instead, although Tarantino briefly considered playing the role himself. Tarantino's friend, Oscar nominee and Jedi Master Samuel L Jackson, cameos as 'Rufus', the piano player in the 'El Paso Massacre' flashback. It's a much smaller role than one would these days associate with an actor of Jackson's fame and calibre. Michael Madsen (Budd) had been in *Reservoir Dogs*, and *Vol. 2* gives him his best screen time since that picture. Christopher Alan Nelson, who makes a remarkable impression in such a short time as The Bride's beau Tommy, is actually make-up artist and occasional actor Chris Nelson, whose credits in the former capacity include *Austin Powers in Goldmember* (Jay Roach, 2002). Tarantino favourite, exploitation movie legend and *Jackie Brown*-featured player Sid Haig appears as a bartender. Michael Parks, who reprised *From Dusk Till Dawn*'s Earl McGraw in *Kill Bill – Vol. 1* plays a completely different character, the pimp Esteban, in *Vol. 2*. It's a marvellous demonstration of his versatility. Like Gordon Liu he receives two photo/caption cards in the long versions, one featuring each role, almost as if the director is daring the audience to notice. Perla Haney-Jardine, who makes such an impression as Bill and The Bride's daughter BB, has since appeared in the Walter Salles-directed American remake of Hideo Nakata's *Dark Water* (which is probably the scariest film ever).

KEY SHOTS: The whole of the first fifteen minutes of *Vol. 2* are in black and white. The beautiful silvers and blacks of the photography bely the fact that the sequences were shot on colour film and then merely developed as black and white rather than shot on actual black and white stock. When making *Ed Wood* in 1993 Tim Burton insisted that Disney, the studio ultimately making the film, pay out for the actual black and white stock (black and white stock is, perhaps counter-intuitively, more expensive than colour film these days and has become a specialist trade) because he refused to countenance shooting in colour and then developing black and white because of the differences in lighting. What

Burton was unprepared to attempt, Tarantino pulls off with aplomb. To call these scenes pseudo-expressionist (the style preferred by most people who shoot black and white film for vanity these days) would be wrong, even given the sharp, beautiful contrasts in the monochrome. They lack the shadows and odd angles associated with the form and are instead – especially in exterior scenes – reminiscent of the classic deep-shot westerns of the 40s (think *My Darling Clementine* (John Ford, 1946)).

Inside the chapel the palette is grey rather than intensely silver and black, reflecting the lack of light. Tarantino gets great tension out of shooting lots of point-of-view shots. For example, the audience sees the Reverend and Mrs Harmony as The Bride would, and then The Bride as the Reverend and Mrs Harmony would. Tarantino plays his old trick of not establishing how many characters there are in a scene by avoiding the traditional wide shot and allows Samuel L Jackson's Rufus to become a sudden presence in the picture.

Rufus is often shot from the right, resulting in shots of Jackson's strong right profile dominating the screen. The massacre, like most of the deaths in the movie, takes place off screen *after*, rather than during, one of Tarantino's most impressive long takes. This starts in the chapel during a conversation and pulls back outwards through the chapel door (the audience see the DiVAS standing there, but only from the back) before the camera lifts into the sky on a crane and the massacre is then completed using only sound effects. Similar in its chilling tenor to the killing of Beaumont in *Jackie Brown*, the scene demonstrates a use for the 'long take' which is neither showy nor possibly designed to save film and editing time by avoiding cutting, but instead simply achieves a dramatic purpose not achievable in any other way. (Tarantino has of course often used long takes to allow actors' performances to build and 'breathe' as they would on stage.)

Once the film switches into colour, the landscape of El Paso takes on the smoking gold and brown pallor of the landscapes of a classic studio western, with The Bride emerging out of the smoke and dust out of focus like Henry Fonda in *Once Upon a Time In The West* (Sergio Leone, 1968) and limping away from Budd's trailer like John Wayne in *The Searchers* (John Ford, 1956). As Bill and Budd talk, the number of cuts increases, but the film never becomes 'fast cutting'; it's just that the takes are generally shorter. This makes the conversation more straightforwardly tense.

In a neat bit of directorial *legerdemain* Tarantino switches from the film's usual widescreen ratio to the TV ratio of 4:3 when The Bride is buried alive. He disguises this switch by having the screen go black as the coffin lid is closed. The effect is to make the scene become deeply claustrophobic. The former effect continues this process, something the laboured breathing of Uma Thurman and the crunching noise of the sound effects assist with greatly.

The Pei Mai flashback is shot in a bleached out, flatly lit manner that recalls the slightly faded prints of chop-socky movies that tend to be shown in rep cinemas or on television. The alarming sound-effects, wide shots and recurrent close-ups are all borrowed from the kind of film being pastiched, making this section feel like it's clipped out of another film entirely.

Perhaps Tarantino's most dramatic achievement in the direction of *Vol. 2* is the almost insanely and mythic, colour-drenched, heroic way he shoots Bill's death. It's an old man walking slowly across some grass in the dark (and on a sound stage to boot) and then stumbling over; yet the audience buys it. It works. It's even exciting. Bravo.

VERNITA GREEN'S BABY: Nikki Green, Vernita Green's daughter, says that she's four years old but, as she arrives home from school on a state yellow bus, she must actually be nearer her fifth birthday than her fourth (children are taken into the American state school system when 'rising five'). At the point that she kills Vernita Green, The Bride hasn't seen her for four years and six months i.e. it is that long since the massacre the audience sees in *Vol. 2*. This probably means that Nikki was born before Vernita took part in the massacre in El Paso and Vernita was pregnant when The Bride fled the DiVAS. This means that The Bride is wrong when she says that Vernita got 'knocked up . . . in the past four years' and that Vernita's pregnancy was a secret, at least from The Bride and possibly from some of the rest of the squad too. (It is more than possible for a woman not to be 'visibly' pregnant until late on in the pregnancy after all.)

This doesn't undercut The Bride's choice to foreswear her life of danger and excitement and murder on discovering she's pregnant; it illustrates that, while it is something that she feels compelled to do, the compulsion and the decision are entirely her own, as another pregnant woman in exactly the same situation didn't feel compelled to do the same thing. If Nikki is not nearer five than four when Vernita is killed – even if she is *exactly* four years old – then Vernita was three months pregnant during the massacre at the El Paso wedding chapel, as far along as The Bride was in fact. In terms of its impact on the films themes and characters, it has exactly the same effect.

SUPERMAN: Bill is (and this is the crux of the film for many) fundamentally wrong in his analysis of Superman as a character. Bill argues that Superman is different from all other superheroes in that he does not have a secret identity. He really is Superman and Clark Kent is who he pretends to be during the day. Whereas The Flash is really Wally West, Green Lantern is truly John Stewart and Batman is *really* Bruce Wayne (and this last example, which Bill himself does use, is itself an arguable point, incidentally), Clark Kent is really Superman, it's Kent, not Superman who is the mask. This is not so.

'Clark Kent is who I am, Superman is what I do' is a sentence John Byrne – perhaps the most influential writer of

Superman stories other than the character's creator Jerry Siegel – wrote for the character to say; and it's the most accurate rendition of the character's essential self. While Superman is an alien he was raised on a farm by two farmers in a small town in Kansas. They may not be his biological ancestors, but Superman's parents are Jonathan and Martha Kent: Ma and Pa.

Superman is a lot of things as a character. Partially he's a Messianic figure created by two Jewish cartoonists at a time of profound anti-Semitism both far away in Europe and at home in America. Partially he's a reflection of the American immigrant experience – he wasn't born in America, he came to America as an infant, but he's as American as something can be. (Interestingly *Superman* writer/editor Mort Weisenger went further in his use of the idea of Superman as an immigrant – he used the results of psychoanalysis and counselling sessions in which he himself participated as raw material to create new elements for the *Superman* stories. These include some of the most enduring aspects of the mythos, including the Bizarro Superman, Kryptonite and the bottle city of Kandor.)

This may sound like I'm over-egging the point, but the truth of the matter is this: Bill is wrong about Superman and, if he's wrong about Superman, then the analogy he goes on to make between Clark Kent and Beatrix Kiddo – Superman and Black Mamba – is also, very simply, *exactly* wrong.

It could not be *more* wrong, and this is very interesting in terms of what it tells us about Bill as a character. Bill doesn't understand Superman and through his failing analogy he also shows that he doesn't understand The Bride. For Bill, Superman is a superior creature above the rules that 'guide' ordinary people, and 'Clark Kent is Superman's critique on the whole human race' in that he's weak and cowardly and inept. Well, no, he just isn't.

Bill sees him this way because he sees himself as superior to those around him and cares nothing for their wants and needs. How could he run a death squad if it were otherwise?

How could he have failed to notice that Superman doesn't kill? It is this selfishness that makes Bill incapable of understanding a character as fundamentally selfless as Clark Kent.

Ultimately it is this, rather than his actions, that reveals a very simple thing: Bill is a villain. He's not a bad man because he doesn't understand Superman, but he doesn't understand Superman because he is a bad man.

MUSICAL NOTES: The Robert Rodriguez track that closes the film is disappointing, unmemorable and generic and doesn't quite provide the rousing musical send-off the movie deserves. Elsewhere there are signs of life but there's nothing as astoundingly surprising as the Santa Esmerelda track used in *Vol. 1*. Well, not quite (the use of Issac Hayes' 'Three Tough Guys' as The Bride fights Pai Mei comes close).

The use of Ennio Morricone's music from lesser-known spaghetti westerns such as *Un Dollaro A Testa* (aka *Navajo Joe*) (Sergio Corbucci, 1966) and *Mercenario* (Sergio Corbucci, 1968), as well as the more iconic, Sergio Leone-directed westerns like *Per Un Pugano di Dollari* (1964) helps create the atmosphere of a revisionist Western without ever straying into tracks that would be instantly familiar to a casual moviegoer (except maybe the drift into 'Il Tramonto', a piece from *Il Buono Il Brutto Il Cattivo* (1966) as Bill and Budd talk). The most impressive use of Morricone is probably the refrain from *Mercenario,* which is used as The Bride escapes her coffin; either that or Bill dying to the theme from *Un Dollaro A Testa*. Both scenes achieve an odd combination of empowerment and release from the use of these ambiguously, sentimentally epic pieces of Morricone score.

It's not all western music though: the main theme from kung-fu pole-fighting classic *Wu lang ba gua gun* (Chia-Liang Liu, 1983) is used while The Bride is trained by Pai Mei (*Wu lang ba gua gun* starred Gordon Liu, who plays Pai Mei).

The most interesting and evocative use of a piece of music in the movie is the use of Malcolm McLaren's trip-hop 'About Her', a record that uses so much of the Zombies' 'She's Not There' (written by Rod Argent) that most people hearing it are likely to assume it's a cover version of it rather than a separate record. The words of Argent's song echo The Bride's story uncannily – the basic refrain 'No one told me about her' obviously refers to her daughter BB; while 'It's too late to say I'm sorry, how could I know, why should I care?' clearly makes the audience think of all the people that The Bride has killed, partially because she believes that her daughter died in the massacre at El Paso and never had the chance to be born. It also references the lack of regret she experiences, knowing that O-Ren, Budd and Vivica deserved to die anyway. Most impressive is the recontextualisation of the lyric 'the way she lies'. In Argent's song this refers to a woman who is not telling the truth; in the film it plays while The Bride looks at her comfortably sleeping daughter. No one told her what her daughter looked like while sleeping, the lyric seems to say. It's remarkably affecting. As a cap to the story it's as appropriate as 'Bang Bang (My Baby Shot Me Down)' is as an opener.

CRITICAL REACTION: 'Tarantino knocks it out of the park . . . You watch and think, "I get it now" ' wrote Peter Travers in *Rolling Stone*. He had particular praise for how 'the actors hold their own against the flying swords and fists of fury', with Michael Madsen in particular 'killer good', while Thurman gave 'an electrifying performance that busts your chops and breaks your heart with no mercy'. '*Vol. 2* is not exactly a zephyr breeze but it's pretty sotto voce' wrote J Hoberman in the *Village Voice*. He felt the need to emphasise the difference between *Vol. 1* and *Vol. 2*, saying that one should call *Vol. 2* 'the ethereal yin to *Vol. 1*'s visceral yang'. As a whole, *Kill Bill* was 'one wacky magnificent assemblage'. Tarantino's great admirer, Roger Ebert, was also happy. 'An exuberant celebration of moviemaking', he wrote, 'a masterful saga . . . Tarantino remains the most brilliantly oddball filmmaker of his generation . . . one of the best films of the year'.

VOL. 3?: In the run up to the release of *Vol. 2* Tarantino was asked more than once if there would be a *Vol 3*. It's a natural enough question in a cinematic world increasingly dominated by sequels, prequels and serial films. On separate occasions he quoted three possible follow-ups to *Vol. 2*, two of which were prequels and the third a sequel. The sequel would be a live-action film he'd make at some point in the distant future, but the star of it wouldn't be Beatrix Kiddo: 'the star will be Vernita's daughter, Nikki'. When pushed for further details, he revealed that Sophie Fatale (Julie Dreyfuss's character from *Vol. 1*) would inherit '. . . all of Bill's money. She'll raise Nikki, who'll take on The Bride'. The two prequels would be animé films devoted to the backstories of the Deadly Viper Assassination Squad.

SPURIOUS INTERTEXTUALITY: Pai Mei, who becomes Beatrix's cruel master but who teaches her the 'five point palm exploding heart technique' is a character who appears in numerous films made at the Shaw Brothers studios – notably *Hung Wen Tin San po Pai Lien Chiao* (Lieh Lo, 1980) in which he is the villain. Chapter Seven is 'The Lonely Grave of Paula Schultz'; there's a 1968 comedy called *The Wicked Dreams of Paula Schultz* in which one of the major characters is called Bill. *Kill Bill*'s Bill, like David Carradine's character of Caine in *Kung-Fu*, plays a wooden flute – a suspiciously familiar one, in fact. As she thrashes around blind, Darryl Hannah seems to be doing her best to ape the death scene she performed in *Blade Runner* (Ridley Scott, 1982). *The Road to Salina* is mentioned – that's also the title of a Rita Hayworth movie. 'If he's the man you want then go stand by him' says Bill, obviously referencing the song made famous by Tammy Wynette. He also deadpans, when asked 'When will I see you again?' by The

Bride, that that is the title of his favourite soul song of the 70s. Larry refers to an 'asshole right here' while pointing to his elbow. Something very similar is said in Bret Easton Ellis's *The Rules of Attraction*, made into a terrific 2002 film by Roger Avary, a pre-fame friend of Tarantino's. Budd drinks Oak Ridge Coffee; Oak Ridge is a town near Tarantino's birthplace of Knoxville, Tennessee. Bill uses the phrase 'natural born killer' to describe The Bride, which is obviously the title of a previous Tarantino script. Tarantino's invented brand Red Apple cigarettes are visible on the table when Beatrix sits down to talk to Esteban. It seems more than probable that the gorgeous eyepatched killer Elle Driver is based on Patch from *Switchblade Sisters* (Jack Hill, 1974). Bill also says, 'So, swordfighter, if you want to swordfight . . .' which has the same rhythm as Joe Cabot and Seth Gecko's 'Okay, ramblers, let's get rambling . . .' Right at the very end of the film, BB is watching a cartoon in which a character is heard to intone, 'the magpie deserves your respect'. Is this a bit of self-referencing from Tarantino, so often accused of being a filmic pasticher, cannibal, magpie? If so, then the only sensible response must be 'Yes, yes he does.'

THE NUMBERS: Released on 16 April 2004 in the US *Vol. 2* took $25,104,949, after release to 2,971 screens. In the UK it opened four days later, where it took £2.7 million on 411 screens. Its final US take was just over $66 million.

FINAL COMMENT: 'Just long enough for me to finish my point.' *Vol. 2* divides audiences almost equally. There are those who claim it as a masterpiece and those who miss the fast-paced trash aesthetic and endless violence of the first part. Some people who loved *Vol. 1* dislike *Vol. 2* and vice versa; this is because *Vol. 2* is so different to its predecessor. It's slow, it's talky. There are few action scenes and much sitting around. The diametrically opposite things are true of the first film. The primary difference, though, is of emotional content. Whereas *Kill Bill – Vol. 1* is a rollercoaster of adrenaline rushes with little or no emotional context, *Vol. 2* consists almost entirely of that kind of context. *Vol. 2* recontextualises and deconstructs *Kill Bill – Vol. 1,* forcing an audience to reassess and re-evaluate so much of the earlier film. That the entire audience knows, about five seconds before it happens, that Beatrix's face is going to appear underneath a caption card saying 'Mommy' is the clearest possible indication of the real human beauty at the centre of this half of The Bride's story. *Kill Bill* really does work better as two instalments – perhaps fate was on Tarantino's side.

Casino Royale

While serving as the president of the jury at the Cannes Film Festival in 2004 Quentin Tarantino expressed the desire, also previously expressed by Steven Spielberg, to direct a film in Eon's James Bond series. Tarantino had bumped into Bond star Pierce Brosnan at the festival and the two had begun talking about the possibility. 'I've always wanted to do it,' Tarantino told the BBC on 16 May that year. He went to explain that ideally he'd like to direct a straight adaptation of Ian Fleming's first Bond novel *Casino Royale* which was published in 1954. An adaptation of the book had been made for TV in 1954 and a spoof version shot by Charles K Feldman's company in 1967 but it had never been made as part of the official Bond series. After Eon, the producers of the Bond series which began with 1962's *Dr No* acquired the film rights to the novel – until then the only Bond novel they didn't already own the screen rights to. Pierce Brosnan had repeatedly publically expressed a desire to play Bond in an adaptation of it, perhaps because he was conscious that of all the actors to play James Bond he was the only one who had never had the opportunity to play the character in a story penned by his creator. While *Casino Royale* is a much smaller-scale story than people more familiar with the screen than the page Bond would expect, Tarantino was still certain it was possible to make a film of the book that would be entirely faithful to the source material saying he'd 'do it more or less the way the Ian Fleming book is' and that he'd be contacting the Bond film copyright holders to let them 'know I'm interested'. Whether Tarantino did contact Eon or not isn't known, but on 4 February 2005 Eon announced that the next James Bond film, scheduled to be released in 2006, would indeed be *Casino Royale*. Tarantino would not be involved in the project, with the screenplay coming from regular Bond writers Neal Purvis and Robert Wade and the hired director being Martin Campbell (who had previously directed the 1995 Bond film *GoldenEye*).

Inglorious Bastards

A World War Two epic, *Inglorious Bastards* was the film that Tarantino set aside in order to make both volumes of *Kill Bill*. Although reports in 2001 led people to believe that the film's screenplay was already complete, Tarantino told reporters in March 2005 that this was not, in fact, the case at all. He said, 'I've written *scenes*. I've written a lot of it but now I have to sit down and start putting it together in a script that I can start shooting. And that's a different thing.'

The basic idea for the film, as suggested in interviews, is that it should be a war film in the same mould as *The Dirty Dozen* (Robert Aldrich, 1967) or one of its (less-impressive) sequels or imitators. *The Dirty Dozen* concerns a US Army Major Reisman (Lee Marvin) who is assigned to train a dozen convicted murderers to kill Nazi officers during World War Two. Tarantino has intimated that *Inglorious Bastards* will star Michael Madsen in the similar role of 'Babe' Buchinsky (Buchinsky being Charles Bronson's real name) and has called the planned film 'an epic', saying 'More so even than *Kill Bill* – it will be my true spaghetti western-influenced film, but set in Nazi-occupied France instead of the Old West. I see it as a time when you had these no-man's lands in Europe that really did resemble the western landscapes of Sergio Leone.' Little else is known about the film, but Tarantino has suggested that he has written a part for former *Saturday Night Live* star Adam Sandler, whom he worked with on the film *Little Nicky* (Steven Brill, 2000). He has also confirmed that *Vol. 2*'s Bo Svenson will feature. Svenson also appeared in a 1977 Italian film called *Quel maledetto treno blindato*, the title of which is often given as both *Deadly Mission* and *Inglorious Bastards* when distributed in the United States and other English-speaking countries. This *Inglorious Bastards* was directed by Enzo G Castellari and was also a World War Two movie about convicts fighting Nazis, although Tarantino has made clear that his *Inglorious Bastards* film is not a remake of Castellari's.

Friday the 13th Part 12?

In early March 2005 reports appeared in usually reliable American trade publications such as the *Hollywood Reporter* (9 March 2005) that Tarantino was in negotiations to direct – and perhaps also write – the twelfth or thirteenth instalment in the *Friday the 13th* slasher horror movie series. This series had debuted with some style with *Friday the 13th* (Sean S Cunningham, 1980) and continued well with *Friday the 13th Part 2* (Steve Miner, 1982) but had quickly faltered, with *Friday the 13th Part VIII: Jason Takes Manhattan* (Steve Hebben, 1989) being a notoriously poor example of the series (and indeed genre) of which it was a part. This was especially frustrating considering the fact that the original *Friday* film, built around effects wizard Tom Savini's gory set-pieces, effectively created that genre. (Savini, of course, appeared in Tarantino's *From Dusk Till Dawn* and both its sequel and prequel.)

The *Friday* series initially concerned a series of murders being carried out at Camp Crystal Lake with a group of teens being menaced and slaughtered by a killer who turned out to be a middle-aged lady with a grudge, although later instalments moved further afield both in terms of setting and in terms of the kind of horror story they were. The sequels concentrated on the more supernatural figure of Ma Voorhees' dead, re-animated son, Jason – the assumed, ostensible killer in the original film before the twist conclusion (and further twist).

The series rallied creatively in the early 1990s with the excellent *Friday the 13th Part IX: Jason Goes to Hell: The Final Friday* (Adam Marcus, 1993) but a further film in the series would not be made for nearly a decade. *Jason X* (James Isaac, 2001) kick-started the series again financially and creatively and led to the hugely enjoyable, and long-mooted, *A Nightmare on Elm Street* (Wes Craven, 1983) crossover *Freddy vs Jason* (Ronny Yu, 2003), which was technically *Jason 11*. *Jason X* was a science-fiction comedy horror featuring a cameo from maverick film director David Cronenberg as a manic American general. *Freddy vs Jason* featured pop star and sex symbol Kelly Rowland (of Destiny's Child) in a major role, which certainly helped its box office takings, but both films have a claim to being the best in the series.

Only a few days after the report, however, Tarantino was denying that he would helm the film, although he did concede that some discussions had taken place. 'I like Jason [the character] and everything,' he told reporters, 'but I've no intention of directing a movie. [Rights holders] New Line talked to me about it, but it was a complete fabrication, that article.' While this is a disappointment to people who are fans of both Jason and Tarantino, perhaps the sensible thing for New Line to do would be to ask Cronenberg to shoot the film?

Sin City (2005)

Comic-book writer/artist Frank Miller, best known for his work on *Batman* ('Year One' and 'The Dark Knight Returns') and *Daredevil* comics, devoted much of the 1990s to producing the independent series *Sin City*. This noir-influenced, sometimes nightmarish set of short – often interlinked – tales set in a fictional city has proved influential in itself and remains one of the defining works of the comic-book medium.

Miller had tried working in Hollywood in the early 90s, writing a screenplay for *Robocop 2* (Irvin Kersnerr, 1991), which was rewritten out of all recognition. He developed a distrust of Hollywood methods and was unwilling to part with the rights to any of his self-created material as a result. (Ironically Miller's *Robocop 2* screenplay has since been adapted as a comic book.)

At the end of the 90s Robert Rodriguez managed to persuade Miller that he had the writer/artist's best intentions and interests at heart and acquired the right to produce a motion picture based on some of Miller's Sin City stories. He even shot an audition showreel for Miller, in which actors Josh Hartnett and Marley Shelton acted out Rodriguez's adaptation of the *Sin City* short story 'The Customer is Always Right' from the 'The Dame Wore Red' collection.

Rodriguez's film of *Sin City* adapts elements or stories from the original 'Sin City' itself (since retroactively subtitled 'The Hard Goodbye' by Miller), 'The Big Fat Kill' and 'That Yellow Bastard'.

Tarantino was invited by Rodriguez to direct a small portion of the movie (which he is co-directing with Miller himself) and Tarantino accepted the assignment for the fee of a mere $1. This was the same dollar, probably the same actual bill, that Rodriguez had charged him for providing some music for *Vol. 2*.

Rodriguez had an ulterior motive in signing up his friend. *Sin City* was being shot on digital videotape rather than film. This innovative production method is something that Rodriguez is strongly in favour of and has already used on some of his films including *Spy Kids 3-D* (2003). Tarantino had publicly doubted that High Definition videotape shooting, as pioneered by George Lucas, could be effective on big-budget films of the kind he would like to make. Working on *Sin City* would entail using such cameras and Rodriguez hoped that Tarantino would be converted by the process of actually working with them. Tarantino's verdict? 'Mission accomplished'.

CSI: Crime Scene Investigation

It was announced in the *Hollywood Reporter* of 24 February 2005 that Tarantino had signed up to direct an episode of the fifth season of CBS ratings-winning crime series *CSI: Crime Scene Investigation*, which stars William Petersen. A long-time fan of the show and its spin-offs, Tarantino acquired the assignment after striking up a relationship with CSI co-creator/executive producer Anthony Zuicker after they met by chance at an awards ceremony.

The episode, the twenty-third episode of the fifth season, would be written by Zuiker, Carol Mendelsohn and Naren Shanker, all members of the regular CSI writing staff, but based upon a story and outline by Tarantino.

Due to be shot in April and to air on 19 May as the fifth-season finale, Tarantino's episode marks his second time behind the cameras for hour long serial television (see ER – 'Motherhood').

An earlier attempt at a return to television had been thwarted when the Director Guild of America, of which Tarantino is not a member, indicated it would be very displeased should he direct the episode of *The X Files* ('Never Again' by Glen Morgan and James Wong) which had been specially written for him to shoot. Tarantino withdrew under the pressure. The episode was eventually directed by TV regular Rob Bowman – who later directed *The X Files* film (1998) and action movies *Reign of Fire* (2002) and *Elektra* (2004) – and aired as the thirteenth episode of *The X Files* fourth season on 4 February 1997.

Icon of the Decade

At the Sony-sponsored 2005 *Empire* Awards, the movie magazine of the same name, long-quoted by Quentin Tarantino as his favourite movie magazine, presented the writer/director with an award that named him 'Icon of the Decade'. Such acclamatory prizes have a habit of coming back to haunt either the recipient of the award or body that awarded it (*Time* twice made Joseph Stalin 'Man of the Year', John Lennon was the BBC's 1960s 'Man of the Decade' just before his life entered its most controversial phase) but Tarantino and *Empire* seem a sensible fit. His populist sensibility and anti-snobbery, combined with his enthusiasm, even love, for film in all its forms fits the magazine's declared modus operandi. Equally, it's easy to see how, with his back catalogue and presence, Tarantino's contribution to film over the last decade would fit him for such a title. He is not necessarily the best American film director of the past ten years (although that's not an unfair label either) but certainly is the one whose work, even his lesser work, exemplifies that decade in American film above all others. From his championing of retro music to the films that have been made in imitation of him, via the simple fact that *Pulp Fiction* is taught not only in film, but also literary, courses in universities in both Britain and America, all the signs are that Tarantino is, and will continue to be seen to be, massively important to the public perception of film and filmmaking.

To reiterate the introduction to this book, Tarantino is the film director as superstar; this award is more than mere recognition of this fact, it cements it. For someone who has only directed five full-length movies, written two (not *really* three) more and dabbled on the fringes of television and acting, that's a remarkable achievement – and a testament to the quality and inevitable endurance of all of his work.

Index of Quotations

75   'Tarantino and Scott . . .' Sragow, Michael, 'True
      Romance', New Yorker, September 1993
75   'a vibrant . . .' Maslin, Janet, 'Desperadoes, Young at
      Heart With Gun in Hand', New York Times, 10
      September 1993
75   'thought of . . .' Ebert, Roger, 'True Romance',
      Chicago Sun-Times, 10 September 1993
75   'savagely funny . . .' Rolling Stone, September 1993,
      via www.rollingstone.com

Natural Born Killers
79   'I really didn't want . . .' Tarantino quoted by Sean
      O'Hagen in Magazine, May 1994

Pulp Fiction
89   'I just finished . . .' Tarantino, quoted in the
      introduction to the UK
      edition of the Reservoir Dogs screenplay (Faber &
      Faber, 1994)
89   'what I'm prepared . . .' Tarantino, quoted in
      Hirschberg, Lynn, 'The Two Hollywoods: The Man
      Who Changed Everything', New York Times, 16
      November 1997
89   'They were scared . . .' Tarantino, quoted in
      Hirschberg, Lynn, 'The Two Hollywoods: The Man
      Who Changed Everything', New York Times, 16
      November 1997
89   'very disillusioned' Tarantino, quoted in Hirschberg,
      Lynn, 'The Two Hollywoods: The Man Who Changed
      Everything', New York Times, 16 November 1997
90   'it's not like . . .' Tarantino, quoted in Corliss, Richard,
      'A Blast to the Heart', Time, 10 October 1994
102   'I went to . . .' Tarantino, speaking on MTV, 17
      December 1997
102   'I don't know . . .' Tarantino, speaking at the Jackie
      Brown Press Junket, December 1997
105   'he has an . . .' Jackson, quoted in Svetsky, Benjamin,
      'Jackie, Oh!', Entertainment Weekly, 19 December 1997

ER – 'Motherhood'

Four Rooms

From Dusk Till Dawn

150 'wish I'd have . . .' Rodriguez, interviewed by Film
Four.

165 'so much mesh . . .' Rafferty, Terence, *From Dusk Till
Dawn*', *New Yorker*, February 1995, via the *New
Yorker* online film file

165 'high-stakes poker . . .' Maslin, Janet, 'Enough Blood to
Feed the Thirstiest Vampires', *New York Times*, 19
January 1996

Jackie Brown

173 'What I might . . .' Tarantino, on the *Charlie Rose
Show*, 14 October 1994

175 'his style *dictated* . . .' Ebert, Roger, 'One on One with
Quentin', *Chicago Sun-Times*, 21 December 1997

175 'it just kind of . . .' Tarantino, appearing on MTV, 17
December 1997

175 'That same movie . . .' Tarantino, quoted in Svetsky,
Benjamin, 'Jackie, O!', *Entertainment Weekly*, 19
December 1997

176 'You're the filmmaker . . .' Leonard, quoted in Ressner,
Jeffrey, 'Back in the Action', *Time*, 17 August 1997

178 'He's gonna write . . .' Grier, quoted in Busack,
Richard Von, 'Grier Window', *Metro*, 24 December
1997

179 'Jackie had to be . . .' Tarantino, quoted in Busack,
Richard Von, 'Grier Window', *Metro*, 24 December
1997

179 'It's like putting . . .' Tarantino, quoted in Busack,
Richard Von, 'Grier Window', *Metro*, 24 December
1997

179 'assertive yet feminine . . . and emotionality . . .' Grier,
speaking on MTV, 17 December 1997

180 'just get *ten per cent* . . .' Forster, quoted in Busack,
Richard Von, 'Grier Window', *Metro*, 24 December
1997

181 'This is the best part . . .' Tarantino, quoted in the *New
York Times* DATE??

181 'a real conniving bitch' Fonda, speaking on MTV, 17 December 1997

181 'In that kind . . .' Fonda, speaking on MTV, 17 December 1997

183 'he was more confident . . .' Jackson, quoted in Svetsky, Benjamin, 'Jackie, Oh!', *Entertainment Weekly*, 19 December 1997

183 'It's not an epic . . . underneath it' Tarantino, quoted in Svetsky, Benjamin, 'Jackie, Oh!', *Entertainment Weekly*, 19 December 1997

183 'moment by moment . . .' Tarantino, quoted in Busack, Richard Von, 'Grier Window', *Metro*, 24 December 1997

185 'She ain't none . . .' Tarantino, speaking on MTV, 17 December 1997

185 'real woman . . .' Grier, speaking on MTV, 17 December 1997

187 'ice-cold Hitchcock . . .' Lane, Anthony, '*Jackie Brown*', *New Yorker*, 12 January 1998

196 'shows Quentin . . . payoff' Siskel, Gene, speaking on *Siskel and Ebert at the Movies*, 22 December 1997

196 'do quite enough . . .' Lane, Anthony, '*Jackie Brown*', *New Yorker*, 12 January 1998

196 'a brilliantly cast homage . . .' Hoberman, J, *Village Voice*, 20 December 1997

196 'Knockout, loaded with action . . .' Travers, Peter, '*Jackie Brown*', *Rolling Stone*, 22 January 1998

197 'It's a love story . . .' Tarantino, quoted in Svetsky, Benjamin, 'Jackie, Oh!', *Entertainment Weekly*, 19 December 1997

200 'You're belittling . . .' Tarantino, quoted in Ebert, Roger, 'One on One with Quentin', *Chicago Sun-Times*, 21 December 1997

202 'I think they lost . . .' Tarantino, quoted on onetimes.com, 27 August 2004

Kill Bill – Vol. 1

208 'full-on, lurid . . .' Tarantino, in *Kill Bill* electronic press pack

208 'I didn't really . . .' Thurman, quoted in Smith, RJ, 'Faster, Pussy Wagon! Kill! Kill!', *Village Voice*, 1 October 2003

209 'If Joseph Von Stenberg . . .' Tarantino, quoted on BBCi, 11 October 2003

214 'whatever I did . . .' Thurman, quoted in the *Kill Bill* electronic press pack

215 'I thought Bill . . .' Tarantino, quoted on BBCi, 7 October 2003

215 'It's a sad cliché . . .' Tarantino, quoted in Smith, RJ, 'Faster, Pussy Wagon! Kill! Kill!', *Village Voice*, 1 October 2003

216 'one of the things . . .' Tarantino, speaking on the *Charlie Rose Show*, 14 October 1994

217 'I wanted to see . . .' Tarantino, quoted in Smith, RJ, 'Faster, Pussy Wagon! Kill! Kill!', *Village Voice*, 1 October 2003

218 'shit they can't . . .' Tarantino, quoted in Smith, RJ, 'Faster, Pussy Wagon! Kill! Kill!', *Village Voice*, 1 October 2003

219 'probably the most . . .' Smith, RJ, 'Faster, Pussy Wagon! Kill! Kill!', *Village Voice*, 1 October 2003

220 'This is definitely . . .' Tarantino, quoted on BBCi, 3 October 2003

220 'Yuen Wo-Ping . . .' . . .' Tarantino, quoted on BBCi, 9 October 2001

221 'The finest actor . . .' *True Romance*, Quentin Tarantino, Faber & Faber

221 'I was only safe . . .' Thurman, quoted in Smith, RJ, 'Faster, Pussy Wagon! Kill! Kill!', *Village Voice*, 1 October 2003

221 'I have done violence' Tarantino, quoted on BBCi, 3 October 2003

224 'It's a slasher . . .' Christopher, James, *The Times*, 9 October 2003

225 '. . . made me so . . .' Smith, Kevin, www.viewaskew.com, 30 September 2003

225 'above all an exercise . . . musical number' Scott, AO, *New York Times*, 10 October 2003

225 'virtuoso violinist . . . makes sense' Ebert, Roger, *Chicago Sun-Times*, 14 October 2003

225 'I had no idea . . .' Wilder, Matthew, *Village Voice*, 15 October 2003

225 'more exhausting than . . .' Hoberman, J, 'Enter the Dragon Lady', *Village Voice*, 1 October 2003

226 'neither is there . . .' Hoberman, J, 'Enter the Dragon Lady', *Village Voice*, 1 October 2003

226 'a grindhouse Ulysses . . . new kennel' Powers, John, 'Once Upon A Time in the East', *LA Weekly*, 10 October, 2003

228 'I wouldn't have had . . .' Tarantino, quoted in Smith, RJ, 'Faster, Pussy Wagon! Kill! Kill!', *Village Voice*, 1 October 2003

228 'pretentious . . . overdose' Tarantino, quoted in the *Kill Bill – Vol. 1* press pack

228 'Cutting the film . . .' Powers, John, 'Once Upon A Time in the East', *LA Weekly*, 10 October, 2003

229 'I'm giving you . . .' Tarantino, quoted in Powers, John, 'Kill Bill . . . or else!', *Village Voice*, 16 April 2004

Vol. 2

250 'Tarantino knocks . . .' Travers, Peter, *Rolling Stone* #947, 29 April 2004

250 '*Vol. 2* is not . . .' Hoberman, J, 'Vengeance is Hers', *Village Voice*, 13 April 2004

251 'the star will be . . .' Tarantino, quoted on BBCi, 10 April 2004

Index